More-with-Less Cookbook

Consume less of the world's food resources, eat better, and save money.

This collection of more than 500 international recipes majors on the use of simple, natural ingredients — healthy and cheap! Recipes include unusual breads, soups, casseroles and main dishes as well as mouth-watering desserts, snacks and cakes.

We live in a world where food resources are stretched to the limit — and squandered by many in affluent countries. *More-with-Less Cookbook* brings together recipes from around the world, and shows how to produce delicious and filling meals without using more than our fair share of the world's resources. Also included are dozens of practical hints, useful charts and basic dietary information.

Doris Longacre compiled this exciting cookbook with help and suggestions from hundreds of Christian people throughout the world who shared her concern that diminishing food resources should be used wisely and fairly. She held a degree in home economics and served for a while as a dietician. With her husband, Paul, she worked in Vietnam and Indonesia. Before her death in 1979 she lived in Pennsylvania, USA, with her husband and two daughters.

We are prepared
with all our hearts
to share our possessions,

gold,
and all that we have,
however little it may be;

to sweat and labour
to meet the needs
of the poor,
as the Spirit
and Word of the Lord
and true brotherly love
teach and imply.

—Menno Simons (1496-1561)

More
WITH
Less
COOKBOOK

DORIS LONGACRE

A LION PAPERBACK

Oxford · Batavia · Sydney

Copyright © 1976 Herald Press, Scottdale, Pennsylvania, USA

Published by
Lion Publishing plc
Sandy Lane West, Oxford, England
ISBN 0 7459 1262 1
Albatross Books Pty Ltd
PO Box 320, Sutherland, NSW 2232, Australia
ISBN 0 86760 875 7

First edition 1977
Second edition 1981
Reprinted 1983, 1984
This edition 1987
Reprinted 1989, 1990

Cover photograph by ZEFA (UK) Ltd

Printed in Great Britain by
Cox and Wyman, Reading

Contents

Preface

The needs of the hungry and the uneven distribution of the world's limited resources cause us all concern. One group of Christians, the Mennonites, produced this cookbook as a practical expression of their concern. Its aim is to show people how to enjoy God's good gifts and eat better—but at the same time free more of the world's food resources for the hungry.

The Mennonites are descended from the sixteenth-century Christian followers of Menno Simons, who travelled through North Germany and the Low Countries preaching the Christian message. More radical than Luther or Calvin, they stressed the importance of Christian community, adult baptism, and non-involvement in politics, and refused to bear arms. They tried to base all their beliefs and practices directly on New Testament patterns.

Today there are many Mennonite communities in USA and Canada, where some Mennonites were driven from Russia by persecution in the nineteenth and early twentieth centuries. Mennonites hold orthodox Christian beliefs, and also forbid the taking of oaths, holding public office, and military service. Like the Quakers, they stress peace and have provided medical and relief services in two World Wars and in Vietnam. This book is a natural outworking of their joyful use of God's good gifts, their unostentatious life-style, and concern for justice and peace.

Introduction

Who does it really help if I cut back? Many people are saying that it does not really matter whether we eat more or less. The argument goes something like this:

If I eat less meat this week will more grain be available in Bangladesh next year? If we stop buying sugared cereals and TV snacks the food industry will come up with something even worse. We may decide not to eat out so often but what difference will that make? The basic problem is bad government policy and import-export agreements—or snail-pace family planning programmes and corrupt governments in the Third World.

All these arguments have elements of truth. But they smack heavily of a common attitude—that it doesn't really matter what one person does; or that what one family can do is so small that it has no over-all effect. In our complex world it is difficult to see how a few families' struggles to save food will help. Yet eating less is an obvious first step. The complexity that frustrates easy answers also means that in the global family our decisions are interrelated. 'Life is like a huge spider's web so that if you touch it anywhere you set the whole thing trembling,' says Frederick Buccher.

How can we continue to overeat, knowing that people are starving in other parts of the world, and be at peace with ourselves and our neighbours? 'The destitute suffer physically, the overindulged morally,' writes one Mennonite relief administrator. Jesus recognized the desire to get more and more as a destructive force when he asked, 'Will a person gain anything if he wins the whole world but loses his life?'

When Jesus was surrounded by 5,000 hungry people he commanded his disciples to see that they were all fed. The disciples obeyed. They shared what was available, although it seemed inadequate. Their act of faith was to share and let God take responsibility for the rest.

Eating less is only a start. Concerned Christians will want to get involved in food production and distribution schemes. They will challenge government policies. But these matters are being dealt with elsewhere. If it was only other people who stood to gain from our changes, hopefully we would go ahead, inspired by Christ to share with them. But we, too, stand to gain. Happily, the whole-grains and legumes, vegetables and fruits and moderate quantities of animal products that make sense in the light of world food-needs are also best for our health. With a few exceptions, they are also the cheapest. When we reduce our intake of heavily grain-fed meat, over-processed foods and sugary products, we not only release resources for the world's hungry, but also protect our own health and purses. In other words we get more for less.

Changing our eating habits

Change takes time, but here are some hints on how to change eating habits:

1. Keep the basic commitment to eat responsibily very much in mind. Study the Bible to see what Jesus and early Christian writers had to say about living in Christ's kingdom, and

about sharing. Study world food needs and solutions. Always remember that our direction comes from Jesus who said, 'Give to the person who begs from you.' 'Give as freely as you have received!' 'Give them something to eat!' 'Give and it will be given to you.'

2. Expect eating habits to change slowly. Often you'll find you like a new dish better the second time around. Don't try to change too many things at once—this will only get the family against changes. A slower approach will give people time to adjust their tastes more smoothly.

3. Be honest about reasons for change. Give matter-of-fact explanations that express an honest desire to share with the hungry. Often children are willing to go further than we expect, if they understand our reasons and are involved in our decisions.

4. Let children help with planning. One mother wrote about her fourteen-year-old son. He complained when she cut down on meat and other foods that he enjoyed, so she let him plan the family menus for a week. To her surprise she found he shared her motivation and planned economically. What they ate was not very different when he planned. But he felt better about the meals and was involved in the family's aims.

5. Be willing to celebrate. The Gospels show that Jesus entered wholeheartedly into times of joy and feasting. Even people who live on monotonous diets in poor countries manage an occasion celebration. Celebrations bring enjoyment by varying from the daily routine. But don't expect food to do everything. 'More-with-less' means saying that faith and relationships are the basis for celebrating: food plays its part alongside.

Building a simpler diet

*God's people wander
in the supermarket
    among chemical frozen pies
    overprocessed instant dinners
    nutritionless snack foods
    soft drinks in throwaway bottles
Like manna in the wilderness
hold fast
    vegetables from
    sun-warmed gardens
    protein-rich beans
    oven-fresh whole-grain breads
    Home-bottled fruit in preserving
    jars.*
    —Jane Short, Elkart, Indiana

How to free resources

What should we eat (and what should we not eat) to free resources for hungry people and to improve our own health? These general guidelines take into account world food and energy needs, good nutrition and food costs. More detailed information is given in *Diet for a Small Planet* by Francis Moore Lappé (Ballantine Books Inc.)

1. Eat more:

whole grains—rice, wheat, barley, rye, oats, corn, millet.

legumes—dried beans (including soy beans), dried peas, lentils, peanuts.

vegetables and fruits—cheaper locally-grown varieties—or home-grown and preserved nuts and seeds.

2. Use sparingly:
   meat,
   poultry,
   seafood,
   milk, cheese, yoghurt,
   eggs.

3. Avoid if possible:
   overprocessed foods and convenience foods,
   packaged foods,
   foods heavy in refined sugar and saturated fats.

Is there enough protein in vegetables?

It is often said that the quality of protein in meat is higher than in vegetable sources, or that meat contains complete protein whereas plants don't. Is there any truth in this?

Twenty amino-acids make up the protein our bodies use. Of these twenty, eight have to come directly from the food we eat. These eight are called the 'essential amino-acids'. The other amino-acids our bodies can synthesize.

All the essential amino-acids must be present at the same time and in the right proportions for our bodies to make use of them. If one is missing, even temporarily, the body's ability to use protein will drop accordingly.

Complete protein foods contain all eight essential amino-acids. Animal products—eggs, milk and meat—provide all eight essential amino-acids in the proportions our bodies require. Eggs come closest to the ideal pattern; milk is a close second, and meats follow. Soybeans and whole rice are almost as good as meats for protein quality. Other grains, the legumes, seeds and nuts are also good sources of protein, but each lacks one or more of the essential amino-acids.

How to combine plant proteins

Although plant proteins lack some essential amino-acids, we don't need to rely solely on animal products for a complete protein supply. The amino-acids lacking in one plant can be made up from another. Plant proteins complement each other when eaten together. This chart shows how this works.

Milk Products
should always be served with **Grains**

cereal with milk
   bread and milk
      cheese sandwiches
         macaroni with cheese
            rice-cheese casserole
               lasagne (pasta and cheese)
                  pizza (crust and cheese)
                    cheese fondue
                       granola or grape nuts made with milk
                    baked goods containing milk
                  rice pudding (rice and milk)

1 c. skim milk	complements	¾ c. rice
¼ c. grated cheese	complements	¾ c. rice
½ c. skim milk	complements	1 c. whole wheat flour
3 T. dry milk powder	complements	1 c. whole wheat flour
1 c. milk	complements	5 slices bread
1 c. milk	complements	1 c. dry macaroni
⅓ c. grated cheese	complements	1 c. dry macaroni

Legumes
should always
be served with **Grains**

peanut-butter sandwiches
   soybean salad with bread
      bread containing soy flour
         lentil soup and muffins
            lentils or split peas (dhal) with rice
               rice-bean casserole
                  baked beans with brown bread
                    beans and tortillas
                      refried beans and rice
                        beans and corn bread
                          bean soup and bread

1 c. beans	complements	2⅔ c. rice
¼ c. soybeans	complements	2½ c. rice
½ c. beans	complements	3 c. whole wheat flour
¼ c. soy flour	complements	1 c. whole wheat flour
¼ c. beans	complements	1 c. cornmeal or 6 tortillas

In her book *Diet for a Small Planet* Francis Lappé says: 'Eating a mixture of protein sources can increase the protein value of the meal; here's a case where the whole is greater than the sum of its parts . . . Such mixes do not result in a perfect protein that is fully utilizable by the body (remember that only egg is near perfect). But combinations can increase the protein quality as much as fifty per cent above the average of of the items eaten separately.' In other words, we get more with less as we plan menus involving plant protein.

How to add extra protein

1. In baked foods:
use part or all whole wheat flour;
add wheat germ—2 T. per cup of flour;
add dry milk powder;
use soy flour—replace 2 or more T. per cup of all-purpose flour with soy flour (2 T. low-fat soy flour has 14 gr. protein).

2. In vegetables, casseroles, soups, main dishes:
add cheese
use a sauce made with milk;
add extra dry-milk powder;
use soybeans;
use ground soybeans as extender;
add hard-boiled eggs.

3. In salads:
add grated cheese or cottage cheese;
add chilled marinated soybeans;
sprinkle with roasted sunflower seeds or nuts;
whip cottage cheese or yogurt into dressings;
add hard-boiled eggs.

4. In desserts:
use yogurt, milk, eggs or cottage cheese;
add extra dry milk powder;
add soy flour;
add nuts;
sprinkle with granola.

Recommended daily protein requirements

	Age (years)	Weight (stones)	Energy (calories)	Protein (grams)
Children	1- 3	2	1300	23
	4 6	3	1800	30
	7-10	4½	2400	36
Males	11-14	7	2800	44
	15-18	9½	3000	54
	19-22	10½	3000	54
	23-50	11	2700	56
	51+	11	2400	56
Females	11-14	7	2400	44
	15-18	8½	2100	48
	19-22	9	2100	46
	23-50	9	2000	46
	51+	9	1800	46
Pregnant			+300	+30
Lactating			+500	+20

(Adapted from *Recommended Dietary Allowances* 8th Edition, 1974
Food and Nutrition Board, National Academy of Sciences—NRC, USA.)

Calorie needs and physical activity

A: Most household chores, typing, assembly-line work, sales work, walking, golf, dancing, driving tractor.
B: heavy housecleaning, digging, moving or lifting of heavy packages, masonry, military drilling, active sports.

C: very heavy manual work, training for professional athletics.
D: dressing, reading, knitting, working at desk with little movement, driving car, spectator at games.

	Weight (stones)	Activity	Calories	Protein (grams)
Male	11	D	2300	48
		A	2850	48
		B	3650	48
		C	4250	48
Female	9	D	1900	39
		A	2400	39
		B	3000	39

Protein and Calorie Content of Protein Foods

	Portion Size	Calories	Protein (Grams)		Portion Size	Calories	Protein (Grams)
Cereals				Pinto beans, dry	⅓ c	349	22.9
All-Bran	⅓ c	70	3.0	Split peas, dry	½ c	348	24.2
Cornflakes	1 c	95	2.1	Peanut butter	1 T	86	3.9
Cream of wheat,				Peanuts, shelled	1 T	86	4.0
cooked	1 c	130	4.4	Soybeans, dry	½ c	403	34.1
Oatmeal, cooked	1 c	148	5.4	Soybeans, immature,			
Oatmeal, dry	1 c	312	11.4	cooked	½ c	88	7.4
Special K	1 c	60	3.2	Soybeans, mature,			
Wheat germ	¼ c	103	7.5	cooked	½ c	130	11.0
Dairy Products and Eggs				**Meats and Fish**			
Eggs, large	1 egg	88	7.0	**Beef, raw**			
Cottage cheese	½ c	120	15.3	Ground beef	¼ lb	304	20.3
Natural cheddar				Ground beef, lean	¼ lb	203	23.4
cheese	1 oz	115	7.2	Chuck steak,			
Natural Swiss cheese	1 oz	106	7.7	choice grade	¼ lb	337	15.5
Processed cheese	1 oz	107	6.5	Chuck steak,			
Milk, whole, fresh	1 c	162	8.6	good grade	¼ lb	288	16.7
Milk, skim	1 c	88	8.8	Sirloin steak,			
(same as buttermilk from skim milk or				choice grade	¼ lb	229	17.8
reconstituted nonfat dry milk)				Steak, choice grade	¼ lb	216	22.1
Nonfat dry milk solids	1 c	215	21.4	Liver	¼ lb	159	22.6
Ice cream	⅛ qt	186	3.6	**Chicken, raw**			
Yogurt, from skim				Whole, ready-to-cook	½ lb	191	28.7
milk	1 c	122	8.3	Breasts	½ lb	197	37.3
Yogurt, from whole				Drumsticks	½ lb	157	25.6
milk	1 c	151	7.3	Thighs	½ lb	218	30.8
				Livers	¼ lb	146	22.4
Flours				**Fish**			
White, all-purpose	1 c	400	11.6	Cod, flesh only, raw	¼ lb	89	20.0
Whole wheat	1 c	400	16.0	Haddock, flesh only,			
Soy, low fat	1 c	356	43.4	raw	¼ lb	89	20.8
Rye	1 c	268	7.5	Mackerel, canned	¼ lb	208	21.9
				Perch, flesh only, raw	¼ lb	108	21.6
Grains and Pasta				Salmon, canned	¼ lb	160	27.0
Barley, pearled dry	¼ c	196	4.6	Tuna, canned in			
Cornmeal, dry	¼ c	135	2.9	water	¼ lb	144	32.0
Rice, white dry	¼ c	178	3.3	**Pork**			
Rice, brown, dry	¼ c	176	3.7	Bacon, raw	¼ lb	667	9.3
Egg noodles, dry	¼ c	70	2.3	Ham, picnic, raw	¼ lb	265	15.6
Macaroni, dry	¼ c	101	3.4	Ham, canned,			
Spaghetti, dry	¼ c	140	4.8	boneless	¼ lb	189	20.9
				Loin chops, raw	¼ lb	266	15.3
Legumes				Sausages, raw	¼ lb	565	10.7
Kidney beans, dry	½ c	343	22.5	**Miscellaneous meats**			
Lentils, dry	½ c	340	24.7	Frankfurters, all-meat	¼ lb	361	14.9
Lima beans, dry	½ c	345	20.4	Luncheon meat,			
Navy beans, dry	½ c	340	22.3	canned	¼ lb	334	17.0
				Salami	¼ lb	352	19.9

Protein values

	Grams of protein per pound
Beef	
Liver	90.3
Mince	81.2
Ground chuck	93.9
Chuck steak, bone-in	71.6
Sirloin steak	71.1
Steak	88.5
Pork	
Ham, smoked, picnic	68.3
Pork chops, loin	61.1
Ham, canned	83.0
Sausages	42.6
Boiled ham, sliced	103.5
Bacon	38.1
Lamb	
Leg of lamb	67.7
Lamb chops	58.9
Chicken	
Whole	57.4
Breasts	74.5
Thighs	61.6
Legs	51.2
Turkey	65.9
Fish	
Perch, frozen	87.5
Cod, frozen	79.8
Fish sticks	74.7
Haddock, frozen	83.0
Mackerel, canned	87.5
Sardines, canned	89.3
Tuna, canned	109.8
Salmon, canned	93.0
Miscellaneous Meats	
Frankfurters, all meat	59.4
Salami	79.4
Luncheon meat, canned	68.0

	Grams of protein per pound
Legumes	
Navy beans, dry	101.2
Lentils, dry	112.0
Split peas, dry	109.3
Baby limas, dry	92.5
Kidney beans, dry	103.9
Pinto beans, dry	103.9
Marrow or pea beans, dry	101.2
Large limas, dry	92.5
Baked beans, tinned	27.7
Soybeans, dry	154.7
Textured veg. protein meat extender	240.0
Peanut butter	114.3
Peanuts, shelled	118.8
Grains and Pasta	
Spaghetti	56.7
Egg noodles	58.1
Rice	30.4
Brown rice	34.0
Cereals	
Wheat germ	144.0
Oatmeal	64.4
Cream of wheat	54.4
Special K	9.6
All-Bran	48.0
Cornflakes	32.0
Flours	
White	47.6
Whole wheat	60.3
Soy	196.9
Dairy Products and Eggs	
Whole milk, one pint	17.2
Nonfat dry milk powder	162.4
Cottage cheese	61.7
Processed cheese	105.2
Cheddar cheese	113.4
Swiss cheese	124.7
Eggs, large (per doz.)	58.2
Miscellaneous	
Pizza, frozen	40.4

Equivalent Measures

		Weight — yields —	Approx. Measure
Dairy	nonfat dry milk solids	1 lb.	4 c.
Products	cheese	1 lb.	4 c. shredded
	cottage cheese	1 lb.	2 c.
	cream cheese	8 oz.	1 c.
	butter or margarine	1 lb.	2 c.
			Approx. measure, cooked
Dried	kidney	1 lb. (1½ c.)	6 c.
Beans	lima	1 lb. (2⅓ c.)	6 c.
	navy	1 lb. (2⅓ c.)	6 c.
	soybeans	1 lb. (2⅓ c.)	6 c.
	spilt peas	1 lb. (2 c.)	5 c.
	lentils	1 lb. (2⅓ c.)	6 c.
			Approx. measure
Flour and	enriched white	1 lb.	4 c. sifted
Grains	enriched cake	1 lb.	4½ c. sifted
	whole wheat	1 lb.	3½ c.
	rye	1 lb.	4 c.
	soy	1 lb.	6 c.
	cornmeal	1 lb.	3 c.
	oatmeal	1 lb.	4¾ c.
Nuts	almonds	1 lb. in shell	1¾ c. shelled
		1 lb. shelled	3½ c.
	pecans	1 lb. in shell	2¼ c. shelled
		1 lb. shelled	4 c.
	peanuts	1 lb. in shell	2¼ c. shelled
		1 lb. shelled	3 c.
	walnuts	1 lb. in shell	1⅔ c. shelled
		1 lb. shelled	4 c.
	coconut	1 whole	2-3 c. shredded
		1 lb. shredded	5 c.
			Approx. measure, cooked
Rice and	rice	1 lb. (2 c.) dried	6 c.
Pasta	macaroni	1 lb. (4 c.) dried	8 c.
	spaghetti	1 lb. (5 c.) dried	9-10 c.
	noodles	1 lb. (6 c.) dried	10½ c.

			Approx. measure
Sugar	**granulated**	1 lb.	2 c.
	brown	1 lb.	2¼ c.
	confectioners	1 lb.	3½ c.
	molasses	1 lb.	1⅓ c.

Misc.	**1 pkg. dry yeast**	1 T.
	1 envelope unflavored gelatin (enough to jell 2 c. liquid)	1 T.
	1 lemon juice	2-3 T.
	rind, grated	1½-3 t.
	1 orange juice	⅓-½ c.
	rind, grated	1-2 T.
	1 lb. bananas (3-4)	2 c. mashed
	1 lb. dates	2½ c. pitted
	1 lb. seedless raisins	2¾ c.
	1 lb. raw potatoes	2 c. cooked and mashed

Metric Conversion Table

	when you know	you can find	if you multiply by
Weight	ounces	grams	28
measured in grams (G)	pounds	kilograms	0.45
1 gram = 1/28 ounce	grams	ounces	0.035
= 1/1000 kilogram	kilograms	pounds	2.2
Liquid Volume	ounces	milliliters	30
measured in liters (L)	pints	liters	0.47
1 liter = 1.06 quarts	quarts	liters	0.95
	gallons	liters	3.8
	milliliters	ounces	0.034
	liters	pints	2.1
	liters	quarts	1.06
	liters	gallons	0.26

	Fahrenheit (°F)	Metric: Centigrade (°C)
Temperature	32°	0°
	212°	100°
	98.6°	37°

Substitutes

For	Use
*1 t. baking powder	⅓ t. baking soda plus ½ t. cream of tartar
	or ¼ t. baking soda plus ⅓ c. sour milk, buttermilk, or yogurt
1 T. cornstarch	2 T. flour
2 T. tapioca	3 T. flour
2 egg yolks	1 whole egg
1 c. whole fresh milk	½ c. evaporated milk plus ½ c. water
	or ⅓ c. dry milk solids plus 1 c. water
1 c. sour milk	1 c. buttermilk
	or 1 c. yogurt
	or 1⅓ T. vinegar or lemon juice plus milk to make 1 c.
*1 c. sour cream (in baking)	⅞ c. buttermilk, sour milk, or yogurt plus 3 T. margarine
1 c. sour cream (in casseroles, salad dressings, desserts)	1 c. yogurt
*1 c. sugar	¾ c. honey, molasses, or corn syrup; reduce liquid in recipe by ¼ c., add ¼ t. soda, and reduce oven temperature by 25°
1 c. brown sugar	see p. 190
1 c. confectioners sugar	see p. 199
*1 c. margarine, butter or shortening	¾ c. bacon fat
	or ¾ c. chicken fat
	or ⅞ c. lard
	or ⅞ c. oil
1 square (1 oz.) unsweetened chocolate	3 T. cocoa

*May not yield perfect results
in products of fine texture
such as light cakes, generally
acceptable in breads, many cookies,
and moist cakes.

Key

c.	cup=8 fl. oz. (**NB** 1 British cup=1 ¼ US cups)
gr.	gram
lb.	pound
oz.	ounce
pkg.	packet
pt	pint
qt	quart
t.	teaspoon
T.	tablespoon
TS	time-saver

All measurements are level (not heaped) and standard measuring utensils should be used. An American yeast packet contains ¼ ounce of yeast.

Most of the recipes do not call for convenience products. In some cases you may want to use them. For example, when a recipe calls for cloves of garlic, garlic salt may be used with similar results, except in stir-fried Chinese dishes. Such options could not all be given because of limited space. Experience teaches a careful cook when and how to substitute.

Glossary

beet	beetroot
bologna	polony
broil	grill
bulk sausage	sausagemeat
bun	soft roll
canning	bottling
cornstarch	cornflour
dhal	split peas
eggplant	aubergine
enriched white flour **enriched cake flour**	} use plain flour
garbanzo beans	chick peas
Graham crackers	digestive biscuits
griddle	circular iron plate used for baking (a heavy frying-pan can be used instead)
hamburger	minced meat
Ice milk	dairy ice cream
link sausage	butcher's sausages
Mason jars	preserving jars
napkin	cloth
scalded milk	milk which is starting to boil
scallions	shallots
skillet	frying-pan
sweet potatoes	yams
Wiener	frankfurter
zucchini	courgettes

Many of the ingredients mentioned in this book are unusual, but most can be obtained from health food shops and delicatessens.

Recipes

O God,
We've wasted
we've complained
we've grumbled.
We've misused our resources.
We've confused our needs with our wants.
For these sins
Father forgive us
Help us reset our priorities
according to your will.

Yeast and quick breads

"Here's a new menu idea at our house—bake bread, and you've got a meal!" writes Marian Franz, Washington, D.C.

Home bread-baking is returning to popularity. Creative enjoyment and the real quality of the product are the first reasons people give for baking. The time spent becomes more of a lark than a chore.

Health-wise there are good reasons for baking bread. Increasingly, nutritionists are questioning the effects of eating year after year bread baked with over 25 different chemicals used to retard spoilage or simplify the manufacturing process. Further, they are asking whether the U.S. and Canadian practice of enriching, or putting back synthetically the vitamins and minerals lost in processing, really works. Initial reports of a recent Canadian nutrition survey show about half the population with thiamine intake below recommended levels and moderate deficiency for a substantial number of adults. These people eat thiamine-enriched bread.[1]

Home-baked bread with whole-grain flours and bran adds fiber lacking in North American diets. Specialists in diseases of the digestive tract writing in the *Journal of the American Medical Association* say many of the diseases of Western civilization have appeared only in the past century and are caused, at least in part, by removal of fiber from flour and cereal. Fiber has no calories or nutritional value, but is needed for bulk and for its effect on chemical and bacterial processes in the intestine.[2]

My cost calculations for whole wheat bread show that when you purchase flour and yeast in bulk, when you use dry milk, and when you bake three to four loaves at once to conserve heat, homemade bread costs about half as much as commercially baked bread. In terms of taste appeal, nutritional value, and creative experience the home-baked product is worth more than its dollar-and-cents value.

Baking bread, like all other worthwhile activities, takes time and a certain amount of practice. For large families, it may not be possible to bake all the bread at home. The saving factor is four or five loaves baked at once and a freezer for storing them. Bread dough can also be mixed one day and baked the next.

Baking Yeast Bread
Essential Equipment:
— Large metal or glass bowl
— Measuring utensils
— Wooden stirring spoon
— Large wooden board or durable surface set at comfortable height for kneading
— Bread pans or casserole dishes for baking

Ingredients:
Yeast
— Cheaper purchased in jar or can; divide with a friend
— 1 T. dry yeast is equivalent to 1 package.

— Store in refrigerator, tightly covered.
— Dissolve first in lukewarm water

with pinch of sugar for speedy rising.

— Needs *warm* liquid (120-130°) for quick rising, but *hot* liquid kills it.

Liquids

— Use warm water, milk, potato or other vegetable water, or whey from making cheese.

— Scald and cool raw (unpasteurized) milk before using.

— Substitute water for milk and add dry milk powder with flour.

Sweeteners

— Use sugar, brown sugar, honey, or molasses interchangeably in most recipes.

Fat

— Yeast breads need only small amounts—use lard, shortening, oil, margarine, fresh meat drippings, or rendered chicken fat.

White flour

— Flour from hard winter wheat, sometimes called Western or Occident flour, works best.

— Unbleached flour is satisfactory.

— Most recipes call for ⅓ to ½ white flour for light texture.

Whole wheat or graham flour

— Look for straight-run whole wheat flour directly from mills.

— Hand or electric grinders are available for home use.

— Use up to ½ whole wheat flour in any baked product.

— Some heavier but delicious breads are made with all whole wheat.

— Store whole wheat flour in refrigerator or freezer in hot weather.

Soy flour

— Sold as low-fat or full-fat soy flour; interchangeable in recipes.

— Has 40-60 grams high-quality protein per cup.

— More expensive per pound than wheat flour, but one of the cheapest *protein sources* currently available

— Contains no gluten to hold gas produced by yeast; cannot be used alone to bake bread.

— Excellent for adding protein to any baked product; for each cup replace 2-4 tablespoons other flour with soy flour.

— Add to soups, stews, casseroles, hot cereals, loaves, and patties to raise protein content.

Other flours: rye, rye graham, buckwheat, corn, millet, oat

— Combine with wheat flour in breads.

— Millet, rolled oats, and wheat can be whirled in a blender to produce flours.

Wheat germ

— Buy raw or untoasted from mill or health food store; toasted is available in supermarkets at higher price. Avoid sweetened wheat germ.

— Add to baked goods to increase protein, vitamins, and minerals.

Processes:

1. Dissolve yeast in warm water with pinch of sugar. Some recipes now omit this step and combine yeast with flours.

2. Making a sponge: Most recipes omit this step but many experienced bakers still believe in it. Mix liquid, dissolved yeast, sugar, and about half the flour to a smooth batter; beat well. Allow to rise until light and bubbly. Stir down and add salt, fat, and remaining flour; proceed with kneading.

3. How much flour? Since flours vary in moisture content, experience alone tells exactly how much flour you need. Dough will be sticky at first, but as kneading progresses, add just enough flour so dough no longer sticks to hands and board.

4. To knead: Fold dough over toward you, press down with heel of hand, give a slight turn, fold over,

and press again. Dust board lightly with flour as needed, and repeat process until dough is smooth, satiny, and no longer sticky.

5. Rising: Place dough in greased bowl, flop over once to grease top surface, cover with clean cloth and allow to rise at 75-80° if possible. To speed the rising process in a cool kitchen, put stopper in the sink and fill with several inches very hot water. Place an empty bowl upside down in the sink and set bowl with dough on top of empty bowl just so that bowl with dough does not touch hot water. Cover dough and entire sink with large tea towel to hold steam in. Allow dough to rise this way about 1 hour, but punch down and turn after 20-30 minutes. Allow dough to rise only until doubled in bulk before punching down or coarse, dry bread may result.

6. Forming loaves: Roll or press out each piece of dough into a rectangle, about 9x12" for a 9x5" bread pan. From 9" edge, roll up tightly and place in greased pan with seam down and ends tucked under if necessary to fit into pan. Bake bread in any oven-proof utensil—coffee cans, casseroles, round cake pans, etc. Cover with cloth and allow to rise again until doubled.

7. Baking and cooling: For a shiny crust, just before baking brush carefully with beaten egg mixed with a little water; sprinkle with sesame or poppy seed if desired. See recipe instructions for baking. Bread is done when it shrinks from the side of the pan, looks nicely browned, and sounds hollow when you tap the bottom of a loaf. Experience tells. Remove from pans immediately and brush with margarine for a soft crust.

To mix now, bake later
— Any yeast dough containing at least 1 T. sugar per cup of flour can be refrigerated up to 3 days. Immediately after kneading, grease top of dough and cover with waxed paper or plastic, then a damp cloth. Refrigerate until ready to use. Punch down occasionally as necessary. About 2 hours before baking, remove dough from refrigerator, shape into rolls or loaf, and let rise until doubled (1½ to 2 hours for cold dough). Bake as directed.
— White or whole wheat bread dough with less sugar can be refrigerated 2 to 24 hours. After dough is put in the pans, brush with oil and cover with plastic. Refrigerate until ready to bake. Preheat oven. Uncover dough carefully, and let stand at room temperature 10 minutes. Puncture any gas bubbles with greased toothpick. Bake as directed.
— Sunday dinner hint: Make rolls according to favorite recipe and put on pans. Cover and freeze immediately. When you leave for church, remove rolls from freezer and leave at room temperature. When you return they will have risen and be ready to bake (takes about 3 hours). Fresh rolls for dinner! Do not freeze longer than 3 weeks.
—Mary Kathryn Yoder,
   Garden City, Mo.

Notes
   1.
Ross Hall, "Nutrition: An Ailing Science," *Atlas World Press Review*, Vol. 22, No. 2, February, 1975, p. 24.
   2.
D. P. Burkitt, A. R. P. Walker, and N. S. Painter, "Dietary Fiber and Disease," *Journal of the American Medical Association*, Vol. 229, No. 8, Aug. 19, 1974, p. 1071.

Honey
Whole Wheat Bread

Makes 2 loaves
375°
40-45 min.

Combine in mixer bowl:
  3 c. whole wheat flour
  ½ c. nonfat dry milk
  1 T. salt
  2 pkg. dry yeast
Heat in saucepan until warm:
  3 c. water or potato water
  ½ c. honey
  2 T. oil
Pour warm (not hot) liquid over flour
mixture. Beat with electric mixer 3
minutes. Stir in:
  1 additional c. whole wheat flour
  4-4½ c. white flour
Knead 5 minutes, using additional white
flour if necessary. Place in greased bowl,
turn, let rise until double in bulk. Punch
down, divide dough in half and shape
into loaves. Place in greased 9x5" bread
pans. Cover and let rise 40-45 minutes.
Bake at 375° for 40-45 minutes.

Options:

Replace 1 c. whole wheat flour with soy
flour.

Add ¼ c. wheat germ.

Bonnie Zook, Leola, Pa.
Bob Friesen, Fresno, Calif.

High Protein
Whole Wheat Bread

Makes 2 loaves
375°
35 min.

Dissolve:
  2 pkg. dry yeast in
  ½ c. warm water
  1 t. sugar
Warm in a saucepan to 130°:
  1 c. water
  1 c. milk
  3 T. sugar
  2 T. margarine
  1 T. salt
Pour into large mixer bowl. Add:
  yeast mixture
  ⅔ c. dry milk powder
  ⅓ c. soy flour
  3 T. wheat germ
  1½ c. whole wheat flour
  1 c. white flour
Beat at medium speed 3 minutes. By
hand stir in:
  1½ c. whole wheat flour
  1 c. white flour
Turn out onto floured board and knead 10
minutes, using:
  1 additional c. white flour
Let rise until doubled. Punch down and
knead briefly. Let rest 10 minutes. Divide
dough and place in two 9x5" greased
loaf pans. Let rise until almost doubled.
Brush with beaten egg and sprinkle with
sesame seeds. Bake at 375° for 35
minutes.

Jean Miller, Akron, Pa.

**Flours vary widely in moisture
content. A good practice with
any kneaded bread is to reserve
the last cup to add as
necessary, a little at a time,
during kneading.**

Easy No-Knead Whole Wheat Bread

T·S

Makes 2 loaves
375°
35-40 min.

Combine in large mixer bowl:
    3 c. whole wheat flour
    ½ c. sugar
    2 T. salt
    3 pkg. dry yeast
Heat in saucepan until very warm
(120-130°):
    2 c. water
    2 c. milk
    ½ c. oil
Add to dry ingredients:
    warmed liquids
    2 eggs
Blend at low speed until moistened. Beat 3 minutes at medium speed. Stir in by hand:
    5-6 c. white flour
Use enough flour to form a stiff batter. Cover and let rise until double. Stir down and spoon into 2 greased 9x5″ bread pans. Bake immediately at 375° for 35-40 minutes. Remove from pans and cool on rack.

Elsie Dyck, Akron, Pa.

Pilgrim's Bread

A light bread with a lovely blend of flavors.

Makes 2 loaves
375°
45 min.

Combine in a bowl:
    ½ c. yellow cornmeal
    ⅓ c. brown sugar
    1 T. salt
Stir gradually into:
    2 c. boiling water

Add:
    ¼ c. oil
Cool to lukewarm.
Dissolve:
    2 pkg. dry yeast in
    ½ c. warm water
Add yeast to cornmeal mixture.
Beat in:
    ¾ c. whole wheat flour
    ½ c. rye flour
By hand stir in:
    4¼-4½ c. unbleached white flour
Turn onto lightly floured surface. Knead until smooth and elastic. Place in a lightly greased bowl, turning once to grease surface. Cover and let rise in warm place until double. Punch dough down; turn out onto lightly floured surface. Divide in half and knead a second time for 3 minutes. Shape dough into 2 loaves and place in greased pans. Cover and let rise again in warm place until double in bulk. Bake at 375° about 45 minutes.

Ruth B. Hess, Akron, Pa.

Ruggenbrot (Rye Bread)

Makes 2 loaves
350°
35-40 min.

Dissolve in large bowl:
    1 pkg. dry yeast in
    1 c. warm water
Add:
    1 c. scalded milk, cooled
    1 T. salt
    2 T. melted fat or oil
    2 T. molasses or brown sugar
    2 c. fine rye flour
Beat until smooth. Slowly blend in:
    4½ c. white flour
Turn dough onto floured surface. Knead 5-10 minutes. Let rest 20 minutes. Punch down and divide dough into 2 equal portions; shape into loaves. Place in greased bread pans, cover and let rise until double. Bake at 350° for 35-40 minutes. Butter tops after removing from oven.

Lena Schmidt, Newton, Kan.

Heidelberg Rye Bread

Makes 2 loaves
400°
25-30 min.

Combine in large mixer bowl:
3 c. flour
2 pkg. dry yeast
¼ c. cocoa
1 T. caraway seeds (optional)
Heat in a saucepan until warm (120°):
2 c. water
⅓ c. molasses
2 T. margarine
1 t. sugar
1 t. salt
Add to dry mixture in mixer bowl, beating at low speed ½ minute, scraping sides of bowl constantly. Beat 3 minutes at high speed.
Stir in by hand:
3-3½ c. rye flour
Turn onto floured surface; knead until smooth, about 5 minutes. Cover; let rest 20 minutes. Punch dough down; divide in half. Shape each half into a round loaf, place on greased baking sheets or 8" pie plates. Brush surface of loaves with a little oil and slash with sharp knife. Let rise until double, 45-60 minutes. Bake at 400° for 25-30 minutes.

Kathy Hostetler, Akron, Pa.

Three-Flour Bread

Makes 3 loaves
450°/350°
25-30 min.

Dissolve in large bowl:
2 pkg. dry yeast in
1 c. warm water
Stir in:
1 T. salt
¼ c. vegetable oil
¼ c. honey or molasses
3 c. warm water
Mix in:
1 c. dry milk powder
1 c. rye flour
¼ c. soy flour
¼ c. wheat germ
4 c. whole wheat or graham flour
5 or more cups white flour
Turn out on floured surface and knead until smooth, adding more flour if needed. Place in greased bowl, turning once. Cover and put in warm place to rise until doubled, about 2 hours. Turn out onto floured surface, knead, and place in 3 greased 9x5" pans. Let rise until almost double; place in cold oven and set at 450° for 10 minutes. Turn down to 350° and bake 25-30 minutes.

Marcia Beachy, DeKalb, Ill.
Rosemary Moyer, North Newton, Kan.

Oatmeal Bread
Oatmeal bread makes delicious toast.

Makes 2 loaves
350°
30-40 min.

Combine in large bowl:
1 c. quick oats
½ c. whole wheat flour
½ c. brown sugar
1 T. salt
2 T. margarine
Pour over:
2 c. boiling water

Be gentle
when you touch bread.
Let it not lie
uncared for, unwanted.
So often bread
is taken for granted.

Stir in to combine.
Dissolve:

**1 pkg. dry yeast in
½ c. warm water**

When batter is cooled to lukewarm, add yeast.
Stir in:

5 c. white flour

When dough is stiff enough to handle, turn onto floured board and knead 5-10 minutes. Place in greased bowl, cover, and let rise until doubled. Punch down and let rise again. Shape into 2 loaves and place in greased 9x5x3" pans. Bake at 350° for 30-40 minutes. Cool on rack, brushing loaves with margarine for a soft crust.

*Ella Rohrer, Orrville, Ohio
Carol Ann Maust, Upland, Calif.*

Cornmeal Yeast Bread

Makes 2 loaves
350°
30-45 min.

Dissolve:

**2 pkg. dry yeast in
½ c. lukewarm water**

Combine in mixing bowl:

**½ c. sugar
1½ t. salt
⅓ c. butter or margarine**

Pour over:

¾ c. milk, scalded

Cool to lukewarm. Stir in:

**1 egg
1 c. white flour
¾ c. cornmeal
yeast mixture**

Beat well. Stir in enough additional flour to make a soft dough:

3-3½ c. flour

Turn dough onto lightly floured board and knead until satiny, about 10 minutes. Place dough in greased bowl; cover and let rise in warm place until double in size, about 1 hour. Punch dough down. Divide in half and place in 2 greased 8" loaf pans. Brush with melted margarine.

Cover and let rise in warm place until nearly double, about 45 minutes. Bake at 350° for 30-45 minutes or until golden brown.

Kathy Hostetler, Akron, Pa.

Round-Loaf Herb Bread

Deliciously fragrant and moist; slice and serve warm with bean soup.

Makes 2 loaves
350°
45 min.

Dissolve:

**2 pkg. dry yeast in
½ c. warm water**

Sauté in small skillet until onion is tender:

**3 T. cooking oil
½ c. chopped onion**

Combine in mixer bowl:

**sautéed onion
1⅔ c. evaporated milk (1 can)
    OR 1½ c. milk plus ½ c. nonfat
    dry milk powder
½ c. chopped parsley
3 T. sugar
1 t. salt
½ t. dried dillweed
¼ t. thyme**

Beat in:

**yeast mixture
1 c. cornmeal
2 c. whole wheat flour**

Stir in by hand:

2½ c. additional whole wheat flour

Turn out on lightly floured surface. Knead 5 minutes. Place in greased bowl, turning once to grease surface. Cover and let rise till double, about 1 hour. Punch down; divide in half. Place in 2 well-greased 1-pound coffee cans. Cover and let rise until double, 30-45 minutes. Bake at 350° for 45 minutes, covering loosely with foil if bread becomes too brown.

Author's Recipe

Pinto Bean Bread

Makes 2 loaves
350°
50 min.

Blend in large bowl:

**2 c. scalded milk, cooled to
lukewarm**
2 pkg. dry yeast

Add:

**2 c. cooked, mashed, unseasoned
pinto beans**
2 T. sugar
2 t. salt
2 T. shortening

Stir in:

5-6 c. flour

Add enough flour to handle dough easily. Turn onto floured board and knead until smooth and elastic. Place in greased bowl, turning once. Cover and let rise in warm place until double in size, about 1 hour. Punch down, cover, let rise again until almost double. Divide dough into two portions and shape into loaves. Place in greased pans; cover, let rise until almost double in bulk, about 45 minutes. Bake at 350° about 50 minutes.

Elaine Schmidt, Greeley, Colo.

Dill Bread

Makes 1 loaf
350°
30 min.

Dissolve:

1 pkg. yeast in
¼ c. warm water

Combine in mixing bowl:

1 c. cottage cheese
2 t. dill seed
2 t. salt
¼ t. soda
1 unbeaten egg
1 T. melted butter or margarine
½ T. minced onion
2 T. sugar

Add:

yeast mixture
2¼-2½ c. sifted flour

Stir well to combine. Let rise in greased bowl to double in size. Punch down. Put into two 7x3″ or one 9x5″ well-greased bread pans. Let rise again, about 45-50 minutes. Bake at 350° about 30 minutes. Remove from pans and brush with melted margarine.

Option:

For a finer grain, add enough additional flour to handle easily and knead 5-10 minutes.

Selma Johnson, North Newton, Kan.
MCC Dining Hall, Akron, Pa.

---

*When mixing baked goods, put
in the bottom of each cup of
flour called for:*
1 T. soy flour
1 T. dry milk solids
1 T. wheat germ
*Fill cup with flour and proceed
with recipe. OR, when pouring 5
pounds of flour into kitchen
canister stir in 1½ c. of each of
the three enriching ingredients.*
*—Jean Liechty Jordan,
Goshen, Ind.*

*There is so much beauty
in bread—*
Beauty of sun and soil,
Beauty of patient toil.
*Winds and rains have caressed it,
Christ often blessed it.*
*Be gentle
when you touch bread.*
—Author unknown

Easy French Bread

Commercial French bread is expensive. You can make 3 or 4 loaves for the price of purchasing one.

Makes 2 loaves
400°
20 min.

Dissolve:
 2 pkg. dry yeast in
 ½ c. warm water
 ½ t. sugar
Combine:
 2 T. sugar
 2 T. fat
 2 t. salt
 2 c. boiling water
Cool to lukewarm and add yeast mixture.
Stir in:
 7½-8 c. flour
Knead 10 minutes, or until smooth and elastic. Place in greased bowl, turning once. Let rise until doubled. Punch down and let rest 15 minutes. Divide dough in half. On floured surface, roll each half to a 12x15″ rectangle. Roll up, starting at 15″ edge. Place loaves on greased cookie sheets and make 4 or 5 slashes diagonally across tops. Let rise until double.
Mix and brush on:
 1 egg, beaten
 2 T. milk
Sprinkle on, if desired:
 poppy or sesame seeds
Bake at 400° for 20 minutes.

Ernestine Lehman, Akron, Pa.

Make hot dog buns from unsliced bread. Cut thick slices of bread, cut each slice in half, and make a slit for the hot dog.
—Gayle Gerber Koontz and Karen Harvey, Leola, Pa.

White Bread

Makes 4 loaves
350°
30-35 min.

Dissolve:
 2 pkg. dry yeast in
 ½ c. warm water
 1½ t. sugar
Combine in large mixer bowl:
 ½ c. sugar
 1 T. salt
 ¼ c. lard or shortening
 3 c. warm water
 yeast mixture
Add:
 5 c. flour
Beat with electric mixer 3 minutes.
Stir in by hand:
 6 c. flour
Turn onto floured board and knead 5 minutes. Place in greased bowl, turning once, cover and let rise ½ hour. Punch down; turn over and let rise again until double. Knead a few minutes, then shape into 4 loaves and place in greased 9x5″ loaf pans. Cover loaves with damp cloth and let rise until doubled. Bake at 350° for 30-35 minutes. Brush tops with margarine if desired.

Louetta Hurst, Lancaster, Pa.

Whole Wheat Rolls

Makes 4 doz. rolls
375°
20-25 min.

Dissolve:
 2 pkg. dry yeast in
 ¾ c. lukewarm water
Combine in large bowl:
 3 c. warm water
 1 c. dry milk powder
 ½ c. soft shortening, margarine, or oil

2 eggs
⅓ c. sugar
2 t. salt
yeast mixture

Have ready:
6 c. white flour
4 c. whole wheat flour

Add 5 c. flour and beat thoroughly, by hand or with electric mixer. Stir in an additional 3 c. flour. Turn dough onto floured board and use 2 more c. flour to knead until smooth and elastic. Let rise in greased bowl until doubled in bulk. Punch down and shape into dinner or cinnamon rolls. Let rise and bake 20-25 minutes at 375°.

MCC Dining Hall, Akron, Pa.

High-Protein Rolls

Makes 2 doz. rolls
350°
20-25 min.

Dissolve:
2 pkg. dry yeast in
½ c. lukewarm water

Heat until lukewarm:
2 c. cottage cheese

Combine in large bowl:
cottage cheese
¼ c. sugar
2 t. salt
½ t. baking soda
2 eggs, slightly beaten
yeast mixture

Gradually add:
4-4½ c. sifted flour

Turn onto floured board and knead 5 minutes. Put dough in a greased bowl, turning once. Let rise in warm place until doubled, about 1½ hours. Punch down. Turn dough onto lightly floured surface. Divide dough into 24 equal pieces and shape into balls. Place balls in two greased 9" baking pans. Bake at 350° for 20-25 minutes or until golden.

Option:

Replace 1-2 c. white flour with whole wheat flour.

Gladys Longacre, Susquehanna, Pa.

Edna Ruth Byler's Potato Dough Baked Goods

100 doughnuts or rolls
375° deep fat/400° oven

Dissolve:
3 pkg. dry yeast in
1 c. lukewarm water

Mix in large bowl:
1 qt. scalded milk
2 c. mashed potatoes (no milk added)
1 c. fat (half butter, half margarine)
1 c. sugar

Let cool to lukewarm, then add:
yeast mixture
6 c. flour

Let stand until mixture foams up (about 20 minutes).

Add:
2 eggs, beaten
1 T. salt
11-12 c. additional flour

A little more flour may be needed, but dough should be soft. Turn out on floured board and knead until satiny. Let raise in warm place until doubled in bulk.

Doughnuts: Roll out dough, cut doughnuts, place on trays and let raise until not quite double. Fry in hot shortening (375°). When drained and while still hot dip in glaze mixture. Insert a stick through holes and let a number of doughnuts drain over glaze bowl until next ones are ready to do.

Glaze:
Combine:
1 lb. powdered sugar
1 T. margarine
1 t. vanilla
dash of mace
enough rich milk to make thin icing

Cinnamon buns: Prepare a mixture of butter and margarine and a mixture of sugar, brown sugar, and cinnamon. Roll a piece of dough to about 18x9". Spread dough with butter mixture and sprinkle over some of the sugar mixture. Roll up the dough as for jelly roll. Cut 1½" chunks and place in greased pans, pressing down lightly on each chunk. Cover and let raise in warm place until nearly double. Bake at 400° for 15-20 minutes or until browned. These may be iced with doughnut glaze as soon as they are taken from the oven.

Sticky buns: Handle dough same as for cinnamon buns, except make a mixture of brown and white sugar, cinnamon, and a little white corn syrup and water. Spread in bottom of heavily greased pans with nuts, if desired, before putting in rolls. Immediately after baking, invert pans over trays and let syrup run down before removing pans.

Dinner rolls: Shape dough as desired, place on greased pans, and bake at 400° starting on a lower rack and changing to upper rack about halfway through for 15 minutes of baking time. Brush tops lightly with butter to remove any floury appearance.

Coffee cake: A good way to use all the leftover bits of dough—put dough in greased pan, dab or punch holes in it, and spread leftover sugar, syrup, or butter mixtures over. Let raise and bake as for cinnamon buns.

To freeze: Let baked goods cool. Wrap or place in large plastic bags and freeze the same day.

Edna Ruth Byler, Akron, Pa.

Raised Coffee Cake (Blechkuchen)

Traditional among Prussian Mennonites when guests come for Sunday afternoon coffee. "Blech" is a large baking pan.

Makes 2 large cakes
375°
20 min.

Scald and cool to lukewarm:
 3 c. milk
Stir together to dissolve:
 2 pkg. dry yeast
 1 c. warm water
Combine in large bowl:
 lukewarm milk
 yeast mixture
 1½ c. soft shortening or lard
 ½ c. sugar
 4 t. salt
 1 egg
 6 c. flour
Beat well until dough is smooth and satiny.
Stir in:
 1 c. raisins combined with
 ¾ c. flour
Cover and let rise in a warm place until doubled. With back of spoon spread dough thinly onto 2 greased 10x15" cookie sheets. Brush generously with melted margarine and sprinkle with sugar.
Bake 20 minutes at 375°.

Elsie Epp, Marion, S.D.

Brown Breadsticks

Makes 6 doz. breadsticks
325°
30 min.

Dissolve:
 1 pkg. dry yeast in
 1 c. warm water

Mix in large bowl:
1 c. melted shortening or oil
3 T. honey
2 t. salt
1 c. boiling water
When lukewarm, add:
2 beaten eggs
1 t. honey
dissolved yeast
Stir in gradually:
6 c. whole wheat flour
Mix well, but do not knead. Place in refrigerator to chill one hour or more. When chilled, break off pieces of dough with well-floured hands. Make into balls the size of a baseball, then roll the ball between hands to form a long roll. Divide each roll into 8 pieces and roll each pencil-thin. Place thin rolls on greased cookie sheets. Let rise until double in bulk. Bake at 325° until crisp, about 30 minutes. Serve plain or with dips.

Options:
Roll thin rolls into sesame or sunflower seeds, or sprinkle with garlic salt.
Add 1 c. shredded cheese when mixing dough.

LaVonne Platt, Newton, Kan.

English Muffins

Makes 18 muffins

Heat in a saucepan until very warm (130°):
1½ c. milk
¼ c. margarine
In large mixer bowl, combine:
2 T. sugar
1 t. salt
1 pkg. dry yeast
1½ c. flour
With mixer at low speed, gradually beat liquid into dry ingredients. Increase speed and beat 2 minutes, or beat vigorously by hand.
Beat in:
1 egg
1 c. flour

With spoon, add:
2 c. flour, or enough to make
stiff dough
Turn dough onto lightly floured surface and knead just until well mixed, about 2 minutes. Shape dough into a ball and place in greased large bowl, turning once. Cover; let rise in warm place until doubled, about 1½ hours. Punch down. Turn onto lightly floured surface; cover with bowl 15 minutes, and let dough rest. Meanwhile, place cornmeal in a pie plate. Roll dough about ⅜" thick. Cut dough into 3" circles; reroll scraps to make 18 circles in all. Dip both sides of each circle in cornmeal; place circles on cookie sheets. Cover and let rise in warm place until doubled, about 45 minutes. Brush large skillet with salad oil and heat. When medium hot, put in 6 muffins, cook 8 minutes on each side or until brown. Repeat until all are cooked. To serve, split muffins horizontally with tines of fork and toast.

Ruth Detweiler, Akron, Pa

Master Baking Mix

Makes 8 or 4 lbs.

8 lbs.	4 lbs.
Sift together 3 times:	
5 lbs.	**10 c. flour**
¾ c.	**6 T. baking powder**
3 T.	**1½ T. salt**
1 T.	**1½ t. cream of tartar**
½ c.	**¼ c. sugar**
Cut in to consistency of cornmeal:	
2 lbs.	**2 c. vegetable shortening**
Stir in:	
4 c.	**2 c. dry milk powder**

Store in covered container at room temperature. To measure baking mix, pile lightly into a cup and level off with spatula.

Options:
Replace ⅓ of the white flour with whole wheat flour.

Add 2 c. untoasted wheat germ to large recipe, 1 c. to small recipe.

Replace 3 c. flour in large recipe or 1½ c. flour in small recipe with soy flour.

Dry milk powder in the mix is optional, but assures higher protein products.

June Suderman, Hillsboro, Kan.
Roberta Kreider, Osceola, Ind.

Corn Bread

Serves 8
400°
20-25 min.

Preheat oven to 400°.
Stir together in a bowl:
1½ c. Master Mix
2 T. sugar
½ t. salt
¾ c. cornmeal
1 t. chili powder (optional)
Combine in a separate bowl:
1 egg
¾ c. milk
1 c. cream-style corn
Stir liquids into dry ingredients just until flour is all moistened. Pour into greased 9″ square pan and bake 20-25 minutes.

Options:

Add ¼ c. chopped green pepper.

For crunchy topping, sprinkle on ½ c. grated cheese and 2 T. sesame seed before baking.

Add ¼ c. bran.

Pancakes or Waffles

Serves 4

Beat together in a bowl:
1 c. milk
1 egg
Stir in:
1½ c. Master Mix
Bake on hot griddle or waffle iron. For lighter waffles, separate egg; add yolk with milk. Beat egg white until stiff and fold into batter just before baking.
Increase milk for thinner batter if desired.

Biscuits

Makes 8 biscuits
450°
10 min.

Preheat oven to 450°.
Combine in bowl:
1½ c. Master Mix
⅓ c. milk
Add milk all at once, stirring 25 strokes. Knead lightly on floured board. Roll ½″ thick, cut, and place on ungreased baking sheet. Bake 10 minutes.

Options:

Add grated cheese, chopped herbs.

Increase milk to ½ c. for drop biscuits.

Use as topping on casseroles, cobblers, meat and vegetable pies, or wherever biscuit dough is called for.

Coffee Cake

Serves 6
375°
25 min.

Preheat oven to 375°.
Beat together in a bowl:
⅓ c. milk
1 egg
Add:
¼ c. sugar
2¼ c. Master Mix
Stir until well blended (about 1 minute). Pour into greased 8″ square baking pan. Combine and sprinkle over:
½ c. brown sugar
3 T. margarine
½ t. cinnamon
¼ c. chopped nuts (optional)
Bake 25 minutes. Serve warm.

Muffins

Makes 12 muffins
425°
20 min.

Preheat oven to 425°.
Beat together in a bowl:
- **1 egg**
- **1 c. milk**
- **2 T. sugar**

Add:
- **3 c. Master Mix**

Stir just until dry ingredients are moistened. Spoon into greased muffin pans and bake 20 minutes.

Options:

Add drained fruit, chopped nuts or chopped dried fruit.

Replace one third of mix called for with quick-cooking oatmeal or all-bran cereal.

Add chopped dried fruit and/or nuts to muffin recipe and bake as a fruit bread; use greased 5x8" loaf pan and bake 40 minutes at 350°

Graham Gems

An old recipe and still perfect to fill out a skimpy meal.

Makes 12 muffins
375°
15 min.

Preheat oven to 375°.
Combine in mixing bowl:
- **1 c. graham or whole wheat flour**
- **1 c. white flour**
- **1 t. soda**
- **¼ c. dark brown sugar**
- **¼ t. salt**
- **½ c. raisins (optional)**

Make a well and add:
- **1 egg, beaten**
- **1 c. buttermilk or sour milk**
- **3 T. melted fat**

Stir only until blended. Fill greased muffin tins half full and bake 15 minutes. Serve hot.

Elizabeth Showalter, Waynesboro, Va.

Refrigerator Bran Muffins

These are delicious hot or cold. Bake and serve as cupcakes by adding a sprinkling of brown sugar and nuts of granola before putting in the oven.

T·S

Makes 4-5 doz.
400°
20 min.

Place in bowl:
- **2 c. ready-to-eat bran cereal**

Pour over:
- **2 c. boiling water**

Set aside to cool.
Cream together in large mixing bowl:
- **1 c. shortening or margarine**
- **1½ c. sugar**
- **4 eggs**

Add and beat in:
- **1 qt. buttermilk**
- **soaked bran mixture**

Sift together:
- **5 c. flour**
- **5 t. soda**
- **1 t. salt**

Add dry ingredients to creamed mixture and fold until flour is moistened.
Fold in:
- **4 c. additional *dry* bran cereal**

Store batter in covered containers in refrigerator. Keeps 3-4 weeks. When ready to bake, preheat oven to 400° and fill well-greased muffin tins ⅔ full. Bake 20 minutes.

Option:

Add raisins and/or nuts just before baking.

Carol Welty, Akron, Pa.
Faye Brenneman, Palmer Lake, Colo.

Crumb Muffins

Makes 12 muffins
375°
25 min.

Preheat oven to 375°.
Combine in mixing bowl:
   1 large egg, slightly beaten
   1 c. milk
   ¼ c. melted margarine
   1 c. dry bread crumbs
Stir and set aside.
Sift together:
   1 c. flour
   1 T. sugar
   ½ t. salt
   1 T. baking powder
Fold dry ingredients into liquids. Stir just
until all is moistened. Fill greased muffin
tins ⅔ full. Bake 25 minutes.

Sandra Miller, Akron, Pa.

Cinnamon-Topped Oatmeal Muffins

Makes 12 muffins
425°
15 min.

Preheat oven to 425°
Sift together into mixing bowl:
   1 c. sifted flour
   ¼ c. sugar
   3 t. baking powder
   ½ t. salt
Stir in:
   1 c. quick or old-fashioned oats
   ½ c. raisins
Add:
   3 T. oil
   1 egg, beaten
   1 c. milk
Stir only until dry ingredients are
moistened. Fill greased muffin cups ⅔
full. Sprinkle with cinnamon topping:
   2 T. sugar
   2 t. flour
   1 t. cinnamon
   1 t. melted butter
Bake 15 minutes.

Anna Ens, Winnipeg, Man.

Whole Wheat Pineapple Muffins

Makes 12 muffins
400°
15-20 min.

Preheat oven to 400°.
Sift together:
   1 c. white flour
   1 c. whole wheat flour
   3 t. baking powder
   ½ t. salt
Set aside.
In small bowl, cream together until fluffy:
   ¼ c. sugar
   ¼ c. margarine
Add:
   1 egg
Beat well; stir in:
   1 c. crushed pineapple, undrained
Add dry ingredients to creamed mixture
and stir just enough to moisten flour. Fill
greased muffin tins ⅔ full. Bake 15-20
minutes. Remove from tins at once. Serve
hot.

Alice and Willard Roth, Elkhart, Ind.

Whole Wheat Buttermilk Pancakes

Serves 3

Combine in a bowl and mix with fork:
   1 c. buttermilk
   2 T. vegetable oil
   1 egg
Add and mix only until moistened:
   ½ c. whole wheat flour
   ½ c. unbleached, white flour
      (part soy flour and wheat germ
      can be used)
   1 t. baking powder
   ½ t. baking soda
   ½ t. salt
Fry in hot, lightly greased skillet.

Marcia Beachy, DeKalb, Ill.

Pancake Mix

Costs half as much as commercial mix and milk is included.

2 lbs.	4 lbs.

Combine in large bowl:

6 c. flour	**12 c. flour**
1 T. salt	**2 T. salt**
6 T. baking powder	**¾ c. baking powder**
6 T. sugar	**¾ c. sugar**
2 c. powdered milk	**4 c. powdered milk**

Mix well and store in airtight container on cupboard shelf.

To use:
Combine in a bowl:

1 egg (beat with fork)
1 c. water
2 T. melted fat or oil
1½ c. pancake mix

Fry on hot ungreased griddle.
Serves 3-4.

Options:

Replace one third white flour with buckwheat flour, whole wheat flour, oatmeal, or rye flour and cornmeal.

Replace one sixth of the flour with soy flour.

Add 1 c. wheat germ to small recipe, 2 c. to large recipe.

Karen Rix, Fonda, Iowa

Basic Biscuits

Makes 18-20 biscuits
425°
10-12 min.

Preheat oven to 425°.
Sift together in a bowl:

2 c. sifted flour
3 t. baking powder
½ t. salt

Cut in:

¼ c. shortening

Add all at once, stirring until soft ball is formed:

¾ c. milk

Turn dough onto floured board; knead lightly 20 to 25 times. Roll or pat dough ½" thick. Cut with floured biscuit cutter or glass. Place on ungreased baking sheet and bake 10-12 minutes. Serve hot. Makes 18-20.

Option:

Cheese Drop Biscuits: Stir 1 c. grated cheese into flour mixture before cutting in shortening. Increase milk to 1 c. and drop onto cookie sheet by tablespoonfuls.

Miriam LeFever, East Petersburg, Pa.

For more nutritious cinnamon rolls I sprinkle the dough with wheat germ along with cinnamon and sugar.
—*Pauline Wyse, Mt. Pleasant, Iowa*

Sweet rolls made with yeast dough are economical desserts or snacks because they do not contain as much sugar as cakes and cookies—and they still satisfy the sweet tooth.
—*Elsie Epp, Marion, S.D.*

This Christmas I baked special yeast breads instead of cookies to save sugar.
—*Anna Mary Brubacher, St. Jacobs, Ont.*

Wheat Germ Griddle Cakes

Wheat germ adds vitamins and protein to pancakes without making them heavy.

Serves 6-8

Beat together at medium speed of electric mixer for one minute, or whirl in blender:

1½ c. wheat germ
2¼ c. milk
3 eggs
6 T. salad oil
1¼ c. white flour
4 t. baking powder
1 T. sugar
1½ t. salt
½ t. cinnamon
¼ t. ginger
⅛ t. mace

Bake on hot griddle.

Option:

For crispy waffles, reserve egg whites, beat until stiff, and fold into batter just before baking. Thin batter slightly with milk.

Selma Johnson, North Newton, Kan.

Apple-Walnut Pancakes

Serves 4

Combine in bowl:

1 c. whole wheat flour
1 c. white flour
1 t. salt
2 t. baking powder
1 T. brown sugar

Combine in separate bowl:

2 c. milk
2 eggs, well beaten
2 T. oil

Add liquids to dry ingredients and stir until just mixed.

Add:

1 c. diced apples
½ c. chopped walnuts

Bake on moderately hot, lightly greased griddle.

Options:

Use yogurt or juice in place of milk.

Substitute another whole grain flour or cornmeal for ½ c. whole wheat flour.

Use other fruit, drained and chopped, in place of apples.

Rosemary Nachtigall, Reedley, Calif.

Grandmother's Russian Pancakes (Pflinzen)

Serves 4-5

Combine in mixing bowl:

2 eggs, beaten
2 c. flour
2 c. milk
½ t. salt

Whirl in blender or use rotary beater. Melt and keep hot:

⅓ c. fat or oil

Heat 10" skillet until medium hot. Add approximately 1 t. hot fat to skillet and pour in about ¼ c. pancake batter, tilting skillet with left hand to allow batter to run over entire surface. Turn in a minute or two when underside is browned. Remove to serving plate and keep warm. Repeat with remaining batter, adding small amount hot fat to skillet each time. Finished pancakes should be thin and slightly crisp on the edges. Serve pancakes with cinnamon-sugar, honey, syrup, applesauce or other fruit sauce. Traditionally each person adds filling and rolls the pancake with a fork, then cuts into bite-size pieces.

Option:

Use this whole wheat recipe with same method:

    3 eggs
    1½ c. milk
    ½ t. salt
    1 T. oil
    1 c. whole wheat flour
    1 T. soy flour

Helen and Adam Mueller,
  Cape Girardeau, Mo.
Eleanor Hiebert, Elkins Park, Pa.

Coconut Pancakes

Serve for dessert or a gourmet brunch if you live where fresh coconuts are cheap.

Serves 4-6

Combine in a bowl:

    2 c. flour
    ½ c. sugar
    2 t. baking powder

Add:

    1 egg, beaten
    ¼ fresh coconut, shredded
    ¼ t. cardamom powder
    ½ t. salt
    2½ c. milk

Stir until smooth. Prepare filling. Combine in saucepan:

    1½ c. brown sugar
    ¾ fresh coconut, shredded
    ¾ c. milk
    ¼ c. raisins

Cook, stirring frequently, until mixture is thick and liquid absorbed.
Heat 1 t. margarine in 9" skillet. Pour in a small amount of batter, tilting skillet to spread batter thinly over entire bottom. Cook until nearly dry on top. Add a narrow strip of filling and roll up. Repeat with remaining batter and filling, keeping pancakes warm in oven. Serve hot.

LaVonne Platt, Newton, Kan.

High Protein Pancakes or Waffles

High protein, low calorie. Contributor says "as waffles these are good warmed over in the toaster in case any survive the first round."

Serves 3

Combine in a blender:

    1 c. cream-style cottage cheese
    4 eggs
    ½ c. flour
    ¼ t. salt
    ¼ c. oil
    ½ c. milk
    ½ t. vanilla

Whirl at high speed 1 minute. Bake on lightly greased griddle or waffle iron. Serves 3 as main dish.

Option:

Beat well with mixer or rotary beater instead of in blender.

Danita Laskowski
Alice Lapp, Goshen, Ind.

Whole Wheat Yeast Waffles

Wonderfully light and crisp. Children love them with peanut butter, which makes an extra high protein meal.

Serves 6

Combine in mixing bowl:

    ½ c. water
    2 T. sugar
    1 pkg. dry yeast

Stir and allow to stand 5 minutes. Add to yeast mixture:

    1½ c. sweet or sour milk,
        buttermilk, or yogurt
    3 egg yolks (reserve whites)
    ⅔ c. oil
    ½ c. untoasted wheat germ
        (optional)

Sift in:

    1½ c. whole wheat flour
    ½ c. nonfat dry milk powder
    1 t. salt

Stir to blend. Let rise in warm place 2 hours or longer, stirring down each time batter has doubled in bulk. Just before baking, fold in:

3 egg whites, stiffly beaten

Bake on preheated waffle iron.

Option:

Mix batter in the evening, omitting eggs. Let rise once or twice, stir down and set in refrigerator overnight. Remove from refrigerator 30 minutes before baking. Stir egg yolks into batter, then fold in egg whites just before baking.

Don Ziegler, Lancaster, Pa.

Fruit Syrup For Pancakes

Combine in saucepan:

½-¾ c. sugar
3 T. cornstarch

Add:

2 c. water

Bring to boil, stirring constantly. Add:

2 c. sliced fresh peaches

Simmer until fruit is tender. Remove from heat and add:

2 T. lemon juice.

Serve hot with pancakes.

Option:

Use mangoes, raspberries, strawberries, blueberries, cherries, or pineapple. Canned or frozen fruit may be used—reduce sugar and use juice to replace part of the water.

Norma Johnson, Lobatse, Botswana

Maple Syrup

Combine in saucepan:

1¾ c. white sugar
¼ c. brown sugar
1 c. water

Bring to boil, cover, and cook 1 minute. Cool slightly. Add:

½ t. vanilla
½ t. maple flavoring

Cover saucepan for a few minutes as syrup cooks to melt down crystals; helps prevent syrup from crystallizing later in storage.

Elsie Epp, Marion, S.D.

Pineapple Sauce

Melt in saucepan:

3 T. margarine

Add:

1 c. crushed pineapple
2 T. brown sugar

Heat 5 minutes, stirring until clear and thick. When sauce cooks down a bit, add dash mace or nutmeg.

Use hot or cold.

Makes about 1 cup. Serve with pancakes, waffles, or on ice cream.

Alice and Willard Roth, Elkhart, Ind.

Economy Pancake Syrup

Combine in saucepan:

1 c. brown sugar, lightly packed
3 c. water
5 t. cornstarch

Cook until slightly thickened. Add:

1 t. maple flavoring

Store in refrigerator.

Lois Hess, Columbus, Ohio
Helen Burkholder, St. Catherines, Ont.

Basic Corn Bread

T·S

Serves 9
400°
25 min.

Preheat oven to 400°.
Mix together:
  1 c. cornmeal
  **1 c. flour (may use part or all
    whole wheat)**
  4 t. baking powder
  ½ t. salt
  2 T. brown sugar
  ½ c. dry milk powder (optional)
Make a well and add:
  2 beaten eggs
  1 c. milk
  ¼ c. oil or melted shortening
Stir just until smooth. Pour into a greased
9x9" pan and bake 25 minutes. Serve hot
with butter, syrup, honey or milk.

Options:

Reduce cornmeal to ¾ cup. Add 3 T. soy
flour, 3 T. wheat germ, 3 T. bran.
To use sour milk in place of sweet,
reduce baking powder to 2 t. and add 1 t.
soda.

Esther Landis, Lancaster, Pa.
Eleanor Hiebert, Elkins Park, Pa.

Indian Corn Pone

Serves 2

Combine in a bowl:
  1 c. cornmeal
  ½ t. salt
  1 t. baking powder
Add:
  2 T. fat (bacon drippings are good)
  ½ c. milk
Grease a large, heavy skillet with bacon
drippings. Drop batter from a
tablespoon, shaping into 4 poñes. Brown
on both sides. Serve hot with butter or
margarine.

Option:
Add ¼ c. dry milk powder to increase
protein content.

LaVonne Platt, Newton, Kan.

Southern
Spoon Bread

Serves 6-8
400°
45 min.

Preheat oven to 400°.
Combine in saucepan:
  1 c. cornmeal
  2 T. margarine
  3 c. milk
Bring to a boil, stirring constantly. When
thickened, remove from heat.
Add:
  4 eggs, beaten
  1 c. milk
  ½ t. salt
Beat well. Pour into 2 qt. greased
casserole and bake 45 minutes. Serve
with hot butter or margarine.

Elizabeth Showalter, Waynesboro, Va.

Sopa Paraguaya
(corn bread)

*Usually served by Paraguayans as a
meat accompaniment.*

Serves 8
375°
30 min.

Heat oven to 375°.
Combine in large mixing bowl:
  ½ c. white flour
  2¼ c. fine cornmeal
  1 T. sugar
  1½ t. salt
  1½ t. baking powder
  2½ c. grated cheese (⅔ lb.)
Set aside.
Sauté in skillet until transparent:
  ¼ c. oil
  2 medium onions, chopped

Beat together in small bowl:
2 eggs
1½ c. milk
Add onions with oil and egg-milk mixture to dry ingredients. Stir just until blended. Pour into greased 9x12" pan and bake 30 minutes.

Ruth Brown, Filadelphia, Paraguay

Three-Grain Peanut Bread

Makes 1 loaf
325°
1 hr., 10 min.

Preheat oven to 325°.
Combine in mixing bowl:
1 c. white flour
½ c. quick cooking oats
½ c. yellow cornmeal
½ c. dry milk powder
½ c. sugar
3 t. baking powder
1 t. salt
Cut in:
⅔ c. cream-style peanut butter
Blend and pour in:
1 egg
1½ c. milk
Mix well. Turn into greased and floured 9x5" loaf pan. Spread batter evenly. Bake 1 hour and 10 minutes, or until cake tester inserted in center comes out clean. Cool 10 minutes and remove from pan.

Becky Mast, State College, Pa.

Whole Wheat Orange Bread

Makes 1 loaf
350°
60-65 min.

Preheat oven to 350°.
Combine in large mixing bowl:
1½ c. whole wheat flour
1½ c. white flour
¾ c. sugar

1-2 T. grated orange peel
2 t. baking powder
½ t. salt
Add:
¾ c. fresh or reconstituted frozen orange juice
½ c. milk
½ c. cooking oil
1 egg, beaten
½ c. chopped nuts (optional)
Stir until dry particles are moistened, about 75 strokes. Pour batter into greased 9x5" or 8x4" loaf pan. Sprinkle with mixture of:
1 T. sugar
½ t. cinnamon
Bake 60-65 minutes, or until toothpick inserted in center comes out clean.

Marjorie Ruth, Akron, Pa.

Heirloom Boston Brown Bread

Makes 4 small loaves
350°
45-50 min.

Preheat oven to 350°.
Combine in mixing bowl:
2 c. graham or whole wheat flour
½ c. white flour
2 t. baking soda
1 t. salt
Add:
2 c. buttermilk or sour milk
½ c. dark molasses
1 c. raisins, chopped and lightly floured
¼ c. nuts (optional)
Mix until smooth. Spoon into either 4 well-greased 1 lb. tin cans or a ring mold. Let stand ½ hour. Bake 45-50 minutes. Cool thoroughly on cake rack before removing from cans. Wrap airtight and store 24 hours before serving.

Ruth Herr, Columbus, Ohio

Carrot-Coconut Bread

Makes 4 small loaves
350°
45-50 min.

Preheat oven to 350°.
In large bowl, sift together:
    2½ c. flour
    1 c. sugar
    1 t. baking powder
    1 t. baking soda
    1 t. cinnamon
    ½ t. salt
Combine separately and add:
    3 beaten eggs
    ½ c. cooking oil
    ½ c. milk
Stir just until dry ingredients are moistened.
Stir in:
    2 c. shredded carrots
    1⅓ c. coconut
    ½ c. raisins
    ½ c. pecans or other nuts
Turn into 4 well-greased and floured 16 oz. fruit or vegetable cans, or two 9" bread pans. Bake 45-50 minutes. Remove from cans and cool thoroughly. Wrap and refrigerate overnight or until used.

MCC Dining Hall, Akron, Pa.

Soy-Banana Bread

Soy flour is expensive among flours, but not as a source of protein. One slice has 8 grams protein (10 slices per loaf.)

Makes 1 loaf

Preheat oven to 350°.
Sift together:
    1 c. plus 2 T. soy flour
    1⅓ c. white flour
    2¾ t. baking powder
    ½ t. soda
    ¾ t. salt
    ½ c. sugar
    ⅓ c. dry milk powder
Cut into dry ingredients:
    ¼ c. shortening
Add and mix just until moistened:
    1 egg, beaten
    ⅓ c. water
    1 c. mashed bananas (2-3)
    ½ c. chopped nuts (optional)
Spread in greased 9x5x3" loaf pan. Bake 50 minutes. Remove loaf from pan to cool. Delicious warm or toasted.

Author's Recipe

Dutch Apple Bread

Makes 1 loaf
350°
55 min.

Preheat oven to 350°.
Cream together:
    ½ c. margarine
    1 c. sugar
Add and beat well:
    2 eggs
    1 t. vanilla
Combine separately:
    2 c. flour
    1 t. soda
    ½ t. salt
Add dry ingredients alternately with:
    ⅓ c. sour milk or orange juice
Fold in:
    1 c. chopped apples
    ⅓ c. chopped walnuts
Bake in greased 9x5" loaf pan for 55 minutes, or until loaf tests done.

Options:
Add ⅓ c. chopped raw cranberries.
Serve thin slices spread with whipped cream cheese.

Sandra L. Miller, Akron, Pa.

Rollkuchen

Russian Mennonites must have these
to accompany a watermelon feast.
The salty version also goes well
with soup.

Serves 6-8

Beat together:
   3 eggs
   1 c. cream, whole milk, or mixture
Sift and add:
   2 t. baking powder
   1 t. salt
   3½-4 c. flour
Add a little more flour if necessary to
make a soft dough which can be rolled
out. Roll on floured board to ¼"
thickness. Cut in 2x4" rectangles, cut slit
in each, and fry in ½" hot fat (375°) until
browned, turning once. Drain on
absorbent paper.
   Sprinkle with powdered sugar or salt
as desired.

Susan Duerksen, Killarney, Man.

Navajo Fry Bread

Serves 6

Sift into a bowl:
   4½ c. flour
   ½ t. salt
   2 t. baking powder
Stir in:
   1½ c. water
   ½ c. milk
Knead with hands. Pat or roll into circles
approximately 5" in diameter. With
fingers make small hole in center. Fry in
several inches hot oil at 400°; electric
skillet is convenient. Dough will puff and
bubble. Turn when golden brown. Drain
on absorbent paper and serve hot with
honey, or use while fresh for Navajo
Tacos *see p. 92*

Options:
Use half whole wheat flour.
Add ⅓ c. dry milk powder.

Shirley Kauffman Sager, Arriba, Colo.
Kathryn Leatherman, Goshen, Ind.

Onion Cheese Loaf

Makes 1 loaf
350°
1 hr.

Preheat oven to 350°.
Combine in mixing bowl:
   1 c. white flour
   1 c. whole wheat flour
   1 T. sugar
   3 t. baking powder
   1 t. dry mustard
   1 t. salt
Cut in until mixture resembles coarse
meal:
   ¼ c. margarine
Add and stir lightly:
   ½ c. shredded cheddar cheese
   2 T. grated Parmesan cheese
Combine separately:
   1 c. milk
   1 egg
Add all at once to cheese mixture and
mix with fork just until dry ingredients are
moistened. Turn mixture into greased
loaf pan. Sprinkle over batter:
   ½ c. finely chopped onion
   paprika
Bake 1 hour.

Ruth Gish, Mt. Joy, Pa.

Zucchini Bread

Makes 2 loaves
350°
1 hr.

Preheat oven to 350°.
Combine in mixing bowl and beat well:
   3 large eggs
   ¾ c. sugar

1 c. vegetable oil
2 c. raw, peeled, grated zucchini
1 T. vanilla
Sift together:
   3 c. flour
   1 t. salt
   1 t. baking soda
   ¼ t. baking powder
   3 t. cinnamon
Add to zucchini mixture and stir until blended.
Add:
   1 c. coarsely chopped nuts
Pour into 2 greased 8" bread pans. Bake 1 hour. Remove from pans and cool on rack.

Option:

Frozen zucchini may be used if pureed in blender.

Danita Laskowski, Goshen, Ind.

Chapatis

Indian chapatis (much like the Mexican tortilla) are one way people without ovens turn flour into bread. Traditionally they were baked on a hot rock near an open fire. Serve with rice and a simple vegetable curry, using chapatis Indian-style to scoop up the food.

Serves 4

Combine in a bowl:
   2 c. whole wheat flour
   ½ t. salt
Stir in:
   2 T. melted margarine
   ⅞ c. water (see below)
Add ¾ c. of the water, then sprinkle on an additional 2 T. as needed to make a soft dough that can be kneaded. Knead well; cover with a damp cloth and set aside for 1 hour. Knead again. Break into golf ball-sized lumps, roll into balls, and roll each out on a floured board to ¼" thick. Dust each lightly with flour.

Heat a heavy ungreased skillet. Cook each chapati 2 minutes on a side, then remove from pan, brush chapati with melted margarine, return to pan and fry until lightly browned. Or brush skillet with fat after frying each chapati. Set oven at 200° and keep chapatis warm and puffy by placing directly on lowest rack until ready to serve.

Ruth Eitzen, Barto, Pa.
Herta Janzen, Calcutta, India

Flour Tortillas

Serve warm tortillas with rice and beans, or use to make a variety of Mexican specialties

Makes 8-11 tortillas

Fresh or frozen tortillas, if available, are usually cheap; canned or dry packaged varieties are much more expensive. Flour tortillas may be made at home. A properly cooked flour tortilla remains mostly white, but is flecked with brown and puffed in spots; it has a dry look but is still soft and pliable.
Combine in mixing bowl:
   2 c. unsifted flour
   1 t. salt
Cut in with pastry blender:
   ¼ c. lard or shortening
When particles are fine, add gradually:
   ½ c. lukewarm water
Toss with fork to make a stiff dough. Form into a ball and knead thoroughly on lightly floured board until smooth and flecked with air bubbles. To make dough easier to handle, grease surface, cover tightly, and refrigerate 4-24 hours before using. Let dough return to room temperature before rolling out.

Divide dough into 8 balls for large tortillas, or 11 balls for common 8-inch size. Roll as thin as possible on a lightly floured board, or between sheets of waxed paper. Drop onto a very hot ungreased griddle. Bake until freckled on one side. (Takes only about 20 seconds.) Lift edge, turn, and bake on second side. To serve at once, fold each limp tortilla around small lumps of margarine. Or cool tortillas, wrap airtight, and refrigerate or freeze. To serve later, place in tightly covered baking dish and warm in oven, or fry briefly in hot shallow oil.

Option:
Replace ½ c. flour with cornmeal or whole wheat flour.

Carol Friesen, Reedley, Calif.
Louise Claassen, Elkhart, Ind.

Gather Up the Fragments

1.
Save any leftover bread heels, stale bread, uneaten toast, dry rolls, crusts, and crumbs in a plastic bag in the freezer. When the oven is heated to 300-325° for another purpose, make crumbs or croutons:
Crumbs:
Dry bread *thoroughly* in a slow oven, turning occasionally. Eat as melba toast; let the baby chew it. Put remaining pieces in heavy plastic bag and crush with rolling pin, or whirl in a blender. Put crumbs through coarse sieve. Toss hard pieces to the birds. Dry bread crumbs keep indefinitely on the shelf in a covered container. Add herbs and seasoned salt if desired. Use to bread meat for frying, in croquettes, meat loaves and patties, or to top au gratin dishes and casseroles. Use to make Coating Mix for Oven-Fried Chicken, p. *119* Mix unseasoned crumbs half and half with graham cracker crumbs for a pie shell.
Croutons:
Spread stale bread lightly with margarine or brush with oil; dice into cubes. Sprinkle with seasoned salt, garlic or onion salt, parsley, basil, oregano, or a combination. Toast in a slow oven until thoroughly dry and crisp. Sprinkle on salads, into soup, on casseroles before baking. Use whenever recipes call for herb-seasoned croutons or stuffing mix.

2.
Dice untoasted stale bread to use in meat loaves and patties. A blender quickly turns a handful of stale bread pieces into crumbs.

3.
Dip stale bread in egg and milk and fry for French toast.

4.
Make bread pudding by pouring custard mixture over stale bread; bake at 325° until knife inserted comes out clean.

5.
Freeze leftover corn bread for use in stuffing. See Creamed Chicken with Cornbread Stuffing, p. *126*

6.
To serve leftover pancakes, place a slice of cheese on each and broil until bubbly. Makes a delicious snack or high-protein lunch entrée.

—Flo Harnish, Akron, Pa.

7.
Recipes using stale bread:
—Basic Burger Mix, p. *110*
—Chicken Strata, p. *122*
—Chicken or Turkey Loaf, p. *123*
—Creamed Chicken
  with Corn Bread Stuffing, p *126*
—Tuna Soufflé Sandwiches, p. *128*
—Old-Fashioned Bread Omelet, p. *97*
—Oven Cheese Fondue, p. *99*
—Cheese Strata, p. *100*
—Applesauce Bread Pudding, p. *191*

We grind wheat in our blender. We put about 2 c. wheat in a glass quart jar (wheat might crack a plastic container), screw on the blender blades, and process at high speed about 4 minutes, or until all the wheat is ground up. Then we put it through a sifter or sieve. What goes through we use in baking bread; what doesn't we cook as breakfast cereal. We add raisins and eat the cereal with brown sugar. The fresh wheat flavor is wonderful!
—Martha and Walter Dyck, Danvers, Ill.

Cereals

Few superprocessed foods have established themselves so securely on North American tables as boxed dry cereals. At breakfast each person hides behind a favorite brand.

Controversy rages concerning which cereals are the most nutritious. Box labeling assures consumers that enough nutrients lost in processing are replaced to bring the crunchies back to where so nutritious a food as whole grain normally ought to be. Then someone does a study feeding dry cereal to laboratory animals, and the results indicate that cereals captioned most nutritious on the side of the box are not necessarily the ones that keep a living organism healthy.

A few facts about packaged dry cereals are indisputable:

1. They are a very expensive way to consume grain—more expensive than bread and far more expensive than hot cooked cereals, even instant varieties. Cereal has no magical nutritional qualities not

found in bread. Dry cereal is twice as expensive as breakfast toast (three times as high for those who bake bread). Dry cereals have risen in price to the point where some are more expensive per pound than certain varieties of meat.

2. Dry cereals waste packaging materials, space on shelves, and energy as they are developed, processed, advertised, and delivered to the stores.

3. Most dry cereals are laced with dyes and preservatives of dubious safety. Many are loaded with sugar. They accustom young children to expect heavy sweetening on their foods. Cereal grains in their natural state contain much-needed fibers and are virtually free of fat; dry cereals have most fibers removed in processing and many contain added fats.

4. The dry cereal market brings people under the thumb of mass advertising—and it presses down hard. Few foods are so exploited on children's TV, through box-top games, and even in contests co-opting schools and fire stations. Parents with preschoolers in the cart find the trip down a supermarket cereal aisle the low point of the week if they're trying to save money.

Consider again the cooked cereals, standby of our grandparents. Quicker varieties can be prepared in the time it takes to set the table and fix orange juice. Beyond the usual oatmeal, all sorts of grains are available that cook up into delicious hot cereals if one searches for them. This book doesn't give many as recipes because availability and naming varies widely, but a little experimenting with amounts of water and cooking times will serve to get them onto the table. Look for:

Wheat germ meal or raw wheat germ—at feed mills or health food stores. Cook like cream of wheat or mix with cream of wheat.

Bulgur wheat—widely available.

Cracked, ground, or rolled wheat —feed mills, health food stores, or grind your own in hand mill, in blender (p. 64), or in small electric coffee grinder.

Millet—health food stores.

Rolled oats—widely available.

Barley grits or groats—mills, supermarkets, other stores.

Brown rice or cornmeal—both widely available. Cook with milk to porridge consistency.

Some of these products, if available only in specialty stores, may be expensive; in other areas they are cheap. In any case, compare prices pound for pound with dry cereals before deciding against them.

Several grains can be combined in your own hot cereal mix. Take another hint from the old cookbooks and don't limit hot cereals to breakfast. They make a good fast meal any other time of day, especially appealing topped with fresh or dried fruits, nuts, brown sugar, or honey.

Another cereal hint:

Because breakfast is such a hurry-up time, add instant dry milk to cooked hot cereal, stir, and serve. Good for a family with young children.
—Virginia Birky, Salem, Ohio

Basic
Dry Cereal Formula

300°
30-60 min.

Preheat oven to 300°.
Combine in large bowl:
7 c. dry ingredients, including
    at least 2-3 c. rolled oats, plus
      other grains and nuts as
      desired:
    wheat germ
    whole wheat flour
    wheat bran
    wheat grits
    cornmeal
    soy flour, grits, or roasted beans
    grape nuts
    uncooked cereals (Ralston,
      Wheatena, etc.)
    sunflower seeds
    sesame seeds
    pumpkin seeds, roasted
    fresh grated or dried coconut
    dry milk solids
    chopped nuts
    spices—cinnamon, nutmeg, etc.
Combine separately and pour over dry
ingredients:
1 c. liquids, including as desired:
    honey
    syrup
    molasses
    brown sugar (use 2 T. water with
      ½ c. sugar)
    oil
    melted margarine
    peanut butter
    milk or cream
Bake in large greased baking pans
30-60 minutes, stirring often. Do not
overbrown. Crunchiness depends on
proportions and baking time. For a
chunkier cereal, allow to cool
undisturbed, then break into pieces.
Add when cool, as desired:
    raisins
    chopped dates
    dried apples
    apricots
    other fruits

Mother's
Grape Nuts

Makes 2½ lbs.
350°
25-30/20-30 min.

Preheat oven to 350°.
Combine in large mixing bowl:
    3 c. graham or whole wheat flour
    ½ c. wheat germ
    1 c. brown sugar or ¾ c. corn syrup
    2 c. buttermilk or sour milk
    1 t. soda
    pinch salt
Beat until smooth.
Spread dough on 2 large greased cookie
sheets. Bake 25-30 minutes.
Crumble by one of these methods:
1. While still warm, break into
   chunks and grate on slaw
   cutter, or whirl briefly in
   blender, about a cupful at a time.
2. Allow to cool thoroughly, then
   put through food grinder,
   coarse plate.
Crisp in 250° oven for 20-30 minutes.
Store in airtight container. Eat with milk.
No added sugar needed.

Option:
Omit wheat germ and increase flour by ½
c.

Ada Beachey, Goshen, Ind.
Viola Dorsch, Musoma, Tanzania
Vincent Krabill, Hesston, Kan.

Simple Granola

One of the simplest and cheapest;
easy for small children to chew.

Makes 2½-3 qts.
250°
1 hr.

Preheat oven to 250°.
Combine in large mixing bowl:
    2 c. whole wheat flour
    6 c. rolled oats

1 c. coconut
1 c. wheat germ
Blend together separately:
½ c. water
1 c. oil
1 c. honey or corn syrup
2 t. vanilla
1 T. salt
Add blended liquids to dry ingredients
and mix thoroughly.
Spread out on 2 greased cookie sheets
and bake 1 hour, or until dry and golden.
Store in covered containers.

Option:
With same liquids, use 4 c. quick oats, 3
c. whole wheat flour, 1 c. wheat germ, 1 c.
soy flour (optional), 1 c. coconut, 1 c.
nuts.

Marian Zuercher, Wooster, Ohio
Anna Beth Birky, West Chicago, Ill.

Koinonia
Granola

Choice recipe from a well-known
Christian community. Make up this
huge batch, fill into peanut-butter jars,
tie with ribbon, and use for Christmas
gifts. If ingredients are bought in bulk,
cost is about two thirds that of
commercial "natural" cereals.

Makes 5 qts.
350°
20-25 min.

Preheat oven to 350°.
Melt in large roasting pan:
½ c. oil
½ lb. margarine
2 T. molasses
1 T. vanilla
1 c. brown sugar
1 c. honey
½ t. salt
When mixed, let cool slightly and add:
2 lbs. rolled oats
½ c. sesame seeds
1 c. chopped nuts
2 c. grape nuts
1 c. wheat germ

1 lb. coconut
1 c. sunflower seeds
Stir thoroughly. Bake in shallow pans for
20-25 minutes. Stir every 5-7 minutes.
After granola has cooled, add 1 c.
raisins.

Koinonia Farms, Americus, Ga.

Soybean
Granola

Makes 2 qts.
325°
15 min.

Preheat oven to 325°.
Combine in large bowl:
4 c. rolled oats
1 c. wheat germ
1 c. sliced almonds or other nuts
1 c. sunflower seeds
½ c. whole wheat bran
1 c. roasted soybeans
Heat to boiling in saucepan:
¼ c. oil
½ c. honey
1 t. vanilla
Pour liquids over dry ingredients and stir
thoroughly. Toast on 2 greased cookie
sheets for 15 minutes or until golden.

Jean Miller, Akron, Pa.

Apple Cinnamon
Crunch

Makes 2 qts.
350°
20-25 min.

Preheat oven to 350°.
Combine in large bowl:
4 c. old-fashioned rolled oats
½ c. coconut
1 c. nuts, finely chopped
½ c. sesame seed
¾ t. salt
1 t. cinnamon
Combine separately and add:
½ c. honey

⅓ c. vegetable oil
½ t. vanilla

Mix thoroughly. Spread on 2 large greased baking pans and bake 20-25 minutes, stirring occasionally.
Add:

8 oz. finely cut dried apples

Store in tightly covered container in refrigerator.

Esther Deal, Ft. Wayne, Ind.

Crunchy Granola

Try this granola sprinkled generously over a bowlful of fresh sliced peaches for an outdoor summer breakfast. Some Swiss restaurants offer granola topped with fresh fruit and whipped cream as "Skiier's Breakfast."

Makes 2 qts.
325°
30 min.

Preheat oven to 325°.
Mix together in large bowl:

½-1 c. coconut
4 c. rolled oats
1 c. sunflower seed
1 c. wheat germ
¼-½ c. sesame seed
1 c. peanuts or chopped walnuts

Bring to a boil:

1 c. honey or brown sugar
½ c. oil
1 T. cinnamon

Pour honey mixture over dry ingredients and mix thoroughly. Spread on 2 greased cookie sheets. Bake about 30 minutes, stirring often. Watch closely at the last, not allowing granola to become too dark. Allow to cool undisturbed, then break into chunks.

Options:

If using brown sugar, increase oil to ¾ c. or add ¼ c. water.
Add 1 c. cornmeal to dry mixture. Omit cinnamon.

Pat and Earl Martin, Quang Ngai, Vietnam
Miriam Witmer, Manheim, Pa.
Dale Suderman, Newton, Kan.

Chunky Granola

Makes 2½ qts.
350°
10-15 min.

Preheat oven to 350°.
Place in ungreased 9x13" pan:

6 c. rolled oats

Bake 10 minutes. Remove from oven and stir in:

½ c. sunflower seeds or nuts
½ c. coconut
½ c. wheat germ
½ c. powdered milk

Add to dry mixture:

⅔ c. honey
⅔ c. oil
1 t. vanilla

Stir until thoroughly coated. Bake 10-15 minutes, stirring every 3-5 minutes until uniformly golden. Do *not* overbake.
Let it cool in pan undisturbed, then break into chunks.

Option:

Chopped raisins, dates, or dried fruits may be added.

Granola bars: For this or other recipes containing 6 to 8 c. dry ingredients and 1 to 2 c. liquid, add to liquids: 1 beaten egg, about ⅓ c. milk. Stir liquids into dry ingredients and mix well. Press mixture firmly into 2 well-greased 10 x 15" cookie sheets. Bake at suggested temperature until nicely browned. Cut immediately into bars. Remove from pans when cool. For sweeter bars, increase honey.

Mary Lou Houser, Lancaster, Pa.

Peanut Granola

Makes 5 qts.
325°
30 min.

Preheat oven to 325°.
Combine in saucepan:

1¼ c. honey
⅔ c. oil
1 c. peanut butter
1 T. salt
1 T. cinnamon
½ c. water

Stir over low heat until peanut butter melts.
Combine in large bowl:

10 c. rolled oats
1 c. chopped raw peanuts or other nuts
1 c. wheat germ
1 c. cornmeal
1 c. coconut

Add liquids and mix well. Place in 2 large shallow greased pans and bake about 30 minutes or until crunchy and brown. Stir often to prevent overbrowning. When cool, add:

2 c. raisins

Store in airtight container.

Louise Leatherman, Akron, Pa.

Everything Cereal

Makes 4-5 qts.
300°
45-60 min.

Preheat oven to 300°.
Combine in large heavy roasting pan:

1 c. whole wheat or soy flour
1½ c. dry milk powder
1½ c. unroasted wheat germ
½ c. buckwheat (optional)
1 c. sesame seeds
6 c. rolled oats
1 c. shelled unroasted sunflower seeds

1 c. grape nuts

Combine in saucepan:

1 c. oil
½ c. honey
2 T. molasses
1 t. vanilla

Warm over low heat to blend. Pour into dry mixture, stirring well.
Roast for 45-60 minutes, stirring every 15 minutes at first, then more frequently, until particles are golden (not dark) brown. After mixture has cooled, add:

2 c. raisins
1 c. each chopped prunes, dates, dried apricots, coconut (all optional)
1 c. dry-roasted chopped peanuts or other nuts

Store in tightly covered containers in cool, dry place.

Rosemary Moyer, North Newton, Kan.
Marlin Dick, Swan Lake Christian Camp, Viborg, S.D.

Apple Oatmeal

Serves 4-6

Combine in saucepan:

1 c. rolled oats
2 c. cold water
½ t. salt

Cook 10 minutes on low heat.
Add:

2 chopped apples
dash nutmeg

Cook 5 minutes more, or until apples are done to desired consistency.
Serve with milk or yogurt and honey, brown sugar, or cinnamon-sugar.

Option:
Use raisins or dates in place of apples.

Grace Whitehead, Kokomo, Ind.

Cornmeal Mush

Serves 4-6

Bring to a boil in heavy saucepan or top of double boiler:
3 c. water
Combine and stir in:
1 c. cold water
1 c. cornmeal
¼ c. flour
1 T. salt
Stir constantly as mush thickens. A wire whisk works well. Cook 30 minutes, covered, on very low heat or over hot water. Eat hot from the kettle with milk and sugar, or pour into loaf pan to cool and set. Slice, dust with flour if desired, and fry in well-greased skillet.

Grace Geiser, Apple Creek, Ohio

Ground Wheat Breakfast Cereal

Serves 6

Bring to a boil:
3 c. water
Combine separately and add:
1 c. cold water
1 c. ground wheat
2 t. salt
Stir constantly while thickening to prevent lumps. Reduce heat and cook 15-20 minutes. Serve with milk and sugar, honey or molasses.

Grace Geiser, Apple Creek, Ohio

Coconut-Oatmeal Cereal

Makes 2 qts.
350°
45 min.

Preheat oven to 350°.
Combine in large mixing bowl:
3 c. white or whole wheat flour
2 c. flake coconut
2 c. quick oatmeal
3 T. sesame seed
3 T. water
¾ c. sugar
5 T. cooking oil
Mix well. Bake in 2 or 3 shallow baking pans until browned, about 45 minutes, stirring occasionally to produce crumbles of desired size.
Serve as cold cereal.
Serves 16 (½ c. servings).

Options:

Add for variety:
raisins
brown sugar
sunflower seeds
nuts

Tropical version: Use 1 finely grated fresh coconut to replace flake coconut and omit 3 T. water.

June Suderman, Hillsboro, Kan.

Family Familia

Place a large bowl of rolled oats in the center of the table. All around place small bowls of whatever is available of the following:
coconut
sesame seeds
sunflower seeds
wheat germ
rolled wheat, rye, or barley
sprouts
nuts
dates, raisins, other dried fruits
fresh, frozen, or canned fruits
Each compiles his/her own. Pass honey and a pitcher of hot milk.

Kathy Histand, Sellersville, Pa.

Beans, soybeans, and lentils

Beans or legumes, a food of humble reputation in North America, are usually considered staple diet for the poor. Few cookbooks devote more than a couple of pages to them. Books will include a baked bean recipe or two, and possibly a soup, but that's the end of the matter.

In dismissing legumes so quickly, a whole resource of cheap plant protein is ignored. Prices have risen markedly, but pound for pound dry beans still do very well on the table of costs for 100 grams of protein.

One-half cup cooked white beans has seven grams protein, the same as a whole egg. A half cup of soybeans has eleven grams. Granted the egg has higher quality protein, but by eating beans together with grains (rice or whole grain bread) the quality or usability of protein in both the beans and the grain improves significantly. For a meatless high-protein meal, baked beans and whole grain bread are an excellent choice.

Dry legumes, especially soybeans, are good sources of minerals and B vitamins. As a double bonus to heart-conscious North Americans, soybeans are one of the few high-protein foods containing *no* saturated fats. In fact, they contain lecithin, which helps in the absorption and utilization of any kind of fat, including cholesterol.

Buy legumes in their dry form, in bulk if possible. They come to the kitchen shelf with almost no backlog of energy used in processing or storage and keep well with little attention.

A row of glass jars containing a variety of dry legumes adds color and texture interest to the kitchen and makes it easy to reach for them in meal planning. Visualize the natural color tones of little green split peas, earth-brown lentils, deep-red kidney beans, and creamy-golden soybeans arranged together.

"But they take so long to soak and cook and I can't ever remember to do it ahead of time," many cooks complain. Consider these suggestions for cooking legumes:

Soaking

Presoak all dry beans and peas by one of the methods given below, except for split peas and lentils. Two to three hours soaking is enough for split peas, although longer won't matter. Lentils need no presoaking and only 30 to 40 minutes cooking time.

1. *Overnight Method:* Wash beans, sort, place in kettle in which they will be cooked, and cover with 4 cups water to 1 cup beans (or follow recipe proportions). Cover and let stand 8 hours or overnight. Use soaking water for cooking—do not discard it.

2. *Quick Method:* Follow directions for overnight method but instead of soaking, bring water and beans to a boil and cook 2 minutes. Cover, remove from heat, and let stand 1 hour. Beans are then ready to cook.

Cooking Beans

1. One cup dried beans yields about 2½ cups cooked beans. See p. *14* for more complete information.

2. Cooking time varies according to size of bean and length of time in storage. Peas and smaller beans usually need less than an hour; larger beans 2 to 3 hours, and soybeans 3 to 4 hours. Large dry limas may tenderize in less than an hour, however. Bring beans to boiling in soaking water, cover, and reduce heat to simmer. Test for tenderness by tasting.

3. Add 1 tablespoon fat to cooking beans to control foaming.

4. Beans may be cooked 20 to 35 minutes in a pressure cooker, but some authorities warn against this because beans tend to sputter and foam which can clog the vent. Never fill pressure cooker more than three fourths full. Timetable for pressure cooking:
small beans, split peas, lentils,
    20 minutes
kidney and navy beans, 35 minutes
soybeans, 40 minutes

5. Since beans require long cooking, which uses energy, cook several pounds at once and freeze them. Frozen cooked beans have almost the same convenience as canned; thaw them quickly by setting the container in hot water. Drop a frozen chunk of beans directly into boiling soup, or place chunk in casserole in hot oven and add baked bean seasonings. Stir half an hour later and continue baking.

6. Cooked beans may be canned in jars in pressure canner.

7. Cook beans just until they begin to tenderize, then add seasonings and liquid and bake

slowly for 4 to 8 hours for wonderful browned-in flavor. Native Americans taught New England colonists how to make these famed "Boston Baked Beans" in earthen pots. Use that oven heat to good advantage. Bake rice pudding or plain rice, make granola or roast soybeans.

Soybeans

With the shortfall in world food supply, North Americans are again taking an interest in eating soybeans, the high-protein plant food already relied upon for centuries in parts of Asia. Older people remember eating soybeans during Depression days. Several have said to me, "You know, we ate soybeans when I was young. We just cooked them up, poured on a little milk or butter, and that's what we ate. But somehow we got away from it."

Eva Carper, a Mennonite schoolteacher from Virginia, wrote a food column for the *Rural New Yorker* in the mid-1930s. Here are suggestions she gave regarding soybeans:

We use soybeans any way that we use navy beans. Of course the flavor is different, because they are a protein food instead of starchy. We plant them in the corn at the edge of the field when we see the corn coming up, and they are about the last thing harvested. The beans grow along the stem and after the leaves drop off they may be stripped off the stalk. After they are dry they are put in bags and the children have a "jumping bee." We clean the pods out on a windy day by pouring from one tub to another.

For soybean soup, soak beans overnight, and boil slowly and long to bring out their best flavor. After they have boiled a while I add salt. When soft add whole milk, season with pepper, and heat. Then pour over pieces of dry or toasted bread and pour browned butter over the soup. This is a hearty dish and not much else needs to be served with it. Also, after beans are boiled, I add molasses, mustard, tomato juice, and ham broth or bacon, and bake like baked beans.

As Mrs. Carper notes, soybeans do have a different flavor. Some describe it as bland, needing spicy seasonings. Some call it mildly objectionable and try to cover it up. Others love soybeans just as they are. A dining-hall dietitian who is experimenting with serving soybean dishes said to me recently, "Why is so much attention focused on doctoring up soybeans? The more we use them, the more I like them just as they are. I find myself snitching them out of the kettle as they cook!"

Another way soybeans can be used is as soy flour, which essentially is milled dry soybeans. Soy flour is one of the most highly concentrated protein foods available.

Textured vegetable protein made from soybeans is sold in supermarkets as a meat extender or substitute. If such products are not overpriced and overpackaged, give them a try. Remember, though, that a cup of leftover home-cooked soybeans, mashed or blended will do the same thing if you're stretching ground meat.

Using Soybeans

1. Use any field soybean for eating. Some varieties may be tastier than others, but all are edible by people. Raise your own or buy directly from a farmer or mill.

2. Immature *green* soybeans need no presoaking and only a short cooking time like that of fresh green limas. *See p. 212*

3. Always presoak dry soybeans at least 8 hours or by quick method, then allow 3 to 4 hours slow cooking.

4. Soybeans will become tender though not quite as soft as other beans, and they never get mushy. The skins may separate and float as cooking begins but will dissolve later. Cooked soybeans freeze well and hold their shape when thawed.

5. Mashed soybeans or soybean paste is versatile in many dishes. Drain hot cooked beans, then mash with potato masher or back of slotted spoon, or put through a food grinder. Mashing is easier when beans are hot. Use a blender if there is liquid in

the recipe which can be added to facilitate getting the mixture through the blades. One cup cooked soybeans yields ⅔ cup soybean paste. Use for sandwich spread, as ground beef extender, in loaves, patties, soufflés or casseroles.

Lentils

The convenience food among legumes, lentils cook in thirty minutes with no presoaking. Nutritionally they compare closely to dry beans and, like other legumes, are complemented by grains.

Lentils are an ancient food of the Middle East and as popular there today as they were thousands of years ago when Jacob tricked Esau out of his birthright for "bread and pottage of lentils" Try Middle Eastern Lentil Soup, p. *145* or Kusherie (Egyptian Rice and Lentils), p. *62*, to understand part of the reason Esau gave in.

The mild nutty flavor of lentils is generally appealing, even to people who have never tried them. What may not be so appealing at first is their brownish color in cooked dishes. Try adding tomato sauce or sliced carrots and a sprinkling of chopped scallions to lentil soup. Serve colorful vegetables or salads with lentil casseroles. Lentils are definitely worth a try if you're looking for low-cost, nutritious main dish ideas. Some of our recipe testers became true converts.

Beans with Sweet-Sour Sauce

Serves 4

TS with pressure cooker

Soak and cook until tender:
    ½ lb. white beans, such as navy or great northern
    1 qt. water
Brown lightly in skillet:
    1½ T. fat
    1½ T. flour
Gradually add:
    2 T. brown or white sugar
    2 T. corn syrup
    ¼ t. salt
    2 t. vinegar
Stir until blended. Gradually add:
    1 c. liquid (hot water or bean liquid)
Bring to a boil and cook a few minutes. Pour over hot beans.

Options:

Sauté a chopped onion in the fat before adding flour.

Cook the whole pound of beans and reserve extra for another dish later in the week.

Helen E. Regier, Newton, Kan.

Make your favorite spaghetti sauce using lentils in place of ground beef. Small and dark, they're a good stand-in for meat and give the sauce a nice texture. Sauté onions and garlic in oil, then add lentils, tomato ingredients, seasonings, and cook 30 to 45 minutes until lentils are tender. Lentils will absorb some liquid so make the sauce a little thinner than usual. Serve over cooked spaghetti. (Complementary protein.)
—Bonnie Krehbiel, Madison, Wis.

Basic
Baked Beans

*Long, slow baking develops rich
flavor. Rice pudding (p.190) bakes
at the same oven temperature and
complements protein in beans. Add
a crunchy salad.*

T·S

Serves 6-8
275°-300°
4-8 hrs.

TS—needs time, not attention

Soak overnight or by quick method:
   1 lb. navy beans
   2 qts. water
In same liquid, bring beans to boil and
simmer until tender, about 1½ hours.
Drain, reserving liquid.
Preheat oven to 275-300°.
Combine in 2 qt. casserole:
   cooked beans
   ½ c. molasses
   ¼ c. ketchup (optional)
   1 t. mustard
   2 t. salt
   ¼ t. pepper
   1 onion, chopped
   2 slices bacon, chopped, or ¼ lb.
      salt pork (optional)
   bean liquid to cover
Bake 4-8 hours, adding liquid
occasionally if necessary. Cover during
first half of baking time, then uncover.

Options:

Substitute soybeans or a combination of
bean varieties.

Add 2-3 t. chili powder.

Sarah Grove, Markham, Ont.

Mexican
Chili Beans

Serves 6

Soak overnight or by quick method:
   1 lb. dried red kidney beans
   2 qts. water
Bring to a boil.
Simmer just until tender, about 40
minutes.
Fry in Dutch oven:
   ¼ lb. salt pork, finely diced
When crisp, add:
   2 c. onions, finely chopped
   4 cloves garlic, finely chopped
Saute until golden. Add:
   2 t. salt
   1 t. pepper
   2-4 t. chili powder, according
      to taste
   1 t. dried leaf oregano
   ¼ t. cumin
   ¾ c. tomato paste
   1 c. tomato sauce
Simmer 15 minutes.
Drain beans, reserving liquid. Add
beans to tomato mixture along with 2 c.
reserved liquid. Cover and simmer 1
hour.

Marjorie Ropp, Montreal, Quebec

Calico Baked Beans
For a Crowd

Serves 10-12
325°
1½ hrs.

Use canned beans, or soak and cook dry
beans. Several varieties of dry beans
may be soaked and cooked together.
One cup dry beans usually yields 2½
cups cooked.

Preheat oven to 325°.
Combine in large casserole, reserving
liquids:
   2 c. green limas, cooked and
      drained

2 c. large dry limas, cooked and
    drained
2 c. red kidney beans, cooked
    and drained
1 qt. pork and beans, or leftover
    baked beans

Fry:

6 slices bacon, diced
OR 1 c. leftover ham bits
OR ½ lb. sausage or ground beef

Pour off excess fat.
Add:

1½ c. onions, cut up

Fry briefly.
Add:

¾ c. brown sugar
2 t. salt
1 t. dry mustard
1 clove minced garlic
½ c. vinegar
½ c. ketchup

Cook 5 minutes and pour over beans.
Add enough reserved bean liquid to
barely cover beans. Bake uncovered 1½
hours, adding additional liquid if beans
become too dry.

Options:

Substitute other varieties of dry beans,
including soy—but keep color contrast
for an attractive dish.

Omit meat altogether—still delicious!

Sharon Baker, Larkspur, Colo.
Karin Hackman, Hatfield, Pa.

Mexican Refried Beans

*Use as filling in tortillas, as side dish
with rice or tacos, or on Navajo
Tacos.*

Serves 5-6

Soak overnight or by quick method:

1 lb. dried pinto, pink, or kidney
    beans

Add:

6 c. water
2 onions, chopped (optional)

Bring to a boil, cover and simmer slowly
until beans are tender, about 3 hours.

Mash beans with potato masher.
Add:

½ c. hot bacon drippings,
    margarine, or lard
salt to taste

Mix well; continue cooking, stirring
frequently until beans are thickened and
fat is absorbed. Serve at once or
refrigerate for later use.

Options:

Cook beans with half the onion; heat fat in
skillet, sauté remaining onion, then mash
¼ c. beans into skillet. Fry a short time
and push to side, adding more beans by
¼ cupfuls and mashing. Simmer 10
minutes to finish.

Add chili powder and/or cumin and
tomato sauce to taste. Place in greased
casserole, sprinkle with cheese, and
keep hot in oven until ready to serve.

Use soybeans or chick peas (garbonzos)
for delicious variation.

Carol Friesen, Reedley, Calif.
Anne Rogers, East Petersburg, Pa.

Crusty Mexican Bean Bake

Serves 6
350°
30 min.

Crust:
Combine:

½ c. flour
½ t. salt
½ t. baking powder
2 T. shortening or margarine
½ c. sour cream or yogurt
    (increase flour by 2 T. if
    using yogurt)
1 egg, beaten

Stir together. May be slightly lumpy.
Spread thinly with back of spoon on
bottom and sides of shallow greased
2-qt. casserole. Fill with bean mixture.
(Crust may be stirred together in
advance. Refrigerate until ready to use.)

Filling:
Brown in skillet:
¾ lb. ground beef
½ c. chopped onion
Add:
1 t. salt
2 t. chili powder
½ t. Tabasco sauce
**2 c. undrained cooked kidney
beans**
¾ c. (6 oz.) tomato paste
Spoon into crust and bake at 350° for 30
minutes. Remove from oven. Sprinkle
over or serve alongside:
½ c. grated cheese
1-2 c. shredded lettuce
1 c. chopped raw tomatoes

Evelyn Fisher, Akron, Pa.

Monterey Beans And Cheese

T·S

Serves 6

Fry, drain, and break into pieces:
2 slices bacon
Set aside. Sauté in bacon fat until tender:
½ medium-sized onion, sliced
½ green pepper, diced
Add:
bacon bits
2 c. cooked kidney beans
¼-½ lb. shredded cheddar cheese
2 ripe tomatoes, diced, or
   ¾ c. tomato sauce
¼ c. beef bouillon or tomato juice
1 t chili powder
½ t. salt
dash of pepper
Cook slowly, stirring constantly, until
ingredients are blended and cheese is
smooth—about 5 minutes. Serve with
rice.

Mary Ella Weaver, Lititz, Pa.

Puerto Rican Rice And Pigeon Peas

*"A Puerto Rican favorite of the rich
and poor," says Maria.*

Serves 6-8

Soak, then cook until tender:
**½ lb. pigeon peas, pinto or
kidney beans**
4 c. water
Brown in dutch oven or deep skillet:
**1 lb. pork ribs or cooking ham,
cut in 1" pieces**
Measure accumulated drippings and
add enough vegetable oil to make ½ c.
Return fat to skillet and add:
achiote, if available, OR
¾ c. tomato paste
Stir to coat meat.
Add to skillet:
2 tomatoes, chopped
½ green pepper, chopped
1 large onion, chopped
2 cloves garlic, minced
2 c. cabbage, finely chopped
1 t. oregano
1 T. capers with juice
1 T. salt
Stir-fry briefly just to wilt vegetables.
Add:
2 c. uncooked rice
cooked pigeon peas, drained
Stir well. Add:
6-7 c. bean liquid and water
Cook at moderate heat 15 minutes. Stir
once or twice. Then reduce heat, cover,
and finish cooking slowly until rice is
done.

Option:

Omit meat. Begin by sautéeing
vegetables in ½ c. fat, then add tomato
paste and remaining ingredients.

*Maria Luisa Rivera de Snyder,
Hesston, Kan.*

Caribbean Rice And Beans

Serves 6-8

Soak overnight or by quick method:
  **2 c. dry pigeon peas, pinto beans,
    or kidney beans**
  6 c. water
  1 T. salt
Bring to a boil, reduce heat, and simmer
just until tender—about 40 minutes.
Drain beans, reserving liquid.
Heat in large covered skillet:
  2 T. oil or margarine
Add:
  1 clove garlic, crushed
  2 green onions, chopped
  1 large tomato, chopped
  1 T. lime juice (optional)
  ⅛ t. ground cloves
  1 T. chopped parsley
  ¼ t. pepper
  drained beans
Sauté about 5 minutes.
Add:
  2 c. rice
  **4 c. reserved bean liquid
    (add water if necessary)**
Bring to a boil, cover, reduce heat to
simmer, and cook 20-25 minutes without
stirring.

  *Shirley King, Grande Riviere du Nord,
    Haiti*
  *Abe and Katherine Dyck, Manchester,
    Jamaica*

Brazilian Rice And Beans

*Brazilians like to accompany this
complete meal with manioc flour
sprinkled on top.*

Serves 8-10

Soak overnight or by quick method:
  2 c. pinto or kidney beans
  6 c. water
Cook about 2 hours or until tender.
In saucepan, cook together about 4 c. of
2-4 of the following vegetables in large
pieces:
  potato
  chayote
  cabbage
  pumpkin
  okra
  carrot
Cook just until tender.
Sauté together in a skillet:
  ½ lb. ground meat (beef or pork)
  **¼ lb. smoked meat (bacon,
    sausage, etc.)**
  2 garlic cloves, minced
  1 medium onion, chopped
  **½ green pepper, chopped
    (optional)**
  1 t. Worcestershire sauce
  2 T. tomato paste
  1 t. coriander
  1 bay leaf
  salt and pepper to taste
Simmer 30 minutes.
Join beans, vegetables, and meat
mixture and heat together 2 minutes.
Serve with rice.

  Josefa Soares, Recife, Brazil

Italian Beans And Pasta

Serves 8

Soak overnight or by quick method:
  **1 lb. dried Great Northern or
    marrow beans**
  4 c. water
In large kettle, bring beans to boil, cover
and simmer 1 hour, adding water if
necessary.
Cook and drain according to package
directions:
  8 oz. elbow macaroni
Brown in skillet:
  ¾ lb. sausage, broken up
  1 clove garlic, minced
  1 onion, chopped
Drain off excess fat. Add macaroni and
sausage mixture to bean kettle.
Add:
  4 c. cooked tomatoes
  ¼ c. dark corn syrup

2 T. chopped parsley
2 t. salt
2 t. dried oregano
¼ t. pepper

Bring to boil, cover and simmer about 15 minutes, adding tomato juice if necessary for stew consistency. Serve in soup bowls with a green salad and whole wheat bread.

Option:

Thin with more water or tomato juice for a soup.

Belmont Mennonite Church Low-Cost Collection, Elkhart, Ind.

Scallions And Beans

Serve as summertime meal with whole grain bread and fresh fruit.

Serves 6

Soak overnight or by quick method:
1 lb. dry white beans
2 qts. water

Cook in water to cover until tender. Drain and cool. (Reserve liquid for soup or stew.)
Combine:
4 scallions, chopped, including tops
2 cloves garlic, peeled and pressed
¼ c. fresh lemon juice
½ c. olive oil
salt and freshly ground pepper

Pour dressing over beans. Sprinkle with parsley. Chill several hours before serving.

Option:

Other oil may replace olive oil but won't yield the same flavor.

Louise Claassen, Elkhart, Ind.
Gwen Peachey, Amman Jordan

Savory Baked Limas

T·S

Serves 6-8
300°
About 5 hrs.

TS—Needs time not attention

Wash and soak overnight:
1 lb. dried baby lima beans
6 c. water

Preheat oven to 300°.
Drain beans (reserve liquid) and place in 2 qt. casserole.
Add:
liquid from soaking beans plus water to make 2 c.
2 c. diced, unpeeled tart apples
½ c. chopped onion
¼ c. dark brown sugar
2 T. Worcestershire sauce
¼ c. molasses
2 t. salt
1 t. dry mustard

Stir well. Score or cut up:
¼ lb. salt pork or slab bacon

Bury pork deep in center of beans. Cover and bake about 5 hours. Stir once or twice and add water if needed.

Erma Weaver, Manheim, Pa.

Basic Cooked Lentils

Serves 6

Bring to a boil and simmer 20 minutes:
1 c. lentils
2½ c. water
2 beef bouillon cubes
1 bay leaf
1 t. salt

Flavor options:

Curried Lentils
Sauté together:
¼ c. margarine
1 large onion, chopped
1 clove garlic, minced
Add:
1 t. salt
1-2 T. curry powder
Fry briefly. Add to Basic Cooked Lentils with:
2 T. lemon juice
chopped parsley
Serve over rice.

Sweet-Sour Lentils
Reduce water by ½ c. in preparing Basic Cooked Lentils.
When lentils are cooked, add:
¼ c. apple or pineapple juice
¼ c. cider vinegar
¼ c. brown sugar
1 clove garlic, crushed
⅛ t. cloves
sautéed onion, if desired
Heat to bubbly. Serve over rice.

Easy Lentil Stew
Add to lentils:
½ lb. diced ham, browned sausage, or browned ground beef
¾ c. tomato paste
2 c. water
¼ t. oregano
1 t. salt
1 onion, chopped
2 stalks celery, chopped
1 clove garlic, minced
Bring to a boil, reduce heat, and simmer 20-30 minutes until vegetables are tender. Serve plain or over rice.

Zona Galle, Madison, Wis.
Becky Mast, State College, Pa.
Marian Franz, Washington, D.C.

Baked Lentils With Cheese

Serves 6
375°
1 hr., 15 min.

Preheat oven to 375°.
Combine in shallow 9x13" baking dish:
1¾ c. lentils, rinsed
2 c. water
1 whole bay leaf
2 t. salt
¼ t. pepper
⅛ t. *each* marjoram, sage, thyme
2 large onions, chopped
2 cloves garlic, minced
2 c. canned tomatoes
Cover tightly and bake 30 minutes.
Uncover and stir in:
2 large carrots, sliced ⅛" thick
½ c. thinly sliced celery
Bake covered 40 minutes until vegetables are tender. Stir in:
1 green pepper, chopped (optional)
2 T. finely chopped parsley
Sprinkle on top:
3 c. shredded cheddar cheese
Bake, uncovered, 5 minutes until cheese melts.

Catherine Kornweibel, Easton, Pa.

Honey Baked Lentils

Serves 8
350°
1 hr.

Combine in a dutch oven or saucepan:
1 lb. (2⅓ c.) lentils
1 small bay leaf
5 c. water
2 t. salt
Bring to a boil. Cover tightly and reduce heat. Simmer 30 minutes. Do not drain. Discard bay leaf.
Preheat oven to 350°.
Combine separately and add to lentils:
1 t. dry mustard
¼ t. powdered ginger
1 T. soy sauce
½ c. chopped onions
1 c. water
Cut in 1" pieces:
4 slices bacon
Stir most of the bacon into lentils and sprinkle remainder on top.
Pour over all:
⅓ c. honey
Cover tightly. Bake 1 hour. Uncover last 10 minutes to brown bacon.

Options:

Bacon may be partially precooked if desired. Substitute ½ lb. browned ground beef or sausage, or omit meat completely.

Delicious served with hot baked rice. Pass soy sauce.

Replace ginger, soy sauce, and 1 c. water in second group of ingredients with 2 T. sugar, 1 t. oregano, 2 c. tomato sauce. Omit honey.

Joann Smith, Goshen, Ind.
Larry Gingrich, Monmouth, Ore.

Skillet Beef With Lentils

T•S

Serves 6-8

Bring 1 qt. water to boil in saucepan. Add:

1½ c. lentils, rinsed

Cook 20 minutes. Drain, reserving liquid. In deep skillet, sauté:

2 T. margarine or butter
2 medium onions, chopped
1 clove garlic, minced

Stir in:

1 lb. ground beef

Brown well. Dissolve in 2⅓ c. reserved liquid:

2 beef bouillon cubes

Add liquid to meat mixture; cover and simmer 10 minutes.
Stir in:

reserved lentils
2 T. long-grain rice
1 t. sugar
1 t. salt
1 t. ground cumin
½ t. pepper

Bring to boil, reduce heat, cover, and simmer 30 minutes, or until lentils and rice are tender and liquid is absorbed (add more liquid if necessary). Check seasonings and stir in:

1 T. cider vinegar

Top with parsley sprinkle.

Ellen Lonçacre, Bally, Pa.

Lentil-Barley Stew

Serves 6

Sauté in large pan:

¼ c. margarine
¾ c. chopped celery
¾ c. chopped onion

Add:

6 c. water
¾ c. lentils

Cook 20 minutes. Add:

1 qt. tomatoes, canned
¾ c. barley or brown rice
2 t. salt
¼ t. pepper
½ t. rosemary
½ t. garlic salt

Simmer 45-60 minutes. Add:

½ c. shredded carrots

Cook 5 minutes, and serve.

Option:

Brown ¾ lb. boneless pork shoulder, diced, then add celery and onion and sauté until golden, omitting margarine. Proceed with recipe as given.

S. V. Martin, Duchess, Alta.
Frances Lehman, Goshen, Ind.

Kusherie (Egyptian Rice and Lentils)

Kusherie is surprisingly easy to make and contains high-quality protein. In Egypt plain yogurt is served as a side dish.

Serves 6-8

Rice and Lentils:
Heat in heavy saucepan or covered skillet:

2 T. oil

Add:

1¼ c. lentils

Brown lentils over medium heat 5 minutes, stirring often.

Add:
3 c. boiling water or stock
1 t. salt
dash pepper
Cook uncovered 10 minutes over medium heat.
Stir in:
1½ c. rice
1 c. boiling water or stock
Bring to boil, reduce heat to low, cover, and simmer 25 minutes without stirring.

Sauce:
In a saucepan, heat together:
¾ c. tomato paste
3 c. tomato juice, tomato sauce, or pureed tomatoes
1 green pepper, chopped
chopped celery leaves
1 T. sugar
½ t. salt
1 t. cumin
¼ t. cayenne pepper or crushed chilis to taste
Bring sauce to boiling, reduce heat, and simmer 20-30 minutes.

Browned Onions:
Heat in small skillet:
2 T. oil
Sauté over medium heat until brown:
3 onions, sliced
4 cloves garlic, minced
To serve, put rice-lentil mixture on a platter. Pour tomato sauce over. Top with browned onions.

Option:
Omit the sauce (but not the browned onions) and serve with plain yogurt.

Carolyn Yoder, Cairo, Egypt

Savory Baked Soybeans

T·S

Serves 6
300°
3 hrs.

TS—Needs time not attention

Soak overnight or by quick method:
2 c. dry soybeans
2 qts. water
Cook slowly 3 hours, or until tender.
Preheat oven to 300°.
Combine with beans:
2 c. tomato sauce
1 large onion, chopped
1 green pepper, chopped (optional)
1 clove garlic, minced
1 t. dry mustard
2 t. chili powder (optional)
2 t. salt
¼ t. pepper
2 T. dark molasses
3 strips bacon, diced, or ¼ lb. diced smoked sausage or ham
Bake in large uncovered casserole 3 hours, adding water if necessary. Stir occasionally.

Options:
Use electric slow cooker.
Bake at 375° for 40 minutes—won't have slow-baked flavor, but still a good dish.

Mabel Kreider, Lancaster, Pa.
Estelle Krabill, Hesston, Kan.
Kathryn Seem, Emmaus, Pa.

Use soybeans in a chili recipe and reduce ground beef to just enough for flavoring, using all soybeans or half kidney and half soybeans.
—Clara Brenneman, Waynesfield, Ohio
—Virginia Birky, Salem, Ohio

Soybean Loaf

Serves 6
350°
1 hr.

Preheat oven to 350°.
Combine in large bowl:

2½ c. soybeans, cooked and mashed
½ c. cottage cheese
½ c. fresh or cooked tomatoes, drained and chopped
2 eggs
2 T. oil
1½ t. salt
½ c. bread crumbs

Mix well. Form into loaf and place on greased baking pan.
Pour over:

1 10-oz. can cream of mushroom soup OR equivalent sauce, see p. 70

Bake 1 hour.

Options:

Add herbs to taste—thyme, oregano, chopped parsley.

Add finely chopped onions and celery.

Substitute 1 c. mashed potatoes (no milk added) for 1 c. soybeans.

Use a tomato or creole sauce to replace mushroom sauce.

Goshen College Dining Hall
Alternative Line, Goshen, Ind.
Genevieve Buckwalter, Osahigawa, Japan

Soybean Hamburger Casserole

Serves 6
350°
45 min.

Preheat oven to 350°.
Sauté in large heavy skillet:

2 T. cooking oil
½ c. onion, chopped
1 c. celery, chopped
¼ c. green pepper, chopped (optional)
¼-½ lb. hamburger

When meat is brown, stir in:

1 t. salt
⅛ t. pepper
½ t. seasoned salt
2½ c. cooked soybeans
1¼ c. tomato soup, tomato sauce, or stewed tomatoes
1 beef bouillon cube, dissolved in
1 c. hot water
2 c. cooked rice

Heat and simmer a few minutes. Place in greased casserole and bake 45 minutes. Remove from oven and top with:

½ c. grated cheese or cheese slices

Return to oven a few minutes until cheese has melted.

Doreen Snyder, Waterloo, Ont.

Soybean Casserole

Serves 6
350°
45 min.

Preheat oven to 350°
Sauté in heavy saucepan about 5 minutes:

5 T. oil
2 c. chopped celery
¼ c. chopped onion
2 T. chopped green pepper

Add:

⅓ c. flour

Cook and stir until bubbly. Add:

2 c. milk
1 t. salt

Bring to boiling point, stirring constantly. Add:

2 c. mashed or chopped cooked soybeans

Pour mixture into greased casserole. Cover with:

1 c. whole wheat bread crumbs or ¼ c. wheat germ

Bake 45 minutes or until brown.

Options:

Use fresh green soybeans instead of dried cooked beans. Leave whole or mash as desired.

Add 1 c. grated cheese to white sauce.

Eleanor Kaufman, Newton, Kan.
Irene Claassen, Holmesville, Neb.

Fresh Soybean-Cheese Casserole

Serves 4-6
375°
45 min.

Preheat oven to 375°.
Sauté in heavy saucepan:
  1 medium onion, diced
  ¼ c. margarine
When onion is soft, add:
  **2 c. fresh green soybeans,
    precooked**
  1 c. evaporated milk
  ⅛ t. Tabasco sauce
  1 t. salt
Cook, stirring, until heated through.
Remove from heat and stir in:
  3 eggs, slightly beaten
Pour half of mixture into a greased casserole. Layer with half of:
  1 c. shredded cheddar cheese
Repeat with rest of beans and top with remaining cheese.
Sprinkle over all:
  12 saltines, crushed
Bake 45 minutes.

Mary Lou Houser, Lancaster, Pa.

Soybean Pie

Serves 4
350°
25 min.

Soak overnight, or by quick method:
  1 c. soybeans
  3 c. water

Cook slowly 3-4 hours. Drain beans.
Heat in skillet:
  1 T. oil
Sauté about 5 minutes:
  1 medium-size onion, chopped
  1 clove garlic, minced
  drained soybeans
Add:
  1 c. tomato sauce
  2 t. chili powder
  2 t. Worcestershire sauce
  salt and pepper to taste
Simmer mixture while preparing cornmeal crust:
Preheat oven to 350°.
Combine:
  ½ c. cornmeal
  ½ c. flour
  1 t. salt
Cut in:
  1 T. shortening
Beat together:
  1 egg
  ¼ c. water
Add to cornmeal mixture. Press into 9" pie plate.
Fill pie with soybean mixture. Top with:
  ½ c. grated cheese
Bake about 25 minutes.

Option:

Soybeans may be ground or mashed if desired.

Susan Hurst, Bowmansville, Pa.

Combine cooked beans, minced watercress, sweet pickle relish, and mayonnaise. Spread between slices of whole wheat toast and add a lettuce leaf. Or add chopped onions and diced cheese, spread mixture on hamburger buns, and broil until bubbly. (Complementary protein.)
—Verna Shelly, Brewton, Ala.

Refried Soybeans

Serve as a side dish with rice, or fill into tortilla shells and top with shredded lettuce, chopped tomatoes, and more cheese.

T·S

Serves 4

Heat in skillet:
¼ c. oil
Add and sauté:
1 onion, chopped
1 clove garlic, minced
When onion is soft, add:
2 c. cooked soybeans, mashed
1-2 t. chili powder
salt to taste
Cook in oil, stirring often; when oil is absorbed, sprinkle with:
**¾ c. shredded cheddar or
Jack cheese**
Let stand covered until cheese is melted.

Alice and Willard Roth, Elkhart, Ind.

Soybean Soufflé

Serves 6
325°
45 min.

Preheat oven to 325°.
Combine in heavy saucepan:
**3 c. warm soybean pulp (drained
cooked soybeans forced
through food mill)**
4 egg yolks
Stir together and heat gently, until mixture is slightly thickened. Do not allow to boil.
Stir in:
2 T. grated onion
2 T. chopped parsley
½ t. thyme
¼ t. marjoram
1 t. salt
dash pepper

Beat until stiff but not dry:
4 egg whites
Fold egg whites into soybean mixture. Pour into a well-buttered 1½ qt. baking dish. Bake 45 minutes, or until set.

Option:

Soybeans, egg yolks, onion, and herbs may be whirled together in blender to puree beans. Stop blender several times and push mixture into blades.

Lois Hess, Columbus, Ohio

Sweet and Sour Soybeans

Serves 4

Combine in a bowl and set aside:
1 T. cornstarch
¼ c. firmly packed brown sugar
¼ t. ground ginger
2 T. soy sauce
¼ c. vinegar
**½ c. pineapple juice, drained
from chunks (see below)**
Heat in large skillet:
2 T. oil
Add:
1 c. green pepper, cut in 1" pieces
1 c. onion, cut in wedges
½ c. carrots, cut in ¼" slices
1 clove garlic, mashed
Stir-fry for about 3 minutes until tender-crisp.
Add:
2 c. cooked soybeans, drained
1 c. pineapple chunks, drained
**½ c. tomatoes, cut in 1" cubes,
or 2 T. ketchup**
Fry a few minutes, then add sauce ingredients.
Cook and stir until mixture boils, and all ingredients are coated with sauce (about 2 minutes). Serve over hot rice. Garnish with chopped scallions if available.

Dorothy Liechty, Berne, Ind.
David and Joanne Janzen, Newton, Kan.

Marinated
Soybeans

*Not intended as a main dish—rather as
a tangy sweet-sour accompaniment
to an otherwise bland meal.*

T·S

Serves 6-8

Combine in a bowl:
- ¼ c. salad oil
- ⅓ c. cider vinegar
- ⅔ c. honey
- salt and pepper to taste

Add:
- 3 c. cooked soybeans, drained
- ¼ t. basil
- ½ t. garlic salt
- ½ t. oregano
- ½ c. chopped dill pickles (optional)
- ½ c. chopped celery
- ½ c. chopped onion or scallions
- ½ c. chopped parsley
- ½ c. chopped green pepper
  (optional)
- 1 clove garlic, minced

Mix well and chill several hours before
serving.

*Mary Lou Houser, Lancaster, Pa.
Anna Mary Brubacher, St. Jacobs, Ont.*

Soybean
Sandwich Spread

Makes 3 c.

Combine in large mixing bowl:
- 1½ c. cooked, mashed soybeans
- ½ c. sunflower seeds
- ½ c. pureed tomatoes or
  tomato sauce
- ½ medium onion, finely chopped
- 1½ T. pickle relish
- 2 T. ketchup
- ½ c. wheat germ
- 1 t. salt
- ⅛ t. pepper
- ¼ t. thyme

- ¼ c. finely chopped celery
  (optional)

Mix well. Will keep in refrigerator several
days. When ready to make sandwiches,
add a little mayonnaise to desired
consistency and spread a thick layer on
whole wheat bread.

Lois Barrett, Wichita, Kan.

Basic Soybean
Spread or Dip

Makes 2½ c.

Sauté in small skillet:
- 2 T. margarine
- 1 onion, finely chopped
- 1 clove garlic, minced
- 2 T. parsley, chopped

Combine in a bowl:
- 2 c. cooked soybeans, ground
- sautéed onion mixture
- 1 t. dried oregano
- 1 T. soy sauce
- ⅓ c. mayonnaise
- salt and pepper

Mix well. Add further ingredients to taste:
1. Bacon bits, chopped green
   pepper, chili powder.
2. Celery, mustard, and chopped
   hard-cooked eggs.
3. Pickle relish and ground ham
   or tuna.
4. Ground carrots and peanuts.
5. Grated cheese, sunflower
   seeds, and/or nuts.

Spread on whole wheat bread or toast
and add leaf lettuce or bean sprouts if
desired. Or use as dip with crackers or
raw vegetable sticks.

*Lois Hess, Columbus, Ohio
LaVonne Platt, Newton, Kan.*

Soybean Curd Sauté

Soybean curd (tofu) is actually cheese made from soybean milk. A common food in Asia, it is available in North America only in Chinese groceries or health food stores. Contributor says, "This is a very flexible dish; use more meat and less bean curd at first and then gradually reverse it."

Serves 4

Sauté in skillet:
> **1 T. oil**
> **¼ c. chopped onion**
> **2 fresh red chili peppers, finely chopped (optional)**

Add:
> **⅔ lb. fresh pork, sliced in small bite-sized pieces**

Stir-fry until meat is browned.
Add:
> **4 cakes (4x4") bean curd, cut into bite-size pieces**

Stir-fry briefly.
Add:
> **1 c. tomato sauce**
> **½ c. tomato paste**
> **2 T. soy sauce**
> **2 T. vinegar**
> **1-2 c. water (as needed for gravy-like consistency)**
> **2 c. frozen or lightly precooked green beans**

Simmer 15 minutes. Serve over hot steamed rice.

Jean Hershey, Pleiku, Vietnam

Gather Up the Fragments

1.
Mash leftover beans and heat according to Refried Beans recipe, p. *57.* Serve with rice or tortillas. (Complementary protein.)

2.
Spread Refried Beans on toast, sprinkle with cheese, and broil until bubbly. (Complementary protein.)

3.
Spoon hot leftover beans over slices of bread and top with a strip of bacon. Loved by our children as "bean bread." (Complementary protein.)
—William Snyder, Akron, Pa.

4.
Combine leftover baked beans, cooked rice, and drained crushed pineapple plus ketchup, maple syrup, and dry mustard for flavoring. Heat together and serve. (Complementary protein.)
—Emma Brubaker, Harrisonburg, Va.

5.
Add curry powder, turmeric, and cumin to leftover split pea or lentil soup, simmer until somewhat thickened, and serve over rice. (Complementary protein.)

6.
Freeze leftover bean dishes in casseroles for convenient reheating later. Bake and carry to a potluck.

7.
For a quick spicy soup, add tomato juice and chili powder to any leftover beans or lentils.

8.
Add sautéed onions and green pepper and pineapple chunks to leftover baked beans. Bake until bubbly throughout.
—Jocele Meyer, Brooklyn, Ohio

9.
Slice leftover soybean loaf and fry slowly in margarine until brown and crisp. Serve with ketchup.

10.
Mash leftover beans and add to meat loaf.

Main dishes and casseroles

Early American cookbooks devote few if any pages to main dishes and casseroles. Surely Grandmother often built meals around a kettle of beans or a hearty stew. German cooking has its homey "ein-topf" or one-pot meal. But the hamburger-noodle-mushroom soup mixtures so familiar today are newcomers on North American tables.

Main dishes and casseroles have a reputation for economy, but thrifty cooks, beware! If your so-called economy casserole uses a pound of meat for five servings plus a can of soup, sour cream, mushrooms, frozen vegetables, frozen onion rings, and grated cheese to top it off, you might fare more cheaply and nutritiously with meat loaf, baked potatoes, and buttered carrots. Nor are all casseroles a panacea for saving time. If three or more processes are to be done at

stove-top before the creation goes to the oven, you may be putting in as much time as the average meat-potatoes-vegetable meal requires. Certainly you'll have as many pots to wash. Grandmother's beans or stew might have served you better.

Casserole recipes must be evaluated for what they involve. For example, some people reject old-fashioned gravy because it's too caloric but use commercial sour cream freely. Herb-seasoned stuffing mix is the latest fashionable casserole-topper, while in many homes stale heels mold in a corner of the breadbox.

Check again that casserole recipe everyone raved about at the last potluck. Does it call for several costly convenience foods? Is it loaded with empty calories or is there real nutritive value in the ingredients? Does it duplicate expensive animal protein by using meat, cottage cheese, eggs, and grated cheese all in the same dish?

But let's not throw out all the casseroles. Their biggest bonus is advance cooking. You put a casserole in the oven, clean up the kitchen, and relax until mealtime with nothing more on your mind than making a salad and setting the table. Further this advantage by preparing an extra portion for the freezer, or have the dish again later in the week. A different menu every evening is as unnecessary as a different dress every morning.

Soups and Sauces

Contemporary casserole recipes all seem to call for a can of soup. Will future cooks be born, live, and die without knowing how to stir up a smooth white sauce? Will there finally be only three flavors

identified at a carry-in dinner—cream of mushroom, cream of chicken, and cream of celery?

Buy a wire whisk and break the mushroom soup cycle. Save money and cans by returning to the basic five-minute white sauce. Variations are as infinite as the herbs and seasonings on your cupboard shelf and the cheeses, broths, and vegetables in your refrigerator.

Basic White Sauce

	Thin	Medium	Medium-Thick	Thick
Melt in heavy saucepan:				
margarine	1 T.	2 T.	3 T.	4 T.
Blend in, cooking and stirring until bubbly:				
flour	1 T.	2 T.	3 T.	4 T.
salt	¼ t.	¼ t.	¼ t.	¼ t.
Using wire whisk to prevent lumps, stir in:				
milk, stock, or combination	1 c.	1 c.	1 c.	1 c.

Cook just until smooth and thickened. Makes slightly over 1 cup. Medium-thick compares to undiluted condensed soups, and makes approximately the same amount contained in one 10-oz. can.

Options:

Cheese Sauce: Add ½ c. grated nippy cheese and ¼ t. dry mustard.

Tomato Sauce: Use tomato juice as liquid; add dash each of garlic salt, onion salt, basil, and oregano.

Mushroom Sauce: Sauté ¼ c. chopped mushrooms and 1 T. finely chopped onion in margarine before adding flour.

Celery Sauce: Sauté ½ c. chopped celery and 1 T. finely chopped onion in margarine before adding flour.

Chicken Sauce: Use chicken broth or bouillon as half the liquid. Add ¼ t. poultry seasoning or sage, and diced cooked chicken if available.

Vary flavor with the following:
    curry powder
    garlic, onion, or celery salt
    grated nutmeg
    lemon juice
    Worcestershire sauce
    chili powder
    chopped or blended
        vegetables
    chopped parsley
    chopped chives
    chopped hard-cooked eggs

White Sauce Mix **T·S**

In a bowl, stir together:
    1½ c. nonfat dry milk solids
    ¾ c. flour
    1 t. salt
Cut in until mix resembles small peas:
    ½ c. margarine
Store in refrigerator.
To make white sauce:

	Thin	Medium	Thick
white sauce mix	⅓ c.	½ c.	⅔ c.
cold water	1 c.	1 c.	1 c.

Cook and stir with wire whisk over medium heat until smooth and thickened. Vary as indicated for Basic White Sauce. Sauté onions, celery, or mushrooms in small amount margarine before adding white sauce mix and liquid. Makes slightly over 1 cup, or about 10 ounces.

Joanne Lehman, Apple Creek, Ohio
Roberta Kreider, Osceola, Ind.

Combine cooked green beans and diced cooked chicken and bake as an au gratin dish (see p. 152) topped with buttered bread cubes and grated cheese.
—Bonnie Sharp,
    Lancaster, Pa.

Basic Spaghetti or Pizza Sauce

Double or triple recipe for freezing.

Makes about 1 qt.

Sauté in heavy saucepan until tender:
    2 T. oil
    2 cloves garlic, minced
    ½ green pepper, chopped
    1 onion, chopped
Add and sauté until brown:
    ¼-½ lb. ground beef (optional)
Add:
    2 c. tomato sauce
    ¾ c. tomato paste
    1 t. Worcestershire sauce
    1 c. stock, beef, broth, or bouillon
    ¼ t. each oregano, basil, thyme, and cumin
    salt and pepper to taste
Simmer over low heat for 1 hour
Use for spaghetti, lasagne, or pizza sauce.

Options:

Add 1 c. cooked lentils instead of meat *see p. 60*

If available cheaply, add sautéed fresh mushrooms to sauce just before serving.

Linda Albert, Visalia, Calif.

Cook separately: rice, fresh or frozen peas, and cheese sauce. When cooked, combine rice and peas and serve with sauce. I remember this dish from the cafeteria at Eastern Mennonite College, but never could find it in a cookbook. That might be because it's so easy!
—Dolores Bauman,
    Lancaster, Pa.

Lasagne Roll-Ups

Serves 7-8
350°
1 hr.

Cook and drain according to package directions:
10 lasagne noodles

Filling
Steam until limp:
2 bunches spinach, Swiss chard, or turnip greens, finely chopped
Add and mix well:
2 T. grated Parmesan cheese
1 c. cottage cheese
½ t. nutmeg

Topping
Prepare:
1 c. onions, sliced
2 c. grated Muenster or Jack cheese

Sauce
Combine in a bowl:
4 c. tomato sauce
2 cloves garlic, minced or crushed
½ t. basil
½ t. oregano
½ t. marjoram
Spread noodles with filling, roll up, and stand on end in greased 9x13" baking pan. Sprinkle cheese and onions on top. Pour sauce over all. Bake at 350° for 1 hour.

Anne Rogers, East Petersburg, Pa.

Spaghetti With Zucchini Sauce

T·S

Serves 4-6

Sauté in large skillet:
¼ c. oil
1 medium onion, sliced
Add:
2 medium zucchini, sliced (about 6 cups)

3 c. diced fresh tomatoes
½ t. salt
1 bay leaf
¼ t. pepper
¼ t. basil leaves
¼ t. oregano leaves
Simmer covered for 15 minutes; uncover, simmer 10 minutes. Discard bay leaf.
Cook according to package directions:
8 oz. spaghetti
Serve spaghetti topped with zucchini sauce and grated Parmesan cheese

Eleanor Hiebert, Elkins Park, Pa.

Spaghetti And Cheese

Serves 4

Preheat oven to 350°.
Cook and drain as directed on package:
8 oz. spaghetti or noodles
Place in a greased casserole dish.
Sprinkle with:
¾ c. grated cheese
Combine and beat together
½ c. milk
1 egg, beaten
½ t. dry mustard
½ t. salt
dash pepper
Pour over spaghetti and cheese.
Bake 25-30 minutes. Cover first 15 minutes, then uncover to brown. Garnish with parsley. Serve with broiled tomato halves or fresh sliced tomatoes sprinkled with herbs.

Bobbie Wilcox, LaVeta, Colo.

Hamburger Helper—Home-Style

T·S

Serves 4

Brown in a skillet:
- **¾ lb. ground beef**
- **1 t. salt**
- **½ t. pepper**

Add:
- **1 T. finely chopped onion**
- **1 stalk chopped celery**
- **¼ c. frozen or canned peas**
- **⅔ c. fresh or canned tomatoes, chopped**

While beef is browning, cook in salted water:
- **1 c. crinkly noodles**

Drain noodles and spread over meat mixture. Sprinkle over all:
- **½-¾ c. shredded cheese**
  OR ⅓ c. grated Parmesan cheese

Simmer uncovered 15 minutes to blend flavors. Serve from skillet.

Marie L. Berg, Hillsboro, Kan.

Spanish Noodle Skillet

T·S

Serves 3-4

Cut into 1" pieces and fry until crisp:
- **2 slices bacon (optional)**

Set aside. Sauté in bacon drippings:
- **½ onion, chopped**
- **½ green pepper, chopped**
- **½ lb. ground beef**

Pour off any excess fat. Add:
- **1 t. salt**
- **dash pepper**
- **¼ t. oregano**
- **2 c. pureed or stewed tomatoes**
- **¾ c. water**

Cover and simmer 10 minutes. Bring to a boil and add, a few at a time:
- **1½ c. egg noodles**

Reduce heat, cover, and simmer 10 more minutes. Stir occasionally. Top with reserved bacon and serve.

Options:

Omit bacon. Sauté vegetables with ground beef, adding a little oil if beef is dry.

Stir in ¾ c. shredded cheese with noodles. Top with ¼ c. additional cheese just before serving.

Bonnie Sharp, Lancaster, Pa.
Martha Charles, Indiana, Pa.

Meat and Noodle Skillet

Contributor says, "At our house this has been added to and subtracted from all down the list, but it helps with guests and we find they like it."

Serves 6

In large skillet, brown lightly:
- **½ lb. ground beef**
- **½ lb. pork sausage**

Add:
- **1 onion, sliced**
- **1 clove garlic, minced**
- **1½ t. salt**
- **⅛ t. pepper**
- **1 t. crushed dried basil leaves**
- **¾ c. tomato paste**
- **3 c. water**
- **1 can mushroom stems and pieces (undrained)**

Stir well. Add:
- **2 c. wide noodles**

Bring to a boil; reduce heat. Cover and simmer 15 minutes or until noodles are tender, stirring gently two or three times with a fork. Before serving, stir in:
- **3 T. crumbled blue cheese**
- **¼ c. chopped walnuts**

Serve from skillet.

Ruth Ressler, Sterling, Ohio

Macaroni Tomato Pie

T·S

Serves 4
350°
20 min.

Cook and drain according to package directions:

1 c. macaroni

Grease a 9" pie plate and line sides and bottom with macaroni. Pour into macaroni shell:

2 c. stewed tomatoes

Season with:

¼ t. pepper
dash of oregano
1 t. salt

Sprinkle over top:

¼ c. shredded cheddar cheese
¼ c. buttered bread crumbs

Bake at 350° for 20 minutes or until crumbs are brown.

Option:

Brown and season ¼ lb. ground beef. Add to pie just before shredded cheese.

Mary Ella Weaver, Lititz, Pa.

Cottage Cheese Casserole

Contains 15 grams high-quality protein per serving, and is relatively low in calories.

Serves 8
350°
40 min.

Sauté in a large skillet:

2 T. margarine
½ c. chopped mushrooms
½ c. chopped onion
½ c. chopped celery
1 clove garlic, minced

Stir in:

¼ t. marjoram, crushed

4½ c. water
¾ c. tomato paste
4 c. elbow macaroni
2 t. salt
1 t. sugar

Simmer until macaroni is tender, about 25 minutes.
Have ready:

¼ c. parsley, chopped
2 c. cottage cheese
⅓ c. grated Parmesan cheese

Put half of the macaroni mixture in a greased 2 qt. casserole dish. Top with 1 c. cottage cheese and ½ of Parmesan cheese and parsley. Repeat layers. Bake at 350° for 40 minutes.

Selma Johnson, North Newton, Kan

Tangy Tuna-Mac

Serves 3-4
350°
30 min.

Cook and drain according to package directions:

1 c. elbow macaroni

Add and stir to combine:

1 7-oz. can tuna, drained
1 c. tomato sauce
½ c. cottage cheese
¼ c. yogurt or sour cream
1 small onion, minced
½ t. salt

Pour into greased casserole.
Toss together:

¼ c. bread crumbs
1 T. melted margarine

Sprinkle around border of casserole. Bake at 350° for 30 minutes.

Rosemary Moyer, North Newton, Kan

Chicken-Cheese Casserole

Serves 6
350°
45 min.

Cook and drain according to package directions:

¾ lb. noodles

Sauté in a skillet:

5 T. margarine
1 small onion, chopped
3 T. chopped green pepper
½ c. sliced mushrooms (optional)

Add:

5 T. flour

Cook and stir until bubbly.
Add:

1½ c. chicken broth
1½ c. milk
½ t. dry mustard
salt and pepper to taste

Cook, stirring until thickened.
Combine:

white sauce
cooked noodles
3 c. cooked chicken or turkey

Put in greased casserole dish and top with:

⅔ c. shredded cheese
buttered bread crumbs

Bake at 350° for 45 minutes.

Mona Sauder, Wauseon, Ohio
Marjorie Geissinger, Zionsville, Pa.

Anna Lou's Broccoli-Tuna Casserole

Serves 6
350°
20-25 min.

Cook in boiling salted water until barely tender:

2 lb. broccoli, cut in spears

Combine in saucepan:

1 9-oz. can tuna
1 10-oz. can mushroom soup or equivalent sauce (*see* p. 75 **)**

½ c. milk
½ c. grated cheese

Heat until almost boiling. Place layer of cooked broccoli in shallow greased casserole. Cover with layer of tuna mixture. Repeat.
Sprinkle with:

⅓ c. grated cheese

Bake at 350° for 20-25 minutes.

Rosemary Moyer, North Newton, Kan.

Main Dishes with Rice

In the short term, there is probably nothing anyone can do to forestall mass starvation in some rice-dependent areas. But the very least we can do is to take a symbolic stand and cook rice with reverence, taking care that each precious grain swells to its fullest but stays firm and separate from the rest. Perhaps we could even inaugurate our own rice ritual: a moment of silence for those who are not getting enough.
—Raymond Sokolov

How to cook perfect rice? So many North Americans who knew rice only as pudding during childhood ask this question.

The food industry tried to answer it by giving us minute rice. I have never understood the advantages of that food, which to me is expensive, takes more last-minute fiddling than ordinary rice, and is supremely tasteless. It takes exactly 25 minutes to prepare ordinary rice, and seldom can I manage to fix anything to serve with it and complete other meal preparations in less time than that. And during the last 20 minutes ordinary rice requires no attention at all—in fact, tampering with it is forbidden!

Basic Steamed Rice

Serves 6

Combine in heavy saucepan:
1½ c. rice
½ t. salt
Just enough water to rise above rice level to a depth of one inch; Asians measure using index finger from tip to middle of first knuckle.

Over high heat, bring to a full rolling boil. Stir through with a fork, loosening grains at the bottom of the pan. Reduce heat to simmer, cover with tight-fitting lid, and *do not stir or peek* for 20 minutes. (If electric burner stays too hot and causes rice to boil over, pull saucepan partially off the burner for first 5 minutes of cooking time.) After 20 minutes, turn off heat and let rice stand covered until ready to serve. Flake gently while transferring to serving dish. Yields a tender but slightly chewy dry rice with no gluey moisture at the bottom.

Options:

Measure 1⅔ c. water to 1 c. rice. Use cooking method above, but reduce water when cooking large quantities.

Use brown rice but increase cooking time to 45 minutes.

Omit salt if serving rice with salty or spicy side dishes.

Baked Rice

Preheat oven to 350°.
Combine in covered casserole:
2 c. hot water
1 c. rice
½ t. salt
1 T. margarine
Cover and bake 45 minutes or longer for large quantities.

Reheating Rice

Place rice in heavy saucepan and sprinkle with about 1 T water per cup of cooked rice. Heat, covered, over very low heat 20-30 minutes. Stir lightly several times with a fork.

Savory Rice

T·S

Serves 6-8

Combine in large heavy saucepan:
4 c. rice
1 t. salt
1 T. dry parsley and/or dried celery leaves
2 t. whole thyme or 1 t. powdered thyme
¼ t. coarse ground black pepper
2 T. finely chopped onion
2 T. finely chopped green pepper
3 beef bouillon cubes, dissolved in 7 c. water
Bring to a boil; cover and reduce heat to simmer. Cook 20-25 minutes without stirring or peeking.

Dorothy Slagell, Hydro, Okla.

Savory Rice Loaf

The sharper the cheese, the tastier the loaf.

Serves 6
350°
1 hr.

Grease loaf pan (9x5x3"). Line bottom with waxed paper.
Toss together lightly in mixing bowl:
3 eggs, slightly beaten
1½ c. cooked rice
1½ c. grated cheese
½ c. fine dry bread crumbs
¼ c. chopped celery
2 T. chopped onion
2 T. chopped parsley
2 T. chopped green pepper
¾ t. salt
1 c. milk
¼ c. melted margarine
Pour into loaf pan. Place pan in baking dish which contains 1" hot water. Bake at 350° for 1 hour or until loaf is set in center. Loosen loaf around edge with spatula; turn out onto platter. Remove paper. Serve with tomato or mushroom sauce

Lois Hess, Columbus, Ohio

Coconut Rice

To obtain coconut milk, whirl in blender chunks from one fresh coconut with coconut liquid and 2 c. hot water. Let cool to lukewarm. Strain and press out liquid for this recipe and use remaining grated coconut in baking.

Serves 4

Heat in heavy saucepan:
  2 T. oil or margarine
Add:
  ½ c. chopped onion
  2-3 whole cloves
  2-3 cinnamon sticks
  2-3 bay leaves
Fry until onions are lightly browned.
Add:
  ¼ t. ground saffron or tumeric
  ¼ t. salt
Fry a few seconds.
Add:
  1 c. rice
  2 c. coconut milk (see above)
Bring to a boil, reduce heat, cover, and cook 30 minutes. If desired, whole spices may be removed before serving and a few raisins, cashews, or walnuts added.

Doris Devadoss, Calcutta, India

Liza's Tomato Sauce, Rice and Eggs

Serves 6-8

Prepare:
  hot cooked rice for 6-8 people
  (see p. 76)
  1 hard-boiled egg per person
Tomato sauce
Sauté in heavy saucepan:
  3 T. margarine
  1 onion, finely chopped
Blend in:
  4 T. flour
Add:
  4 c. tomato juice
  1½ t. salt
  2 t. sugar
  chopped parsley
  1 beef bouillon cube
  dash pepper
Cook, stirring until thickened. Simmer 5 minutes. Serve over hot rice and garnish with sliced eggs.

Gladys Rutt, New Holland, Pa.

Brown Rice Skillet

Serves 4-6

Heat in skillet to boiling:
  3 c. water
  1 T. instant chicken bouillon
  or 2 cubes
Stir in:
  1 c. brown rice
Cover skillet, reduce heat to low and simmer 45 minutes.
Hard-boil:
  4-6 eggs
Sauté in small skillet:
  2 T. margarine
  ½ c. sliced mushrooms
  2-4 scallions, sliced
When rice is done, stir in:
  hard-boiled eggs, chopped
  1 c. water chestnuts, drained

and sliced (optional)
sautéed vegetables
Heat through. Serve with soy sauce.

Bonnie Krehbiel, Madison, Wis.

Broccoli Rice

Serves 4
350°
45 min.

Cook ½ c. rice *see p. 76* or have ready
1½-2 c. leftover rice.
Sauté in small skillet:
  ¼ c. margarine
  1 onion, chopped
Add:
  2 c. chopped broccoli, cooked
    and drained
  ⅔ c. grated cheese
  ½ c. milk
  cooked rice
Bake in covered casserole at 350° for 45
minutes.

Becky Harder, Mt. Lake, Minn.

Rice Guiso

T·S

Serves 3-4

Heat in heavy saucepan or covered
skillet:
  1 T. oil or trimmed meat fats
Add:
  ¼-½ lb. pork or beef, cut in
    small cubes
Brown well. Add:
  1 onion, chopped
  1 c. rice
  1 t. salt
  ⅛ t. pepper
Sauté briefly. Add:
  1¾ c. water
  2 T. tomato paste (optional)
Cover, lower heat, and cook very slowly
about 30 minutes or until rice is tender.

Myrtle Unruh, Filadelphia, Paraguay

Pizza Rice Casserole

*Meat and cottage cheese together
yield a high-protein dish.*

Serves 6
325°
30 min.

Cook:
  ⅔ c. rice or have
    ready 2 c. leftover rice
Brown in large skillet:
  ¾ lb. ground beef
  1 onion, chopped
Add:
  2 c. tomato sauce
  ¼ t. garlic salt
  1 t. sugar
  1 t. salt
  dash pepper
  ¼ t. oregano
  1 t. parsley flakes
Cover and simmer 15 minutes.
Combine:
  1½ c. cottage cheese
  cooked rice
Put ⅓ of rice mixture in a buttered 2 qt.
casserole. Top with ⅓ of meat-tomato
sauce. Continue to alternate layers,
ending with tomato sauce. Sprinkle with:
  ½ c. shredded cheese
Bake at 325° for 30 minutes, or until hot
and bubbly.

Myrna Schmidt, Lakewood, Colo.

Rice with Cheese And Tomatoes

T·S

Serves 6

Cook:
**1 c. rice (*see p. 76*) or have
    ready 3 c. leftover cooked rice**
Sauté:
**3 T. fat or oil
1 medium onion, chopped
3 stalks celery, chopped
1 green pepper, chopped**
Add:
**2 c. cooked tomatoes
cooked rice
2 c. shredded cheese
1 t. salt
dash pepper**
Cover and simmer until cheese is melted.

Susan Holland, Hillsboro, Kan.

Vietnam Fried Rice

T·S

Serves 4

Cook 1 c. rice (*see p. 76*) or have ready 3 c. leftover rice.
Heat in large skillet:
4 T. cooking oil
Add:
**¼-½ lb. any cooked or raw meat,
    cut into thin strips
3 cloves garlic, minced
1 large onion, chopped coarsely
1 t. salt
1 t. pepper
1 t. sugar
1 T. soy sauce**
Stir-fry until meat is tender and hot, about 1-2 minutes.
Add:
3 c. cooked rice
Stir-fry 5 minutes. Add:
**1 c. leftover or frozen vegetables,
    such as peas, green beans,
    or carrots**
Stir well into rice-meat mixture.
Just before serving, add:
2 eggs, beaten
Over medium heat, stir carefully through rice until eggs are cooked. Serve piping hot with salad of leaf lettuce, cucumbers, fresh mint and parsley.

Pat Hostetter Martin, Quang Ngai, Vietnam

Kay's Japanese Rice

Serves 5-6

Cook:
1½ c. rice
Prepare:
**2-3 carrots, cut in long thin strips
2 onions, sliced very thin and
    separated into rings
½ lb. raw or cooked meat
    or seafood, cut in thin strips**
When rice is nearly done, heat a skillet and add:
**2 T. margarine or oil
meat, if raw
prepared vegetables
salt and pepper**
Stir-fry quickly just until vegetables are crisp-tender and meat is cooked. If using cooked meat, add at the last minute just to heat through. Put mixture in serving dish. Keep warm.
To hot skillet, add:
1 T. margarine or oil
Beat together:
**2 eggs
1 T. milk
½ t. salt**
Pour egg mixture in skillet and allow to spread out. When partially firm, turn like a large pancake and cook briefly on

Use oven method for cooking rice when oven is already hot for other purposes.

second side. Remove from skillet, roll up, and cut into thin strips. Add egg strips and vegetable mixture to hot rice. Stir gently to combine and return to serving dish. Serve with soy sauce.

Option:

Add 1-2 c. bean sprouts with vegetables.

Marjorie Stucky, Murdock, Kan.

Nasi Goreng (Indonesian Fried Rice)

Serves 10-12

Cook 4 c. rice without salt, according to directions on *p. 76*
Heat in large skillet:
   6 T. oil
Sauté until golden brown:
   2 large onions, chopped
Add and sauté for 1 minute:
   ½ t. black or white pepper
   1 t. paprika
   1 t. garlic powder
   1 t. ground coriander
   1 t. cumin
   1 t. tumeric
   2 t. laos (Java galingale root)
   ½ t. sereh powder (lemon grass or citronella)
   2½ t. salt
   Tabasco, dried chili pepper flakes or fresh hot pepper to taste
While preparing the above, sauté in separate skillet:
   1 lb. ground beef, cubed raw chicken, cubed raw pork or small shrimp
Add cooked rice and sautéed meat to spice mixture.
Sauté over low heat, stirring occasionally, to blend flavors (about 10 minutes).
Beat with fork in small bowl:
   4 eggs
   ½ t. salt
   dash pepper
Using skillet in which meat was fried, fry eggs in several thin layers, turning each layer once and rolling each as you take it

from the skillet. Cut each roll into strips ⅛" wide.
Serve fried rice on a large platter. Put strips of egg on top and garnish with radishes, cucumber wedges, and parsley.

Option:

Sereh powder and laos can be omitted but the dish loses some of its Spice Island authenticity. Check availability in Chinese grocery stores.

Jean Miller, Akron, Pa.

Pakistani Kima

It's just an easy hamburger curry—so quick and so good.

T·S

Serves 5-6

Sauté in skillet:
   3 T. butter or margarine
   1 c. chopped onion
   1 clove garlic, minced
Add:
   1 lb. ground beef
Brown well. Stir in:
   1 T. curry powder
   1½ t. salt
   dash pepper
   dash *each* cinnamon, ginger, and tumeric
   2 c. cooked tomatoes
   2 potatoes, diced
   2 c. frozen peas or green beans
Cover and simmer 25 minutes. Serve with rice.

Ann Naylor, Ames, Iowa

Hamburger Casserole

Serves 6
325°
2 hrs.

Combine in casserole with cover:
   1 lb. hamburger
   1 c. uncooked rice
   1 c. diced carrots
   1 c. onions, finely chopped
   2 10-oz. cans tomato soup
      OR equivalent sauce
      (*see p. 70*)
   1 t. salt
   pepper to taste
   2 c. boiling water
Cover and bake at 325° for 2 hours.

Options:

Substitute 1 qt. tomato juice for tomato soup and water.

Sprinkle with ⅓ c. grated cheese 10 minutes before removing from oven.

Verna Wagler, Baden, Ont.
Fran Sauder, Lancaster, Pa.

Pork Sausage Casserole

Serves 6-8
350°
1 hr.

Brown in a skillet:
   1 lb. bulk pork sausage
   1 onion, chopped
Drain excess fat.
Add:
   2 c. raw long-grain rice
   1 c. chopped celery
   ½ c. chopped onion
   ½ t. poultry seasoning
   chopped parsley
   3½ c. boiling chicken broth
   salt and pepper
Bake at 350° for 1 hour.

Elsie Epp, Marion, S.D.
Mary Lou Houser, Lancaster, Pa.

Mandarin Rice Bake

Serves 6
350°
1 hr., 15 min.

Place in greased 2 qt. casserole:
   ¾ c. raw rice
   1½ c. boiling water
   ½ t. salt
Add over rice:
   1½-2 c. cubed ham or other
      leftover meat
   1½ c. chopped celery
   1 c. chopped onion
   ½ c. chopped green pepper
   ¼ c. chopped pimiento (optional)
Stir in:
   1 can condensed cream of chicken
      or mushroom soup OR
      equivalent sauce, (*see p. 70***)**
   2 T. soy sauce
Cover; bake at 350° for 1 hour and 15 minutes.

Evelyn Bauer, Goshen, Ind.

Quick Chop Suey

T·S

Serves 4-6

Cook rice according to directions on p. 125.
Sauté together:
   ½ lb. ground beef
   1 onion, sliced
   ¾ c. celery, sliced
Add:
   2 c. canned (drain) or 3 c. fresh
      bean sprouts
   1 c. beef or chicken broth
   ½ c. sliced mushrooms (optional)
Cover skillet. Simmer 5 minutes.
Combine:
   1 T. cornstarch
   2 T. soy sauce

Add to beef mixture, stirring constantly.
Cook until thickened and smooth.
Serve over hot rice.

Option:

Diced leftover beef, pork, or chicken may
replace ground beef. Sauté onion and
celery in 2 T. oil. Add meat during last 10
minutes just to heat through.

Helen Hiebert, Winkler, Man.

Chow Mein

*You'll stand over the stove, but not for
long; the result has no comparison in
texture and flavor with what comes
from a can!*

Serves 6-8

Cook rice according to method on p. **76**
Prepare and have ready:
  **1 lb. pork, beef, chicken, or
    shrimp, cut in thin slices
  3 c. celery, sliced diagonally
  2 c. onions, sliced lengthwise
  ¾ c. mushrooms, fresh or canned
    (drain)
  3 c. fresh bean sprouts**
Combine in a small bowl and set aside:
  **1 T. fresh ginger, chopped
  OR ¼ t. powdered ginger
  1 t. sugar
  3 T. cornstarch
  5 T. soy sauce
  ¾ c. soup stock or reconstituted
    bouillon**
Heat in a large skillet:
  1 T. oil
Add meat and stir-fry just until done.
Remove from heat. In another skillet,
stir-fry in 1 T. oil each vegetable just until
slightly cooked. Add each vegetable to
meat skillet after stir-frying. Just before
serving, reheat meat mixture and add
sauce. Cook just until sauce thickens
and clears. Serve hot with rice.

LaVonne Platt, Newton, Kan.

Vegetarian Indian Meal

John Nyce, registrar at Goshen College,
Goshen, Indiana, learned to cook Indian
food while teaching at Woodstock
School, Mussoorie, India. Here he
presents menu and recipes for a
complete Indian meal for 7-8 people.
Although no meat is included, proteins in
the split peas, rice, and cottage cheese
or yogurt complement each other for an
adequate supply.

Menu
  Garden Vegetable Curry*
  Curried Split Peas (Dhal)*
  **Long-Grain Rice
  Tomato Chutney***
  **Small Curd Cottage Cheese
    or Yogurt
  Fresh Fruit Tray
  Hindustani Tea***
*Recipes included

The meal requires little last-minute fuss.
Curried Split Peas, Tomato Chutney, and
Hindustani Tea can be prepared 3-4
hours in advance. Garden Vegetable
Curry should be started 1¼ hours before
serving time, but needs minimal
attention the last half hour. Thirty minutes
before serving time cook 3-4 c.
long-grain rice, according to directions
on p. **76**. One pound of cottage cheese
or yogurt served as a side dish adds
protein and provides a pleasant contrast
to the hot spicy dhal and curry. Another
curry (see p.**113**) could be substituted
for the one given here. Food purchase
and preparation could easily be divided
among several households and then put
together for a feast with minimal time
input for anyone.

Garden Vegetable Curry

Serves 7-8

Heat in 3-4 qt. saucepan on medium heat:

3 T. vegetable oil

Add and fry lightly for 4-5 minutes (do not brown):

2 medium onions, finely chopped
2 cloves minced garlic

Add:

2 T. curry powder
1 t. tumeric
1 t. whole cumin seed

Continue frying 3-4 minutes. Add:

1 c. chopped tomatoes

Cook briefly until a thick sauce results. Add:

1 medium head cabbage, chopped
3 medium carrots, diced
4-5 small potatoes, unpeeled and cut into ¾" cubes
3 c. green beans

Stir until all are covered by sauce. Add:

1 t. salt

Reduce heat and simmer 30-45 minutes. Add water any time sauce is below ⅔ depth on vegetables. 15 minutes before serving time, add:

1 T. lemon juice
additional salt if needed

Options:

Use canned or frozen green beans, but add 15 minutes before serving time.

Substitute 1 c. tomato sauce for fresh tomatoes.

Substitute 2 chopped zucchini squash and 3 chopped green tomatoes for cabbage and carrots. Experiment with adding peas, lima beans, eggplant, and cauliflower.

Top curry with halved hard-cooked eggs.

John Nyce, Goshen, Ind.
Lon and Kathryn Sherer, Goshen, Ind.

Curried Split Peas (Dhal)

Serves 7-8

Soak 3-4 hours or by quick method:

1 c. dried split peas or mung beans
2½ c. water

Add:

1 t. tumeric
½ t. cayenne red pepper
1 t. salt

Bring to boil, reduce heat, cover partially, and simmer 20-30 minutes. Peas should be tender and beginning to disintegrate. Add additional water if needed to maintain thick gravy consistency.

Sauté in small frying pan:

3 T. margarine or butter
1 large onion, thinly sliced lengthwise
1 t. whole cumin seed
10 whole cloves
5 whole black peppercorns

Fry until onions are well browned (10-12 minutes). Add onion mixture to cooked peas and set aside until near mealtime. Reheat before serving. Serve as a sauce to be placed over rice.

John Nyce, Goshen, Ind.
Shirley Yoder, Pati, Java
Ruth Eitzen, Barto, Pa.

Tomato Chutney

Serves 7-8

Combine in a bowl:

2 c. chopped fresh or canned tomatoes
1 medium onion, chopped
3 T. lemon juice
2 T. vinegar
1 T. sugar
pinch of salt
pepper

Garnish with fresh coriander, if available. Serve as a side dish with rice and curry.

John Nyce, Goshen, Ind.

Hindustani Tea (Chai)

Serves 7-8

Heat together in a 3-4 qt. saucepan:
6 c. water
7 t. loose tea
Boil 10 minutes. Add:
6 c. milk
Heat to near boiling. Add to taste:
10-15 t. sugar
Tastes best when prepared 2 or more hours in advance and set aside. Reheat during meal and serve with fresh fruit for dessert.

John Nyce, Goshen, Ind.

Easy Curry

T·S

Serves 3-4

Brown in small amount of fat:
¼-½ lb. chicken or other meat (raw or cooked), finely cut
Add:
2-2½ c. water
Chop and add in order according to cooking time needed:
2 medium carrots
3 stalks celery
1 green pepper
½ medium onion
Add:
1 t. salt
⅛ t. pepper
1 T. curry powder
Blend together and add:
·**1 c. tomato sauce**
⅓ c. milk
2 T. cornstarch
Simmer 45 minutes or until vegetables are tender and sauce is thick and glossy. Stir frequently. Serve over rice, noodles, or biscuits.

Marie J. Frantz, North Newton, Kan.

Cracked Wheat or Bulgar Pilaf

T·S

Serves 6

Sauté in a skillet:
1 T. oil
1 small onion, chopped
1 c. cracked wheat or bulgar
Stir over medium heat until onion is transparent and wheat is glazed. Add:
½ t. salt
2 c. broth or stock
Reduce heat to low, cover and cook 25 minutes or until liquid is absorbed.

Option:

¼ lb. sliced mushrooms may be added when sautéing onion; increase oil to 3 T.

Grace Whitehead, Kokomo, Ind.

Beef-Barley Skillet

T·S

Serves 6

Sauté in skillet:
¾ lb. ground beef
½ c. chopped onion
¼ c. chopped celery
¼ c. chopped green pepper
Drain off excess fat. Stir in:
1¼ t. salt
⅛ t. pepper
½ t. marjoram
1 t. sugar
1 t. Worcestershire sauce
½ c. chili sauce
2 c. canned tomatoes, broken up
1½ c. water
¾ c. quick-cooking or pearl barley
Bring to a boil. Reduce heat to simmer, cover, and cook about 35 minutes for quick-cooking barley or 1 hour for pearl barley.

Marjorie Stucky, Murdock, Kan.
Marjorie Ruth, Akron, Pa.

Campfire Pocket Stew

Charcoal Fire
30 min.

Prepare a good bed of coals.
For each person to be served, wash and slice thinly:

1 potato
1 carrot
1 onion
¼ green pepper
small handful fresh green beans

Add:

several ½" chunks of cheese
salt and pepper

Wrap in:

2 large cabbage leaves

Wrap all in aluminum foil, shiny side in, and cook on the coals, 15 minutes on each side.

Karen Kreider, Goshen, Ind.

Six-Layer Dish

Serves 4
300°
2½-3 hrs.

Layer in order given in a 2 qt. greased casserole, seasoning each layer with salt and pepper:

2 medium potatoes, sliced
2 medium carrots, sliced
⅓ c. uncooked rice
2 small onions, sliced
1 lb. ground beef
1 qt. canned tomatoes

Sprinkle over:

1 T. brown sugar

Bake at 300° for 2½-3 hours.

Options:

Just before ground beef add 1 c. cooked kidney beans, drained.

Substitute browned pork sausage for ground beef.

Garden Supper Casserole

Serves 4
350°
30-35 min.

Mix:

2 c. cubed soft bread
½ c. shredded sharp cheese
2 T. margarine, melted

Spread half the mixture in greased 1 qt. casserole and top with:

1 c. cooked peas or
other vegetable

Sauté until tender:

3 T. margarine
2 T. chopped onion

Blend in:

3 T. flour
1 t. salt
⅛ t. pepper

Cook over low heat, stirring until mixture is bubbly.
Stir in:

1½ c. milk

Cook, stirring constantly, until thickened.
Stir in:

1 c. cooked beef, chicken or pork, diced

Pour over peas. Arrange on top:

1 large tomato, sliced (optional)

Sprinkle with remaining bread mixture. Bake uncovered at 350° for 30-35 minutes.

Judy Classen, Akron, Pa.

Meat, Cheese, and Potato Scallop

Serves 4-6
300°
1 hr., 15 min.

Make a cheese sauce:
- **2 T. butter or margarine**
- **2 T. flour**
- **¼ t. salt**
- **1½ c. milk**
- **¾ c. cheese**

Combine in greased casserole:
- **1 medium onion, sliced**
- **4 medium potatoes, sliced**
- **2½ c. canned luncheon meat or leftover ham, diced**

Pour cheese sauce over meat and potatoes mixture. Cover and bake at 300° for 1 hour. Remove cover and bake 15 minutes longer.

Betty Lou Huber, Atmore, Ala.

El Burgos

Serves 8
350°
30 min.

Cook in small amount of water just until tender:
- **5 large potatoes, thinly sliced**

Drain.
Sauté in skillet:
- **1 lb. ground beef**
- **2 green peppers, chopped**
- **1 large onion, diced**

Combine in a bowl:
- **2 c. shredded cheddar cheese**
- **1 t. salt**
- **1 T. brown sugar**
- **2 c. tomato sauce**

Alternate layers of meat mixture and potatoes in greased 2 qt. casserole. Pour cheese-tomato mixture over all. Bake at 350° for 30 minutes.

Mary Ella Weaver, Lititz, Pa.

Easy Moussaka (Greece)

Traditional moussaka includes meat and a custardy cheese sauce which is delicious, but complicated and costly. Try one of these simplified and cheaper versions.

T·S

Serves 6
350°
40 min.

Preheat oven to broil.
Cut into ½" slices:
- **1 large eggplant, unpared**

Place slices on cookie sheet, brush with melted margarine, sprinkle with salt and pepper, and broil 5 minutes, or until golden. Turn slices, brush and season again and brown second side. Set oven at 350° when broiling is completed.
Meanwhile, fry together:
- **1 lb. ground beef**
- **1 onion, chopped**
- **1 clove garlic, minced**
- **salt, pepper, and dash nutmeg**

Add:
- **2 c. tomato sauce**
- **⅓ c. tomato paste**
- **½ t. oregano**
- **1 T. chopped parsley**
- **1 T. chopped mint (optional)**

In 9x9" baking dish, layer half of eggplant slices and half of meat mixture; repeat with remaining ingredients. Sprinkle with:
- **½-1 c. grated cheese**

Bake 40 minutes.

Option:
Omit meat. Sauté onion and garlic in 2 T oil and proceed with tomato sauce.
Combine separately:
- **1 egg, beaten**
- **2 T. Parmesan cheese**
- **1 c. cottage cheese**

Place half of tomato sauce in casserole, add half of eggplant, all of cottage cheese mixture, remaining eggplant, remaining tomato sauce. Sprinkle layers and top with additional Parmesan. Omit last ½-1 c. grated cheese. Bake as directed.

Yaksoba (Japan)

T·S

Serves 4

Cook and drain according to package directions:
  1 c. thin noodles
(Leftover noodles or spaghetti may be used.)
Slice as indicated and have ready:
  ½-¾ lb. round steak, sliced very thin
  2 medium onions, cut in thin wedges
  2 medium carrots, sliced very thin
  ¼ head cabbage, sliced in strips
  2 c. fresh or 1 c. canned bean sprouts, drained
Heat in skillet:
  2 T. oil
Brown meat. Add vegetables in order as given above, stir-frying each a few minutes, and adding salt and pepper with each addition. Add noodles last and cook just long enough to heat through. Vegetables should be crisp-tender. May be served on rice or alone. Pass soy sauce.

Betsey Zook, Leola, Pa.

Ten-Minute All-In-One Meal

T·S

Preheat broiler.
For each person to be served, place side by side on a cookie sheet:
  2 slices whole wheat bread
Layer on each slice of bread:
  1 slice from a large tomato
  1 thin slice from a large onion
  1 slice favorite hard cheese
Broil until cheese melts and edges of bread are crusty.
Eat with fork or fingers.

Flo Harnish, Akron, Pa.

Sausage-Sweet Potato Bake

Serves 4-6
375°
50-60 min.

Brown in skillet:
  1 lb. bulk sausage
Break up large pieces and drain off excess fat
Arrange in 2 qt. casserole:
  2 medium raw sweet potatoes, peeled and sliced
  3 medium apples, peeled and sliced
  browned sausage
Combine and pour over:
  2 T. sugar
  1 T. flour
  ¼ t. ground cinnamon
  ¼ t. salt
  ½ c. water
Cover and bake at 375° for 50-60 minutes, or until potatoes and apples are tender.

Option:
Use cooked or canned sweet potatoes.

Esther Martin, Lancaster, Pa.

New Potatoes And Peas With Ham

Serves 4-6

Scrub and cook in boiling salted water until partially tender:

8-12 small whole new potatoes

Add:

3-4 green onions, chopped
2 c. fresh peas

Continue cooking until vegetables are tender. Drain, reserving liquid.
Make a white sauce:

2 T. margarine
2 T. flour
1½ c. vegetable liquid and milk
salt and pepper

Pour sauce over vegetables. Add:

1-2 c. cubed cooked ham
½ c. grated cheese

Heat through and serve.

Eunice Gerbrandt, Drake, Sask.

Newfoundland Boiled Dinner

In Newfoundland Boiled Dinner is followed by bread or muffins with jam and tea for dessert.

Serves 4-6

Bring to boil in soup kettle:

1-2 lb. ham pieces, ham hocks or ham bone
1 medium onion, cut in chunks water to cover

Simmer until meat is tender. Remove meat from bone and return to broth. Taste broth and add salt if needed.
Cut vegetables in large pieces and add in this order:

3-4 carrots
3-4 yellow turnips
3-4 potatoes
4-6 small whole onions (optional)
1 head cabbage, cut in large wedges

Cover and cook until vegetables are tender.
Serve from pot onto large plates.

Turkey Apple Casserole

Serves 5-6
400°
20 min.

Sauté in skillet until soft, but not brown:

2 T. margarine
3 T. minced onion

Stir in:

½ t. garlic powder
2 t. curry powder
¼ c. firmly packed brown sugar
1¼ c. turkey broth
2 c. pineapple juice

Heat almost to boiling. Add:

2 c. soft bread crumbs
3 c. diced unpeeled red apples
3 c. cubed cooked turkey

Remove from heat and turn into casserole. Sprinkle with:

¼ c. buttered bread crumbs

Bake at 400° for 20 minutes.

Miriam B. Buckwalter, Salunga, Pa.

Colorado Pie

Serves 4-6
400°
25 min.

Prepare pastry for 2-crust pie, using 1 t. onion salt in pastry if desired. Line 9" pie pan with half the pastry. Roll out top crust.
Brown in skillet:

1 lb. ground beef
½ c. chopped onion

Stir in:

1 T. sugar
¼ t. pepper
2 c. cooked green beans, drained
½ t. salt
⅛ t. oregano
1 10-oz. can tomato soup
OR equivalent sauce (see p. 70)

Pour into pastry-lined pan, add top crust and cut slits in it.
Bake at 400° for 25 minutes.

MCC Dining Hall, Akron, Pa.

Cheese Pizza

Serves 4-6
450°
20-25 min.

Crust:
Combine in large bowl:
   1 c. warm water
   1 pkg. yeast
When dissolved, add:
   1 T. sugar
   1½ t. salt
   2 T. vegetable oil
   1¼ c. flour
Beat until smooth. Add:
   **2 c. additional flour, or enough
      to make stiff dough
      (may use part whole wheat)**
Knead until elastic, about 5 minutes.
Place in greased bowl and let rise until
double, about 45 minutes. Form 2 balls.
Pat and stretch to fill 2 greased pizza
pans. Let rise 10 minutes.

Sauce:
Combine in saucepan:
   1 small onion, chopped
   **2½ c. canned tomatoes, OR 2 c.
      tomato sauce, OR 3 c. fresh
      tomatoes, chopped**
   1 bay leaf
   1 t. salt
   1 t. oregano
   ½ t. basil
   dash pepper
   1 clove garlic, minced
Bring to boil, crushing whole tomatoes.
Cover and cook slowly for 30 minutes or
until sauce is slightly thick. Discard bay
leaf. Pour over crust.
Sprinkle on:
   2 T. chopped onion
   1 finely chopped green pepper
   2 t. oregano
   1 t. basil
   salt, pepper and garlic salt, to taste
Arrange on top:
   **½-1 lb. sliced cheese—mozzarella,
      cheddar, and/or Swiss**
Bake at 450° for 20-25 minutes, or until
crust is golden brown.

Kamala Platt, Newton, Kan.
Jocele Meyer, Brooklyn, Ohio

Mini-Pizzas

T·S
Serves 6

Split and arrange on baking sheet:
   6 English muffins
Combine in bowl:
   2 c. tomato sauce
   1 t. salt
   ½ t. pepper
   ½ t. oregano
   ½ t. Italian seasoning
   ¼ t. garlic salt
Coat muffins with tomato mixture.
Sprinkle on:
   2 c. (½ lb.) grated cheese
Broil until cheese is bubbly. Remove and
serve hot.

Options:
Add browned hamburger, sausage,
chopped salami, green pepper, onion, or
mushrooms.

Egg Salad Pizzas:
   4 hard-cooked eggs, chopped
   ½ c. shredded cheese
   ⅓ c. tomato paste
   ¼ c. mayonnaise or salad dressing
   2 T. finely chopped onion
   **to taste: salt, pepper, basil,
      oregano, garlic powder**
Spread on 4 split muffins. Broil until
heated through.

Joan Manolis, Upland, Calif.

Tuna or Chicken Turnovers

Serve with clear soup and green salad.

Serves 5-6
400°
15 min.

Preheat oven to 400°.
Combine:
  1 c. tuna or diced cooked chicken
  1 c. shredded cheese
  ¼ c. chopped celery
  1 t. chives OR 1 t. onion,
    finely chopped
  mayonnaise to moisten
  salt and pepper
Prepare:
  1 recipe biscuit dough
Roll dough ⅛-¼" thick and cut into four-inch rounds or squares. Place about 2½ T. filling on each; fold over and seal. Brush tops with melted margarine. Bake 15 minutes.

Ruth Heatwole, Charlottesville, Va.

Make a pie with leftover cooked spaghetti and meat sauce as follows: Mix spaghetti with a little melted margarine, Parmesan cheese, and a beaten egg. Form into "crust" in greased pie plate. Spread cottage cheese or grated cheese on crust. Pour in thick spaghetti sauce. Sprinkle with additional shredded cheese and bake at 350° for 20-30 minutes.
—Marcia Beachy, DeKalb, Ill.

Bierrocks

Serves 10
350°
20-30 min.

Prepare as for roll dough: (*see p. 28*)
  2 c. warm water
  2 pkg. dry yeast
  ¼ c. sugar
  1½ t. salt
  1 egg
  ¼ c. margarine
  6-6½ c. flour
Chill dough several hours.

Meat mixture:
Brown in skillet:
  1½ lb. beef
  ½ c. onion
Add:
  3 c. cabbage, finely cut
  1½ t. salt
  ½ t. pepper
  dash Tabasco sauce
Cover skillet and continue cooking over *low heat*, stirring occasionally, until cabbage is tender. Do not add liquid. Cool slightly.
Roll out dough into thin sheets. Cut in 5" squares. Place 2 T. meat mixture on each square, pinch edges together, and place pinched side down on greased cookie sheet. Let rise 15 minutes. Bake at 350° for 20-30 minutes.

Options:
Pizza-flavored filling: To browned beef and onion, add:
  ¾ c. tomato paste
  ¼ c. water
  2 t. sugar
  1 t. oregano
  1 t. salt
  ⅛ t. pepper
Cool slightly. Place several tablespoons meat mixture on half of each square. Sprinkle on each:
  1-2 t. grated cheese
Bake as directed above.

Reduce amount of filling, use any roll recipe, and make just enough for one meal as a treat on baking day.

MCC Dining Hall, Akron, Pa.
Louise Claassen, Elkhart, Ind.

Vareniky

*"Vareniky schmaikt goat!" say the
Low Germans. Try this satisfying
meatless dish from Russian
Mennonite tradition. Some cooks
brown vareniky briefly in butter after
taking them from the boiling water.*

Serves 6

Combine in a bowl:
  1 lb. *dry curd* cottage cheese
  1½ T. onions, finely chopped
    (optional)
  ½ t. salt
  3 egg yolks
Mix well with hands until cottage cheese
is in fine curds. Set aside.
Combine in separate bowl:
  3 egg whites, lightly beaten
  1 c. milk
  2 t. salt
  3-3½ c. flour
Mix together, adding flour as necessary
until dough is stiff enough to roll out. Turn
onto floured board. Roll out half of dough
⅛" thick, and cut into squares or circles
5" in diameter. Use large cookie cutter or
invert small bowl on dough and cut
around with knife. Place 1 rounded
tablespoon cottage cheese mixture on
each circle and fold over to form half
circle; pinch edges firmly. Repeat with
remaining dough and dough scraps.
In saucepan, heat 4-6 c. water to boiling.
Add 1 t. salt. Drop vareniky into boiling
water, several at a time. Cook five
minutes. Remove with slotted spoon and
drain. Keep hot.
Serve with *cream gravy*.
Sauté in a skillet:
  2 T. margarine
  1 small onion, finely chopped
    (optional)
Add:
  1 c. cream
  salt and pepper to taste
Heat slowly, but do not boil.

  Susan Duerksen, Killarney, Man.
  Ruby J. Wiebe, Hillsboro, Kan.

Mexican-American Dishes

A variety of economical but
delicious Mexican-American foods
can be made from basic ingredients
such as tortillas, chili sauce, and
refried beans. Tortillas are usually
cheap if available fresh or frozen;
packaged dry varieties are
expensive. *See p. 43* for flour
tortilla recipe, or look for masa
harina flour mix for home
preparation. Refried beans are
available canned, but home-cooked
beans are easy to make and far more
economical. *See p. 57*.

Quesadillas

Have ready:
  **1 can (7 oz.) California green
    chilies, seeds and pith removed**
  **1 lb. Jack cheese, cut in sticks,
    1x4x½"**
  12 corn or flour tortillas
  **margarine, lard or salad oil for
    frying (optional)**
Place about half a chili and a thick stick
of Jack cheese in the center of each
tortilla. Fold tortilla over cheese and pin
shut with a small toothpick.
Fry in shallow hot fat until crisp, turning
occasionally. Drain on paper towels. Or
heat and soften the tortilla on each side
on a medium-hot ungreased griddle or
frying pan, until cheese has melted.
Chilies may be omitted.

  Carol Friesen, Reedley, Calif.

Chili-Tomato Sauce

Makes about 3 cups

Sauté in heavy saucepan:
2 T. salad oil
1 medium-sized onion, minced
When onion is just yellow, not brown,
add:
3½ c. tomato puree or sauce
2 cloves garlic, minced or mashed
1-2 T. chili powder
¼ t. dried oregano
1 t. salt
Cover and simmer at least 30 minutes,
stirring frequently. Put through medium
strainer. Use for tacos or enchiladas.

Carol Friesen, Reedley, Calif.

Burritos

*Great for eating on the run, camping,
or with small children.*

Spoon refried beans or scrambled eggs
onto heated tortilla.
Top with grated cheese.
Roll up, tucking in ends to keep filling
from falling out.

Marianne Miller, Topeka, Kan.
Carol Friesen, Reedley, Calif.

Navajo Tacos

Spread **Navajo Fry Bread** (p.42) with
Refried Beans (p. 57)
Top with **shredded cheese** and broil
until cheese melts.
Sprinkle generously with **shredded
lettuce.**

Shirley Kauffman Sager, Arriba, Colo.

Enchiladas

Serves 6
350°
15-20 min.

Brown in skillet:
¾ lb. ground beef
1 medium onion, chopped
Stir in:
2 c. refried beans (see p. 57)
1 t. salt
**½ t. garlic powder or 1 clove
garlic, mashed**
Heat until bubbly, cover, and keep warm.
Prepare:
12 tortillas
Dip, one at a time, in shallow hot oil to
soften; drain quickly.
Heat chili-tomato sauce (see p. 92)
pour about half into an ungreased,
shallow 3 qt. baking dish. Place about ⅓
c. beef-bean filling on each tortilla, and
roll to enclose filling. Place, flap side
down, in the sauce in the bottom of the
baking dish. Pour remaining sauce
evenly over tortillas; cover with:
**2 c. (½ lb.) shredded cheddar
cheese**
Bake uncovered at 350° for 15-20
minutes, or until thoroughly heated.

Options:

Bake immediately or assemble and
refrigerate several hours or overnight.

Roll enchiladas as described above, or
spread filling over tortillas and stack
evenly. Cut stack in wedges to serve.

Omit meat. Sprinkle a little shredded
cheese over refried beans before rolling
up each tortilla.

Carol Friesen, Reedley, Calif.

Empanadas (Mexican Turnovers)

Serves 6-8
400°
15-20 min.

Sift together in bowl:
  2 c. flour
  2 t. baking powder
  1 t. salt
Cut in:
  ½ c. shortening
Add:
  ⅓ c. cold milk
Stir into a ball, handling like pie crust. Roll out thin and cut in 4″ rounds or squares. Place a spoonful of filling on one half of a round. Fold over, moisten edges, and press firmly so they seal. Deep fry, or bake 15-20 minutes at 400°.

Fillings:
— ground cooked chicken or beef, sautéed with onion, raisins, and blanched slivered almonds. Add ½ t. cumin, 1 t. chili powder. 1 beaten egg.
— refried beans, grated cheese, and chopped chili.
— tuna or salmon with mushrooms, chopped chives, and chili.
— for sweet turnovers, add 2 T. sugar to dry ingredients while making dough. Fill with 3 oz. cream cheese blended with 3 T. strawberry or apricot preserves, or simply with shredded cheese. Sprinkle fried empanadas with confectioners sugar.

Lois Deckert, North Newton, Kan.
Myrtle Unruh, Filadelphia, Paraguay
Geraldine Lehman Mumaw,
  Santa Cruz, Bolivia

Tacos

To prepare taco shells:
  Fold warm tortillas in half and use as is with fillings below, or fry each tortilla briefly in shallow hot fat (about ¼″), turning once and then folding in half before tortilla becomes too crisp. Drain folded shells on absorbent paper and keep warm until ready to serve.
Fillings:
  refried beans
  browned ground beef
  chopped cooked chicken
  chopped onions, tomatoes,
    radishes, avocado
  finely shredded lettuce
  grated cheese
  hot chilies
  chili-tomato sauce
Serve basket of taco shells with fillings in individual bowls, inviting guests to make their own. Refried beans, chopped onions, shredded lettuce, grated cheese, and chili-tomato sauce would provide enough variety for a delicious meal.

Anne Rogers, East Petersburg, Pa.
Sam, Lois, Jennie, and Sara Miller,
  Harrisburg, Pa.

Cook separately: rice, fresh or frozen peas, and cheese sauce. When cooked, combine rice and peas and serve with sauce. I remember this dish from the cafeteria at Eastern Mennonite College, but never could find it in a cookbook. That might be because it's so easy!
—Dolores Bauman,
  Lancaster, Pa.

Gather Up
the Fragments

1.
"Meat in spaghetti sauce doesn't have to be only ground beef," says my sister-in-law of Italian ancestry. She accumulates odds and ends of any kind of cooked meat, chops it finely, and uses it in her sauce, which is outstanding.
—Helen Peifer, Akron, Pa.

2.
When reheating leftover casseroles, make and pour over a little more of the sauce used, whether tomato, cream sauce, etc. Add a fresh sprinkling of cheese or bread crumbs and bake. Reheated look and dry texture is gone.

3.
Freeze leftover main dishes in small casseroles to heat for one or two persons—handy when parents are going out but must feed children first, or for spouse at home alone.

4.
Whirl small amounts of leftover main dishes in the blender and incorporate resulting sauce into another soup or main dish. For example, leftover macaroni and cheese goes into a cheese sauce.

5.
Use dollops of leftover mashed potatoes with cheese sprinkle to top a variety of casseroles, not just Shepherd's Pie.

6.
Use leftover rice for fried rice (**see recipes, pp. 79, 80**). Stir-fry leftover cooked noodles or spaghetti in the same way with scallions or onions, bits of meat, vegetables, and eggs. Eat with soy sauce.

7.
Some recipes using leftover rice:

Eggs, milk, and cheese

Eggs are a complete protein food containing all the essential amino acids required by the human body. In fact, the amino acid pattern of eggs is closer to matching the ideal pattern than that of any other high-protein food, including meat.

Eggs rank low among animal proteins in amount of grain required in production. But, like other animal protein foods, eggs should be used carefully. An egg contains 7 grams of complete protein. If a meal includes an egg or more per person plus vegetable protein in breads or legumes, let that be enough. Adding deviled eggs or Pennsylvania Dutch red-beet eggs to a meal including meat is a waste of protein. Instead serve these egg specialties occasionally to replace meat.

Eggs team up naturally with milk and cheese. Combinations like scalloped eggs, soufflés, and quiches (cheesy main-dish custard pies) can be as high in protein per serving as several ounces of meat.

Milk and Cheese

Principles that apply to using eggs responsibly also fit milk and cheese. One glass of milk (8 oz.) has 8.5 grams of complete protein, more than 1 egg. A 1-inch cube of cheddar cheese has 7 grams protein, and ½ cup of cottage cheese has 15. Do we need cheese cubes on an appetizer tray, cottage cheese salad, and a glass of milk with a ham dinner? From menus like these come the figures that show North Americans eating 90-plus grams of protein per person daily.

Buying cheese. So many varieties and styles of cheese line the dairy case that a shopper can be thrown into total confusion. Two guidelines are worth remembering: 1) Always check *price per pound*, 2) know the difference between *natural* and *pasteurized process cheese.*

Cheese often comes packaged in odd sizes rather than in 1-pound chunks. Some wrappers show the number of slices in huge print but to read the ounces contained you must find a light and adjust your glasses. Thrifty shoppers find the price per pound no matter what other information is offered.

Sorting out the difference between natural and pasteurized process cheese takes more skill. *Natural cheese,* sometimes called hard cheese, is simply made from coagulating milk and separating curds from whey. Varieties of natural cheese resulting from different ripening processes include cheddar, longhorn, Jack, Swiss, Edam, colby, brick, Muenster, Parmesan, and on and on.

Pasteurized process cheese, often called American, is made from natural cheese by shredding,

melting, pasteurizing, and adding an emulsifier. If the words *cheese food* or *cheese spread* appear on the label, even more liquids and stabilizers than are allowed in pasteurized process cheese have been added.

Pasteurized process cheese is understandably cheaper, because it contains more added liquids. Natural cheese, while a little more expensive, gives you more protein and calcium and fewer additives. Process cheese may be handy for certain recipes, such as Cheese Spread. But for sandwiches and most recipes, you get as much for your money with natural cheese. Commercial cheese foods and cheese spreads are particularly poor buys.

Many recipes in this book do not identify which kind of cheese to use. This is intentional, encouraging you to look for best buys in your community and use what is on hand.

Both eggs and cheese respond best to short cooking time on low-medium heat. High heat and long cooking give tough, rubbery products. Be a gentle cook and save energy while you save the texture of your eggs and cheese.

Puffy Cheddar Omelet

Serves 3

Beat until soft peaks form:
    4 egg whites
In separate small bowl, beat together:
    4 egg yolks
    ¼ c. mayonnaise
    3 T. water
    ½ t. salt
Carefully fold yolk mixture into whites.
Heat in 10″ skillet:
    2 T. margarine

Add egg mixture. Cook without stirring over low heat until egg is cooked through, about 15 minutes. Cover after 5 minutes to insure even cooking.
Sprinkle on:

1 c. finely shredded cheddar cheese

1-2 T. chopped herbs, such as parsley, chives, basil, or tarragon

Cover long enough to melt cheese. Fold omelet in half and slide onto warm plate.

Frances Lehman, Goshen, Ind.

Old-Fashioned Bread Omelet

Contributor says this was her mother's standby when unexpected guests stayed for Sunday evening supper.

Serves 4
325°
10 min.

Combine and soak 15 minutes:

1 c. bread cubes

½ c. milk

Preheat oven to 325°.
Combine in bowl:

4 eggs, beaten

¼ c. grated cheese

½ t. salt

bread and milk mixture

Heat in skillet:

1 T. margarine

Pour in egg mixture and cook over medium heat without stirring, about 5 minutes. When browned underneath, place pan in oven for 10 minutes to finish cooking on top. Turn out onto hot platter, folding omelet in half.

Adele Mowere, Phoenixville, Pa.

Scrambled Eggs And Noodles

Serves 5

Cook and drain according to package directions:

2 c. wide noodles

Heat in a skillet:

3 T. margarine

Add noodles and stir-fry briefly.
Combine and pour over:

3 eggs, beaten

⅓ c. milk, cream or evaporated milk

salt and pepper to taste

Scramble until eggs are set.
Garnish with paprika, chopped parsley, and tomato wedges.

Option:
Sauté chopped scallions or onion in margarine before adding noodles.

Bobbie Wilcox, LaVeta, Colo.

Poached Egg Surprise

Serves 4

Make 1 c. Medium White Sauce (*see p. 70*).
Stir in:

2 T. chopped green pepper

Place on individual serving plates:

4 slices toast

Spread toast thickly with:

soft sharp cheese

Poach until firm:

4 eggs

Place an egg on each slice of toast and pour hot sauce over all.

Elvera Goering, Salina, Kan.

Huevos Rancheros (eggs poached in tomato sauce)

Serve with green salad and corn muffins for supper or late-morning breakfast.

Serves 6

Sauté in skillet:
  3 T. oil
  1 green pepper, thinly sliced
  1 large onion, chopped
  2 cloves garlic, minced
Add:
  2 large fresh tomatoes, finely chopped OR 2 c. stewed tomatoes, drained
  ½ c. tomato sauce
  ½ t. salt
  1-2 T. chili powder
  ½ t. cumin
  ½ t. oregano
Cook over medium heat 20 minutes, occasionally mashing tomatoes.
Break into hot sauce:
  6 eggs
Cover eggs with:
  6 slices mozzarella cheese
Cover skillet and poach eggs over low heat 3-5 minutes, or until as firm as desired.

Elizabeth Yoder, Bluffton, Ohio

Swiss Eggs

T·S

Serves 6
375°
25 min.

Preheat oven to 375°.
Cover bottom of shallow greased casserole with:
  1 c. grated Swiss or cheddar cheese
Make 6 depressions in cheese. Slide an egg into each depression, using:
  6 eggs

Sprinkle with:
  ¼ c. cream or evaporated milk
  salt and pepper
  chopped parsley
Top with:
  ½-1 c. additional grated cheese
Bake 25 minutes or until eggs are firm but not hard.

Ruth Eitzen, Barto, Pa.

Sunny Scalloped Eggs

Serves 4-5
400°
15 min.

Sauté in heavy saucepan:
  ¼ c. margarine
  1 c. diced celery
  2 T. minced onion
Blend in:
  3 T. flour
Cook and stir until bubbly. Add:
  1 t. salt
  1½ c. milk
Cook and stir until thick. Stir in:
  2 T. chopped parsley
Arrange in greased 5-c. casserole:
  6 hard-cooked eggs, halved
Pour sauce over eggs. Toss together:
  2 T. melted margarine
  1 slice bread, cubed
Place on top of casserole. Bake at 400° for 15 minutes.

Options:

Stir ¾ c. shredded cheese into white sauce.

Eggs Florentine: Cook ¾ lb. fresh or 2 c. frozen spinach just until tender. Drain, chop, and season. Place in bottom of 2 qt. casserole. Proceed with recipe as given, placing eggs and sauce on top of spinach. Top with grated cheese and buttered crumbs. Serves 6.

Prepare as in Option 2, but substitute broccoli for spinach. Chop broccoli or leave in spears.

Helen June Martin, Ephrata, Pa.
Janice Wenger, Ephrata, Pa.

Cheese Fondue

With a crisp green salad, cheese fondue makes a hearty meal.

Serves 6

Melt in fondue pot:
2 T. margarine
Add:
3 T. flour
Stir until blended. Add:
2½ c. milk
1 t. caraway seeds, soaked in hot water for 15 minutes (optional)
dash Worcestershire sauce
Add gradually:
1 lb. Swiss or cheddar cheese, diced
Stir until cheese melts. When it begins bubbling, add:
1 t. salt
1 T. lemon juice
⅛ t. nutmeg
Spear cubes of crusty French or rye bread with fondue fork and dunk.

Options:

Make fondue in a heavy saucepan. Keep warm over hot water.

Pour fondue over bread cubes for individual servings.

Kamala Platt, Newton, Kan.
Annie Lind, Windsor, Vt.
Ruth Eitzen, Barto, Pa.

Give more color and flavor to an old standby by layering macaroni and cheese in a casserole with a cup or two of the Basic Spaghetti Sauce (p. 71). Top with shredded cheese and bake until bubbly.

Chili Con Queso (a Mexican Fondue)

Serves 4

Heat in fondue pot:
1 c. stewed tomatoes or tomato sauce
chilies or cayenne pepper to taste
Add slice by slice:
24 slices American cheese
Serve with an assortment of dunkers:
carrot strips
celery
cauliflower
corn chips
tortillas
breadsticks
bread cubes

Kamala Platt, Newton, Kan.

Oven Cheese Fondue

Tester's five-year-old says it tastes like toasted cheese sandwiches.

Serves 5
325°
30 min.

Preheat oven to 325°.
Beat until lemon-colored:
5 eggs
Add and mix well:
1 t. salt
dash pepper
2-3 c. grated cheese
Add:
2½ c. hot milk
1 qt. cubed bread
Pour into greased 7x11" baking pan.
Bake 30 minutes, or until set.
Top with chopped parsley just before serving.

Florence Mellinger, Lancaster, Pa.
Erma Clemens, Chestertown, Md.

Cheese Strata

Serves 6
350°
45 min.

Preheat oven to 350°.
Butter lightly:
   12 slices bread (can be stale)
Arrange 6 slices in bottom of 9x13"
greased baking dish. Cover with:
   6 slices cheese or 2 c. shredded cheese
Top with remaining bread.
Beat together and pour over:
   2⅔ c. milk
   4 eggs
   ¾ t. salt
   ¼ t. dry mustard
Bake 45 minutes or until puffed and
golden. May be prepared in advance
and refrigerated before baking.

Option:

Add a layer of sautéed vegetables
(onion, green pepper, mushrooms) or
leftover cooked vegetables just before
cheese.

Janet Landes, Phoenix, Ariz.
Ruth Magnusen, Glendale, Ariz.
Viola Wiebe, Hillsboro, Kan.

Basic Cheese Soufflé

Serves 4-6
350°
50-60 min.

Preheat oven to 350°.
Make 1 c. Thick White Sauce (**see p. 70**).
Add to hot white sauce:
   ⅛ t. pepper
   ¼ t. dry mustard
   3 egg yolks, slightly beaten (reserve whites)
   1 c. shredded sharp cheese

Stir until cheese melts. Remove from
heat.
Beat until stiff but not dry:
   3 egg whites
   ¼ t. cream of tartar
Carefully fold egg whites into cheese
sauce. Pour into ungreased 1½ qt.
casserole and set in pan of hot water 1"
deep. Bake 50-60 minutes, until puffed
and golden. Serve immediately.

Options:

Corn Soufflé: Omit cheese. Fold 2 c.
fresh grated or home frozen (thawed)
corn into white sauce.
Broccoli or Spinach Soufflé: Cook ¾ lb.
broccoli or spinach. Drain and chop
finely (should yield 1½-2 c.). Omit
cheese. Fold vegetable into white sauce.
Chicken Soufflé: Reduce cheese to ¼ c.
Fold 1 c. finely chopped cooked chicken
into white sauce.

Kitty Collier, Millersville, Pa.
Joann Smith, Goshen, Ind.
Chris Schmidt, Walton, Kan.

Bread and Cheese Soufflé

*Light and delicate as any
traditional soufflé.*

Serves 4-5
350°
30-40 min.

Preheat oven to 350°.
Scald in a saucepan:
   1 c. milk
Add:
   1 c. soft bread crumbs
   1 c. shredded cheese
   1 T. margarine
   ½ t. salt
Stir until cheese melts, heating gently if
necessary.
Separate:
   3 eggs
Add cheese mixture to beaten egg yolks;
beat egg whites until stiff, but not dry and
fold into cheese mixture. Pour into
greased 1 qt. baking dish. Set in pan of
hot water and bake 30-40 minutes, until
puffed and golden.

Jean Horst, Lancaster, Pa.

Cheese and Rice Soufflé

Contributor's teenage son requested this for his birthday dinner. Doris serves it with green beans, garlic bread, and fresh fruit tray.

Serves 5
350°
40 min.

Preheat oven to 350°.
Make a white sauce:
  2 T. margarine
  3 T. flour
  ¾ c. milk
Add:
  2 c. sharp cheese, shredded
Cook over low heat, stirring constantly, until cheese melts.
Add to cheese sauce:
  4 egg yolks, slightly beaten
    (reserve whites)
  ½ t. salt
  dash pepper
  1 c. cooked rice
Remove sauce from heat and pour into large bowl.
Beat until stiff, but not dry:
  4 egg whites
Gently fold whites into cheese mixture. Turn into greased soufflé dish. To form crown, with spoon make shallow path about 1" in from edge all the way around. Bake 40 minutes and serve at once.

Doris Yoder, Newton, Kan

Quiche Lorraine

Serves 8-10
375°
10 min./45-50 min.

Crust
Mix as for pie crust:
  2 c. sifted flour
  ½ t. salt
  ¼ t. sugar
  ½ c. chilled margarine cut into
    ½" bits
  3 T. chilled vegetable shortening
  5 T. cold water
Roll out and fit into 2 9" pie pans. Prick pastry with fork. Bake at 400° for 10 minutes.

Quiche Filling (enough for 2 pies)
Beat until blended:
  6 eggs
  2 c. light cream or
    evaporated milk
  2 c. milk
  1 t. salt
  dash pepper
  dash nutmeg
Add:
  2 c. grated Swiss cheese
Pour into pastry shells. Bake at 375° for 45-50 minutes. Cool 5 minutes before serving.

Option:
Place in pie shells before pouring in egg mixture:
— 1 chopped onion, sautéed
— 4 slices bacon, fried crisp
  and crumbled
  OR 1-2 c. cooked ham, finely
  chopped

Joann Smith, Goshen, Ind.
Eleanor Hiebert, Elkins Park, Pa.

Tomato Quiche

Serves 6

375°
---
10 min./40-45 min.

Preheat oven to 375°.
Prepare 1 9″ pie shell. Bake for 10 minutes.
Place in shell:
  2 c. chopped or sliced tomatoes
Sprinkle with:
  ½ t. basil
  1 t. salt
  ⅛ t. pepper
  ½ t. sugar
  4 scallions, chopped
Spread over tomatoes:
  ½ c. grated Swiss cheese
  ½ c. grated cheddar cheese
Combine:
  2 eggs, slightly beaten
  2 T. flour
  1 c. evaporated milk
Pour over cheese and bake at 375° for 40-45 minutes, or until set.
Cool 5 minutes before serving.

Mary Lou Houser, Lancaster, Pa.
Carry Dueck, Saskatoon, Sask.

Cornmeal Quiche

Serves 6

425°/350°

25-30 min.

Crust:
Combine in bowl:
  ½ c. cornmeal
  ¾ c. sifted flour
  ½ t. salt
  ⅛ t. pepper
Cut in:
  ⅓ c. shortening, soft
Sprinkle over while tossing with a fork:
  3 T. cold water
Stir lightly until mixture will form a ball.
Roll out on lightly floured board. Fit loosely into 9″ pie plate; fold edge under and flute.
Preheat oven to 425°.

Filling:
Lay on bottom of unbaked crust:
  6 slices or 1¼ c. shredded cheese
Spread over cheese:
  2 c. whole kernel corn, well drained
Combine in a bowl:
  5 eggs
  ¾ c. light cream or evaporated milk
  1 t. salt
  ¼ t. cayenne
Beat until well blended. Pour over corn.
Place on bottom rack of oven. Bake for 15 minutes. Reduce temperature to 350° and continue baking 25-30 minutes. Let stand 10 minutes before cutting and serving.

Eleanor Hiebert, Elkins Park, Pa.

Meat-Potato Quiche

Attractive and delicious with its crispy-brown potato edging.

Serves 4-5

425°
---
15 min./30 min.

Preheat oven to 425°.
In 9″ pie pan, stir together:
  3 T. vegetable oil
  3 c. coarsely shredded raw potato
Press evenly into pie crust shape. Bake at 425° for 15 minutes until just beginning to brown. Remove from oven.
Layer on:
  1 c. grated Swiss or
    cheddar cheese
  ¾ c. cooked diced chicken,
    ham, or browned sausage
  ¼ c. chopped onion
In a bowl, beat together:
  1 c. evaporated or rich milk
    (part cream)
  2 eggs
  ½ t. salt
  ⅛ t. pepper

Pour egg mixture onto other ingredients. Sprinkle with:

1 T. parsley flakes

Return to oven and bake at 425° about 30 minutes, or until lightly browned, and knife inserted 1" from edge comes out clean. Allow to cool 5 minutes before cutting into wedges.

Donna Koehn, Blaine, Wash.

Torta Pascualina (Argentine Spinach Pie)

Serves 4
350°
30-40 min.

Have ready:

1 pie shell and crust for top, unbaked

Cook, drain, and chop finely:

1½ c. frozen or 2 qt. fresh spinach

Sauté until tender:

2 T. oil
1 onion, chopped

Combine:

spinach
sautéed onion
¼ t. nutmeg
1 t. oregano
½ t. salt
2 beaten eggs
1 c. grated Swiss cheese

Pour into pie shell. Arrange top crust and seal. Bake at 350° for 30-40 minutes. Serve hot in wedges.

Carol Byler, Montevideo, Uruguay
Jean Gerber Shank, Goshen, Ind.

Eggs Foo Yung

Eggs Foo Yung can be made on an electric griddle or frying pan at the table.

Serves 6-8

Patties:
Brown in skillet:

½ lb. ground beef

Combine in bowl:

¾ c. finely chopped onion or scallions
¼ c. finely diced celery
1 c. canned (drain) or 2 c. fresh bean sprouts
6 eggs, well beaten
1 t. salt

Add beef to egg mixture. Heat in a skillet:

2 T. fat

Fry by ¼ cupfuls. Keep patties shaped with pancake turner by pushing egg back into the patties. When set and brown on one side, turn and brown other side. Serve hot with rice and sauce.

Sauce:
Combine in saucepan:

¼ c. soy sauce
1 T. cornstarch
2 t. sugar
2 t. vinegar
¾ c. water or chicken broth

Cook, stirring constantly, until sauce clears. Keep hot.

Helen Hiebert, Winkler, Man.

Grits and Cheese Casserole

Hominy, a traditional Southern United States favorite, is dried corn with the hull and germ removed.

Serves 8
275°
1 hr.

Bring to boil in saucepan:
4 c. water
Add:
1 c. hominy grits
Cook over low heat 5 minutes, stirring occasionally. Remove from heat.
Add:
⅓ c. margarine
2 c. shredded cheese
1 t. Worcestershire sauce
6 drops hot pepper sauce
1 t. salt
3 eggs, beaten
Turn into 2 qt. casserole. Sprinkle with paprika.
Bake at 275° for 1 hour.

Miriam Bowers, Grantham, Pa.

Creamy Egg and Noodle Bake

Very high in protein—over 20 gr. per serving. Homemade yogurt cuts cost.

Serves 8
350°
25 min.

Cook and drain according to package directions:
3 c. noodles
Sauté until tender:
2 T. margarine
½ c. finely chopped onion
Combine:
sautéed onion
drained noodles
8 hard-cooked eggs, chopped
Combine separately:
2 c. small curd cottage cheese

1 c. plain yogurt
⅓ c. Parmesan cheese
2 t. poppy seed
1 t. Worcestershire sauce
½ t. salt
dash pepper
Fold into noodle mixture. Pour into greased casserole.
Combine and sprinkle over:
¾ c. soft bread crumbs
1 T. melted margarine
Bake uncovered at 350° for 25 minutes.

Becky Mast, State College, Pa.

Cheese Spread

A big saving over commercial cheese spreads!

Makes 5 4-oz. jars

Combine in top of double boiler:
1⅔ c. (1 can) evaporated milk
1 lb. pasteurized process (American) cheese, grated
Heat and stir over hot water until cheese melts. Remove from heat and add:
2 T. vinegar
½ t. dry mustard
½ t. salt
dash cayenne pepper
flavoring (see options)
Stir occasionally as spread cools. Store covered in refrigerator. Keeps several weeks.

Options:

Flavor with crumbled bacon or soybean-based bacon substitute, crumbled blue cheese, chopped pimiento, or onion and garlic salt.

After spread cools, form into ball or rolls. Roll in chopped nuts or parsley. Serve with crackers or celery.

Dorothy King, Dalton, Ohio

Sour Cream Substitute

Makes 1¼ c.

Combine in blender container:
¼ c. water
1 c. cottage cheese
Blend on high speed for 20 seconds, until cottage cheese is liquified.
Add:
1 t. lemon juice
½ t. salt
¾ t. garlic or onion salt
chopped chives, or parsley
Use on salads, baked potatoes, or as a dip with fresh vegetable sticks.

Virginia Birky, Salem, Ohio

Buttermilk (from dry milk powder)

Makes 1 qt.

Pour into quart jar:
3 c. water at room temperature
Add:
1⅓ c. dry milk powder
Stir until dissolved. Add:
½ c. commercial buttermilk
dash of salt if desired
Stir until blended. Let stand at room temperature until thickened. Stir just until smooth; refrigerate. Stir before using. Save ½ c. buttermilk to use as the base for next batch.

Rosemary Moyer, North Newton, Kan.

Cottage Cheese

Makes 1⅓ lb. cheese

Scald with boiling water:
3-quart saucepan
measuring cup
whisk or slotted spoon
Measure into saucepan and mix:
10 c. warm water (110°)
4 c. dry milk solids
1 c. commercial buttermilk or
starter from previous batch
Incubate at 90° constant heat for 11 hours, or until the milk has set to the consistency of custard. (A sharp knife will leave a clean cut.) If when you check the milk you find that the whey is separated, you will know that it has set too long. A good incubating place in most homes is the kitchen oven with *only* the light turned on.

Cut the curd. Dip out one cup of curd with a scalded dipper and put it into a scalded container. Stir. Cover tightly. Set in very cold place in back of refrigerator to keep for your next batch of cheese. With a sharp blade that reaches to the bottom of the pan, cut the curd in ¾″ checkerboard squares. Slash crosswise with the knife to make uniform cubes. Let stand undisturbed 15 minutes.

Cook the curd. Pour hot water (120°) over the curds to a depth of 1 inch. Set pan in a large pot containing hot water (120°). Heat so gradually that the curd temperature rises 3 degrees every 10 minutes. Very gently rotate the curds, tumbling them over with a spoon, trying not to break them up. Repeat this every 10 minutes. At the end of 1¼ hours the curds should be shrunken quite separate from the whey.

Drain the curd. Dip the curds into a cotton bag or cloth. Reserve the whey for cooking and baking. Wash curds with tepid, then very cold water.
Add:
1 t. salt
Mix gently. Hang bag up to drain until cheese has reached the consistency you prefer. Store in a covered container in the refrigerator. For creamed cottage cheese, add:
½ c. cream

Option:

Buttermilk: Prepare milk for fermentation as directed. When curd is set, stir it vigorously with a whisk. Save a starter for future batches.

Used by permission from The No Fad Good Food $5 a Week Cookbook, *by Caroline Ackerman. New York: Dodd, Mead & Co., 1974.*

Making Cheese

Basic directions for soft or hard cheese:
1.
Ripen the milk: Add 1 cup starter to 1 gallon fresh milk. Use buttermilk, yogurt, clabbered milk, or a commercial powdered cheese starter. Cover and set at room temperature overnight.
2.
Add rennet: Add ½ rennet tablet dissolved in ¼ c. cool water and stir thoroughly. Cover and leave 30-45 minutes, or until milk coagulates. This step can be omitted if, in ripening the milk, you let milk set 18-24 hours or until it separates.
3.
Cut the curd: When curd is firm and a little whey appears on the top, use a long sharp knife to cut into ½" strips lengthwise. Then slant the knife and cut crosswise in the opposite direction. Stir carefully with a wooden spoon.
4.
Heat the curd: Place the container of curds and whey into a larger container of water and heat slowly to 100°F. The temperature should rise 2 degrees every five minutes. Hold at this temperature until curd is of desired firmness. Gently squeeze a small handful of curds; curd is ready when it breaks easily and doesn't stick together. This should happen 1½ to 2½ hours after adding the rennet. For cream cheese, curd can be softer than for other types.
5.
Remove the whey: Pour curds and whey into a colander or strainer lined with cheesecloth or a clean dish towel. Stir or work through with your hands until whey has drained off and curds have cooled to 90°F. Save whey.*
6.
Salt the curd: Sprinkle salt to taste throughout the curd and mix well. To make *cottage cheese*, pour curds into a bowl, add a little cream, chill and serve. To make *cream cheese*, put in a cheese press** for 5 minutes to form.
To make *hard cheese*, proceed as follows:

7.
Press the curd: Wrap curd in a circle of cheesecloth. Put in cheese press and insert follower. Start with a weight of 3 or 4 bricks for 10 minutes; drain off any whey, replace follower, and add 2 more bricks. Remove from press after 1 hour.
8.
For *mild cheese*, press the cheese: Remove cheesecloth; rinse the cheese in warm water; smooth any holes in the surface. (If the cheese is not firm do not wash.) Dry with a cloth and replace in press. Let set 18-24 hours. Cheese is now ready to eat.
9.
For *sharper cheese*, cure as follows: Wash and smooth cheese under warm water; put cheese on a shelf in a cool, dry place. Turn and wipe daily for 3 to 5 days, until a rind forms. Heat ¼ lb. paraffin to 210°F. Hold cheese in the paraffin for 10 seconds, covering the whole surface. Put cheese back on the shelf in a cool place and turn daily. Cheese can be cured any length of time up to five months, but taste from time to time to make sure it doesn't get stronger than you want. Each time you make cheese, results may be a little different. Don't let a failure deter you from trying again.

•
Use whey in baking or cooking to replace water. Whey may be recooked to make various kinds of cheese; look for instructions in more detailed cheese-making manuals.

••
Make cheese press from a plastic jug. Cut off both ends and cut two circular boards to fit tightly inside. Punch nail holes in the bottom board for drainage. Place bricks on top of the follower board to make weight.

Kamala Platt, Newton, Kan.

Gather Up
the Fragments

1.
Moldy cheese: Just trim off mold and use remaining cheese—it's perfectly safe.

2.
Hard, dry cheese: Grate finely and sprinkle over spaghetti or other Italian dishes.

3.
Leftover egg yolks: Cover unbroken yolks with water to prevent drying out in the refrigerator.

— Two egg yolks will replace one whole egg in thickening power.

— Don't fret looking for special recipes calling for a few egg yolks; use them to enrich scrambled eggs, fried rice, breads, cakes, cookies, coffee cakes, sauces, puddings, and custards.

— Gently hard-cook unbroken egg yolks in small amount water. Grate over salads, sauces, or vegetables.

— To feed egg yolks to baby, break egg and drop yolk into gently boiling water to hard-cook. Collect whites in container in refrigerator or freezer. (To use whites, see below.)

— Mix one egg yolk with 1 T. water and brush over rolls and bread before baking—gives a lovely glaze.

— Use in these recipes:
Mock Hollandaise Sauce, *p. 154*
Cooked Mayonnaise, *p. 171*
Pumpkin Ice Cream, *p. 195*

4.
Leftover egg whites:

— Use 1 or 2 whites with several whole eggs in scrambled eggs or omelets—recommended for low-cholesterol diets.

— Beat 1 or 2 extra whites until stiff and fold into waffle or cake batter. Yields a higher, lighter product.

— Make a cornstarch pudding without eggs; pour into baking dish. Beat egg whites into meringue, adding 2 T. sugar per egg white. Spread over pudding and brown in oven. Good for cholesterol-watchers.

— Use in these recipes:
Jelly Frosting, *p. 201*
Whipped Topping II, *p. 200*

Meats and fish

Meat could be used more imaginatively in North America. There are ways of serving meat other than placing a three by six-inch slab on every dinner plate.

When our family set up housekeeping in Saigon, I watched our cook unpack her market basket. I could not believe anything special would result from the tiny piece of pork and the little handful of shrimp she unfolded from a banana leaf. In my terms, it was enough to serve one person, and we were having guests. But that little bit of meat flavored a whole array of Vietnamese dishes. Vegetables and meat both tasted more exciting than do the Western each-stewed-in-its-own-juices varieties. This is one reason Oriental cuisine has so many converts.

Most of the recipes in this chapter are for meats as such. Check also the way meats are used together with vegetables in Chapters 4 and 8. No wonder our children will not eat vegetables. We cook them limp and watery and serve them up plain, when they could be stir-fried half crisp, complemented Asian-style with bits of meat and a delicious sauce. Try the Japanese Yaksoba (*on page 87*), given me by a fourth-grade child who usually doesn't like her vegetables either.

In a beautiful way, using meat carefully and creatively also saves money and benefits health.

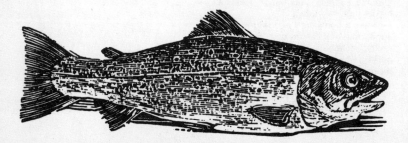

Convenience products which have a long shelf life, such as luncheon meats and hot dogs, contain preservatives. Additives for color, flavor, and texture are also used liberally. These extended meat products may look cheap compared to raw fresh meat. Consider the cost of ingredients, however, to determine if you can do the same thing yourself for less.

Stir bread crumbs or ground soybeans into a meat loaf, and make enough for tomorrow's sandwiches. You pay less for both the meat and the filler than if you buy bologna. Get a sharp knife and slice your own cold cooked meat. Freeze ground cooked meat in convenient-sized containers for spreads. Rely on peanut butter, cheese, egg salad and soybean spreads (*see p. 67*)

Buy cheaper cuts

In the future as much grain as possible must be conserved for people to eat directly. This may mean slightly tougher meat calling for long, slow cooking, but also meat that is lower in price, cholesterol, and calories.

For tougher cuts, learn to make stews and curries. The Chinese Savory Beef (*p. 112*), is a dish I often made in Vietnam where some chunks of beef brought home from the market were dark red, utterly devoid of fat, and tough as shoe leather. I suspect this "beef" originated from the backsides of worn-out water buffaloes who had plowed many a paddy. Savory seasoning and 4-hour stewing turned the shoe leather into delicious tender dishes.

Soy, Cheese, and Meat Loaf

Serves 5

375°

45 min.

Preheat oven to 375°.
Combine in mixing bowl:
- **½ lb. ground beef**
- **2 oz. vegetable-protein meat extender with**
- **¾ c. milk**
  OR ¾ c. ground cooked soybeans, mashed
- **2 eggs**
- **⅓ c. bread crumbs or rolled oats**
- **½ c. grated cheese or cottage cheese**
- **2 T. minced parsley**
- **1 minced onion**
- **1 t. salt**
- **pepper**

Shape into loaf and spread with ketchup or tomato sauce, if desired. Bake 45 minutes. Let cool 5 minutes before slicing.
To mash soybeans easily, whirl in blender together with eggs and cottage cheese.

Christine Swartzendruber, Ft. Wayne, Ind.
Olive Schertz, Tiskilwa, Ill.

Basic Burger Mix

Make up in quantity and freeze patties to save time later.

Serves 6
350°
35 min.

Put through food grinder in order given:
    1 c. cooked soybeans, drained
    1 c. any cooked meat OR raw ground beef (grinding not necessary)
    1 onion, coarsely chopped
    1 c. whole wheat bread pieces
Add:
    2 T. parsley, chopped
    2 eggs, beaten
    1 t. salt
    ½ t. celery salt
    ½ t. garlic salt
    2 t. Worcestershire sauce
    other seasonings to taste
Form into patties and coat with:
    ½ c. dry bread crumbs or wheat germ
Fry in oil, bake at 350° for 35 minutes, broil, or grill over charcoal. Serve in warm buns with lettuce and tomato.

Option:
Omit meat and add 1 c. cooked brown rice.

Lois Hess, Columbus, Ohio

Poor Man's Steak

Serves 5-6
300°
1½ hr.

Combine and mix well:
    1½ lbs. ground beef
    ½ c. fine bread or cracker crumbs
    ½ c. water
    2 t. salt
    ½ t. pepper
Pat out about ¾" thick on cookie sheet. Refrigerate overnight. Cut into pieces, dip into flour, and brown in small amount hot fat.
Preheat oven to 300°.
Lay pieces in baking dish or roaster.
Pour over:
    1-2 c. mushroom or tomato sauce (see p. 70)
Bake 1½ hours.

Anna Petersheim, Kinzers, Pa.
Clara Yoder, Milford, Del.

Hamburger Stew

Serves 6

Brown in heavy kettle:
    1 lb. ground beef
Drain excess fat and add:
    2 c. tomato juice
    ½ c. chopped onion
    1 c. diced potatoes
    1 c. diced carrots
    2 t. salt
Cover and simmer until vegetables are tender.
Make white sauce:
    2 T. butter
    2 T. flour
    2 c. milk
Blend into first mixture and serve.

Option:
Add limas, soybeans, corn, green beans or other vegetables. Increase liquid as needed.

Sarah E. Campbell, Dayton, Va.

Oven Beef Stew

Serves 4
350°
2 hrs.

Shake in a bag:
  2 T. flour
  1 t. salt
  dash of pepper
  1 lb. beef cubes
Heat in heavy skillet:
  2 T. shortening
Brown beef cubes, then place in greased casserole dish.
Preheat oven to 350°.
Add:
  2 c. tomato juice
  1½ c. chopped onion
  ½ t. dried basil
Cover and bake 1 hour.
Add:
  4 medium potatoes, cubed
  4 medium carrots, cut in 1" pieces
Bake 1 hour longer, or until tender.

Bonnie Zook, Leola, Pa.

Five-Hour Stew

Serves 8
250°
5 hrs.

The evening before, brown in Dutch oven:
  2 lbs. stew meat, dredged in flour
Add:
  favorite seasonings (salt, pepper, garlic, basil, parsley)
  3 large potatoes, cut up
  1 medium onion, cut up
  4 carrots, cut in chunks
  1 qt. stewed tomatoes
  ¼ c. tapioca, sprinkled over all
Refrigerate overnight. Bake covered, for 5 hours at 250°.

Lois Zehr, Ft. Dodge, Iowa

Filled Round Steak

Serves 4-5
300°
2 hrs.

Prepare:
  1-1½ lbs. round steak
If 1" thick, cut through horizontally to make thin large steaks. Or pound a ¾" steak to make it large and thin.
Combine for filling:
  1 c. leftover mashed potatoes
  ⅓ c. dry bread crumbs
  1 small onion, diced
  1 egg
  salt and pepper to taste
Spread filling over meat and roll up. Tie with string or secure with toothpicks. Place in baking pan. Baste with bacon drippings or margarine, cover, and bake at 300° for 2 hours, or until tender.
Remove to platter and slice.
Serve with brown gravy:
  Brown in 4 T. meat drippings:
  2-3 T. flour
  salt and pepper
  pinch sugar
Add liquids from cooking vegetables. Cook and stir until thickened.

Susanna Vogt, Drake, Sask.

Hamburger–Onion Pie

Serves 6-8
400°
30 min.

Preheat oven to 400°
Combine with fork.
> **1 c. biscuit mix (see p. 32)**
> **⅓ c. light cream or evaporated milk**

Knead and roll dough to line 9" pie pan.
Sauté:
> **1 lb. ground beef**
> **2 medium onions, sliced**

Add:
> **1 t. salt**
> **¼ t. pepper**
> **1 t. curry powder**
> **2 T. flour**

Spread meat mixture in dough-lined pan.
Combine:
> **2 eggs, slightly beaten**
> **1 c. small-curd cottage cheese**

Pour over meat but *do not* mix. Sprinkle
with paprika.
Bake 30 minutes.

Viola Wiebe, Hillsboro, Kan.

Fiesta Sloppy Joes

Serves 6

Brown in heavy skillet, keeping meat in
chunks:
> **1 lb. ground beef (may use**
> **part soy extender)**

Drain off excess fat. Add:
> **¾ c. uncooked rice**
> **1 c. sliced onion**
> **¼ c. chopped green pepper**
> **1 clove garlic, minced**
> **½ t. sugar**
> **¼ t. dry mustard**
> **¼ t. celery seeds**
> **1 t. salt**
> **¼ t. chili powder**
> **2 c. cooked tomatoes or**
> **1½ c. tomato juice**

Bring to a boil. Reduce heat to low,
cover, and cook 25 minutes without
stirring. Stir and serve hot in buns.

Author's Recipe

Chinese Savory Beef

Serves 8

Heat in heavy skillet or Dutch oven:
> **2 T. oil or minced fat from beef**

Add and quick-fry until brown:
> **2 lb. lean beef, cut in 1½" squares**
> **(may use very tough meat)**

Add and quick-fry a few minutes:
> **3 scallions, chopped**
> **OR 1 onion, chopped**
> **2 cloves garlic, crushed**
> **2 thin slices ginger (optional)**

Add:
> **½ c. soy sauce**
> **2 T. brown sugar**
> **⅛ t. pepper**
> **3 c. water**

Bring to a boil. Reduce heat, cover, and
simmer 3 hours. Add more liquid if
needed. Just before serving thicken with
small amount flour if desired. Serve over
rice or noodles.

Option:

20-30 minutes before serving add ½ lb.
vegetables, such as green pepper,
mushrooms, or carrots.

Author's Recipe

Chinese Meatballs

Serves 8

Cook rice or noodles to serve 8.
Prepare and reserve ready to fry:

**1 cucumber, peeled and sliced
2 stalks celery, sliced
2 green peppers, sliced
1 large onion, sliced
1½ c. frozen peas
2 large tomatoes, cut in wedges
1½ c. pineapple chunks, drained
(reserve juice)**

Season, shape into small balls, and fry:

**1½ lb. ground beef (may use
part soybean extender)**

Combine and pour over meatballs:

**¾ c. brown sugar
¾ c. vinegar
3 T. soy sauce
½ t. ginger
juice from pineapple
2-3 T. cornstarch**

Allow sauce to thicken, then reduce heat and simmer 20 minutes.
In separate skillet, stir-fry vegetables in small amount of hot oil until crisp-tender, adding tomatoes and pineapple last.
Serve on large platter with rice or noodles in center, meatballs around, vegetables over the rice, and sauce over all.

Erma Weaver, Manheim, Pa.

Basic Meat Curry

See also p. 113 for Vegetable Curry and side dish recipes.

Serves 8

Sauté in heavy deep skillet or kettle:

**2 T. fat, oil, or shortening
2 onions, finely chopped
1-2 cloves garlic, minced**

Blend in small bowl:

**2 T. lemon juice or vinegar
2-4 t. curry powder**

Stir curry mixture into sautéed onions and fry lightly 1-2 minutes. This produces a relatively mild curry; if desired, season with additional spices as listed under Option 1 below.
Add *one* of the following:

**1 3-lb. chicken fryer, cut into
12-15 small pieces
2 lbs. beef, cut in 1" chunks
2 lbs. mutton, cut in 1" chunks
2 lbs. boneless fish, cut in chunks
3 c. any leftover cooked
diced meat
2 lbs. meatballs, browned**

Stir-fry briefly to coat meat with spices.
Add:

**1 c. tomato juice or sauce
1 t. salt
1-2 c. broth or water**

Bring to a boil, reduce heat, cover, and simmer about 2-3 hours for beef and mutton, 1½ hours for chicken, 20 minutes for fish and cooked meats. Add more liquid during cooking as needed for thin stew consistency. Thicken slightly with flour just before serving, if desired.
Serve with hot steamed rice and, if desired, a selection of the following condiments placed in small bowls:

**Chop Salad, p. 175
Tomato Chutney, p. 83
peanuts
sunflower seeds
coconut
chopped scallions, onions,
tomatoes, green pepper
pineapple tidbits
diced apples
raisins
banana slices
chopped hard-cooked eggs**

Options:

Ideally all curry powder should be added at the beginning and fried briefly before adding meat. But if later the curry tastes bland, add more. Experience tells. Curry is a blend of spices; among those used are cardamom, cloves, cinnamon, coriander, tumeric, ginger, cumin, and cayenne. Season with these alone or use in combination with curry powder.

About 20 minutes before serving add 2 medium potatoes, cubed.

Egg curry: Replace broth or water with additional tomato sauce. Use 8-10 hard-cooked eggs, halved, to replace meat. Heat through and serve.

Make curry ahead of time and reheat before serving. Freezes well.

Author's Recipe

Genghis Khan

Serves 5-6

Heat in heavy skillet:
   2 T. oil
Add and brown quickly:
   1 lb. thinly sliced mutton or beef
Add:
   2 large onions, sliced
   4 carrots, thinly sliced
   2 green peppers, sliced
   2 stalks celery, sliced
Stir-fry briefly, then add:
   ¼ c. Worcestershire sauce
   ⅓ c. soy sauce
   1 T. sesame seeds
Heat through until vegetables are crisp-tender. Serve over hot rice.

Ruth Zook, Toyoto, Japan

West African Groundnut Stew

Serves 8

In large heavy kettle, heat:
   3 T. oil
Add:
   2 lbs. beef cubes, 1" or smaller, rolled in flour
While browning, add:
   ½ t. nutmeg
   1 T. chili powder
When meat is browned, add:
   4 medium-sized onions, sliced
   1 clove garlic, minced
   ¾ c. tomato paste
   6 c. water
   red pepper, if desired
Simmer until meat is tender.
A half hour before serving, heat in small saucepan:
   ½ c. chunky peanut butter
   2 T. oil
Stir over medium heat 5 minutes. Add peanut-butter mixture slowly to beef stew and simmer over low heat 20 minutes. Serve over rice. May be accompanied with small dishes of condiments. See curry condiments

Options:

Use chicken pieces in place of beef.

To use leftover cooked meat, begin by sautéing onion and garlic, then add meat with tomato paste and water.

Grace Hostetter, Lagos, Nigeria
Alice and Willard Roth, Elkhart, Ind.
Vietta Nofziger, Barberton, Ohio

Liver Fricassee

Serves 6

Pour boiling water over:
1 lb. sliced liver
Let stand 5 minutes. Drain, wipe dry and cut into strips.
Dredge with:
½ t. salt
⅛ t. pepper
¼ c. flour
Brown quickly in hot bacon or other fat.
Add:
½ t. poultry seasoning
½ t. celery salt
1 c. cooked tomatoes
1 onion, chopped
1 c. boiling water
Simmer 45 minutes. Serve with cooked noodles.

Elsie Epp, Marion, S.D.

Stir-Fried Liver

T·S

Serves 4

Cut in strips:
½ lb. partially frozen liver
Combine:
2 slices fresh ginger root, minced (optional)
2 t. cornstarch
2 t. cooking sherry (optional)
1 T. soy sauce
¼ t. sugar
Add to liver and toss to coat. Let stand 20 minutes.
Heat in skillet:
2 T. oil
Add:
2 scallions, chopped
1 clove garlic, minced
½ t. salt
approx. 2 c. of any of these vegetables, sliced:
mushrooms, peas, green beans, celery, carrots, green pepper
Stir-fry just until vegetables are crisp-tender. Remove vegetables from skillet. Add liver and stir-fry 2-3 minutes. Return cooked vegetables to skillet and stir to reheat. Serve over rice.

Option:

Just before returning vegetables to skillet, add a sauce of 1 c. beef broth and 2 t. cornstarch.

Louise Lehman, Wapakoneta, Ohio
Lois Kauffman, West Point, Neb.

Our-Children-Love Liver

Serves 4-5

Cut into sticks about ½" wide and 2-3" long:
1 lb. partially frozen sliced beef liver
Place liver sticks on absorbent paper to catch excess juice as meat thaws.
Fry in a large skillet:
2-4 slices bacon
When crisp, remove and set aside.
Combine in paper bag:
¼ c. flour
1 t. salt or seasoned salt
dash pepper
Shake liver sticks in the bag. Place one by one in hot skillet and fry in bacon fat over medium heat. Turn sticks individually with sharp-tined fork as they brown. Fry only until crisp and golden—5-8 minutes. Remove to platter.

Add small amount oil to skillet if necessary.
Add and fry briefly, stirring constantly:
1 onion, sliced and separated into rings
Sprinkle with salt and pepper. When onion rings just begin to wilt, transfer to platter and arrange over liver sticks with crisp bacon, broken into pieces. Eat as finger food and pass ketchup for dipping.

Author's Recipe

Pork Hocks Pot Dinner

Put the oven heat to good use with a dessert and some baked goods for the week ahead.

T·S

Serves 4
325°
4 hrs.

TS—needs time not attention

Preheat oven to 325°.
Place in large casserole with cover:
4 pork hocks
Cover with:
**2-3 c. drained sauerkraut
(reserve liquid)
1 t. caraway or celery seed
¾ c. sliced onion**
Pour over:
**reserved sauerkraut liquid plus
water to make 2 c.**
Cover and bake 3 hours.
Add to casserole:
**4 medium potatoes, pared and
halved
salt and pepper to taste**
Cover and continue baking 1 hour or until
meat and potatoes are tender.

Lois Kauffman, West Point, Neb.

Wild Game Braise

*"Venison, mutton, goat, or economy cuts
of beef can be transformed into company
fare with this method. The aroma is
wonderful! Bake potatoes and an apple
dessert alongside," says contributor.*

Serves 12
325°
3-4 hrs.

Heat in heavy skillet or Dutch oven:
cut-up fat or tallow from meat
When skillet is well-greased, remove
remaining fat pieces.
Brown in hot fat, a layer at a time:
**3 lbs. meat, sliced ¾" thick
(use less tender cuts)**
Season with:
salt and pepper
Add:
1 c. hot water
Sprinkle over in a layer:
**2 large onions, sliced
salt and pepper**
Bring to boiling point and cover.
Bake at 325° for 3-4 hours. Add more
water if necessary.
Make gravy from pan drippings.

Martha Nafziger, LaCrete, Alta.

Ham Loaf

Serves 8
350°
1½-2 hrs.

Combine in bowl:
**1 lb. fresh pork, ground
1 lb. cured ham, ground
1 c. bread crumbs
1 egg
1 t. salt
⅛ t. pepper
¾-1 c. milk**
Mix well. Shape into a loaf, dust with
flour, and place in baking pan.
Bake at 350° for 1½-2 hours.
At the end of 1 hour pour over the loaf
either
1 c. tomato juice
or this sauce:
**¾ c. brown sugar
1 t. dry mustard
½ c. water
½ t. vinegar**
Bring to boil before pouring over ham
loaf.

*Mennonite Community Cookbook, used
by permission.*

German Pork Chops

T·S

Serves 6
350°
1 hr.

Preheat oven to 350°.
Place in bottom of greased casserole dish:

2-3 potatoes, pared and sliced

Sprinkle with:

salt, pepper, and caraway seed to taste

Add:

2 c. drained sauerkraut

Sprinkle with more caraway seed.
Top with:

6 pork chops
salt, pepper, and caraway seed

Pour over:

⅓ c. water

Bake, covered, 1 hour, or until done.
Uncover last 15 minutes to brown chops.

Danita Laskowski, Goshen, Ind.

Baked Beef Heart

Serves 10-12
300°
2 hrs.

Prepare heart by removing as much fat and tendon as possible. Salt freely with seasoned salt. Fill with moist bread stuffing.

Place heart in a covered roaster and add about ½" water. Bake at 300° for 2 hours. Potatoes and green beans may be added to the roaster, allowing 1 hour cooking time.

Slice through heart and stuffing to serve. Arrange slices on platter with vegetables.

Vietta Nofziger, Barberton, Ohio

Sweet and Sour Pork

Serves 5

Combine in bowl for marinade:

1 egg, beaten
1 T. sugar
1 t. salt
1 T. soy sauce

Add to marinade and let stand 20-30 minutes:

1 lb. lean pork, cubed

Prepare and set aside:

1 clove garlic, minced
4 slices ginger root, finely chopped (optional)
1 green pepper, cut in chunks
1 onion, cut in wedges
1 tomato, cut in wedges
¾ c. pineapple chunks, drained (reserve juice)

Combine and set aside:

3 T. vinegar
3 T. brown sugar
2 T. soy sauce
1 T. cornstarch
¾ c. pineapple juice

Heat in a wok or skillet:

4 T. oil

Dredge pork cubes in cornstarch. Fry on all sides until brown. Remove from skillet and keep warm. Pour off excess fat if necessary, leaving about 2 tablespoons. Stir-fry garlic, ginger, peppers, and onions 2-3 minutes. Add tomato chunks, pineapple chunks, and sauce ingredients. Cook just until sauce thickens and clears. Return pork to skillet, heat to bubbling, and serve immediately with hot rice. Onions and peppers should be partially crisp.

Jessie Hostetler, Portland, Ore.
Bonnie Zook, Leola, Pa.

Pork–Grits Sausage

Groats are hulled and crushed or coarsely ground grains. Buckwheat groats (South Dakota Mennonites say "gritz") are eaten in Russia as kasha. This old recipe from the Freeman community probably originated in Russia.

Makes 3-4 lbs. sausage

Boil until well done:
  3 lb. pork roast in
  several cups water
Place in large bowl:
  2 c. buckwheat groats (grits)
Pour boiling pork broth over groats. Set aside.
Sauté until clear, but not brown:
  ¼ c. fat
  1 large onion, chopped
Grind the cooled pork. Combine:
  groats (drain off some broth
    if necessary)
  meat
  onions
  salt and pepper
Form into patties and freeze.
To serve brown in frypan or broil.

Adina Graber, Freeman, S.D.

Grace's Kitchen-Stove Scrapple

Delicious for lunch or supper as well as breakfast.

Serves 6-8

Brown in skillet:
  1 lb. bulk sausage or
    hamburger-sausage mixture
Drain off some fat, if necessary.
Add:
  1 small carrot, grated
  ¼ c. chopped celery
  ½ c. chopped green onion
Sauté until tender. Season with salt, pepper, onion, and garlic salt as desired.

In large saucepan, bring to a boil:
  3 c. water or stock
Combine and stir slowly into boiling water:
  1 c. cold water
  1 c. cornmeal
Stir constantly over medium heat until thick. Cover and cook 10 minutes longer, stirring occasionally.

Add sausage-vegetable mixture to cornmeal mixture. Rinse loaf pan in cold water, then pour in scrapple. Cover and refrigerate overnight. Slice ½" thick, dip in flour, and fry until crisp. Serve with syrup, apple butter, or ketchup.

Grace Whitehead, Kokomo, Ind.

Cornmeal Scrapple

Serves 6-8

In heavy saucepan, bring to boil:
  3½ c. water, stock or broth
Combine in bowl:
  1½ c. cornmeal
  ⅓ c. flour
  1½ t. salt
  ⅛ t. each savory, sage, and pepper
  1½ c. cold water

Slowly add cornmeal mixture to boiling water, stirring constantly with wire whisk. When thickened, add, bit by bit:

¾ c. raw ground meat (beef or pork)

When well blended, turn into double boiler and cook slowly over hot water for 2 hours. Pour into a loaf pan and chill at least 12 hours. Slice ¼-½" thick, dust with flour, and fry in shallow hot fat until golden. Serve with syrup, jam, applesauce, or apple butter.

Arlie Weaver, Chinle, Ariz.

Coating Mix For Oven-Fried Chicken

T·S

Makes 2⅓ c. mix

350°

1 hr.

Combine in a bowl:

2 c. dry bread crumbs (see p. 44)
1½ t. salt
1½ t. paprika
1 t. celery salt
1 t. onion salt
¼ t. pepper
1 t. poultry seasoning (optional)
¼ c. vegetable oil

Blend ingredients with fork or pastry blender until well mixed. Keeps unrefrigerated in tightly covered container.
When ready to use:
Preheat oven to 350°.

Put ½ c. coating mix in plastic or paper bag. Moisten chicken pieces with water or milk and shake one piece at a time in bag. Add more mix as needed. Lay chicken skin-side up in greased pan and bake 1 hour or until tender. No turning needed.

Option:

Use for fish fillets. Bake 30 min.

Grace Anders, Souderton, Pa.

Baked Herb Chicken

T·S

Serves 6

325°

1¼ hrs.

Preheat oven to 325°.
Arrange in 9x13" baking pan:

1 3-lb. fryer, cut up

Combine and pour over:

1¼ c. thick mushroom sauce (see p. 70)
OR 1 can mushroom soup
1 t. grated lemon rind
2 T. lemon juice
½ t. salt
¼ t. basil
¼ t. oregano

Bake uncovered 1¼ hours. Serve with hot cooked rice.

Option:

Bake at 250° for 2½-3 hours—makes a good Sunday chicken dinner.

Carolyn Weaver, Lancaster, Pa.

Honey-Baked Chicken

Serves 6

350°

1¼ hrs.

Preheat oven to 350°.
Arrange in shallow baking pan, skin-side up:

1 3-lb. fryer, cut up

Combine and pour over:

⅓ c. margarine, melted
⅓ c. honey
2 T. prepared mustard
1 t. salt
1 t. curry powder

Bake 1¼ hour, basting every 15 minutes, until chicken is tender and nicely browned. Good served with rice.

Jan Harmon, Upland, Calif.

Two Meals For Four People From a Three-Pound Chicken

Meal 1: Chicken Stew
Combine in soup kettle:
    5 c. water
    4 chicken bouillon cubes
    ¼ c. wine vinegar
    celery leaves
    1 onion, chopped
    1 chicken, cut in pieces
    salt and pepper
Place in tea ball or spice bag and add:
    4 cloves
    4 peppercorns
    ½ bay leaf
Simmer until chicken is tender. Near end of cooking time, add desired vegetables, such as:
    4 medium potatoes, halved
    4-6 carrots, in large chunks
    1-2 c. fresh or frozen peas
        (add shortly before serving)
Remove spice ball. Remove to serving dish meaty chicken pieces and vegetables. Reserve some meat and most of broth for Meal II. Refrigerate or freeze.

Meal 2: Chicken Soup
Bring stock to boil. Add:
    ½ c. uncooked rice OR 1-2 c.
    leftover cooked rice
Sauté in small skillet:
    2 T. margarine or oil
    2 carrots, chopped
    2 stalks celery, chopped
    1 c. peas (optional)
Just before serving, add reserved meat and sautéed vegetables to stock and rice. Heat and serve.

Norma Fairfield, Singers Glen, Va.

Baked Chicken With Tomato—Rice Stuffing

T·S

Serves 4
350°
1 hr.

Brown in skillet:
    2 lbs. chicken parts
Preheat oven to 350°.
While chicken fries, combine in bowl:
    ⅓ c. chopped celery
    ¼ c. chopped green pepper
    ⅓ c. chopped onion
    ⅔ c. uncooked rice
    1 c. cooked tomatoes
    ½ c. water
    ¾ t. salt
    dash pepper
    ¼ t. powdered sage
Turn into 12x7x2" baking dish.
Arrange chicken on top of rice. Sprinkle with additional salt, pepper, and paprika.
Cover; bake 1 hour, or until chicken is tender.

Linda Grasse, Chambersburg, Pa.

Chicken Pie

Serves 6
400°
20 min.

Place in large kettle:
    1 3-lb. chicken
    5 c. water
    ½ t. salt
Cook until chicken is tender. Drain, reserving broth. Remove meat from bones.
Cook in small amount salted water:
    1 c. sliced celery
    2 c. frozen mixed vegetables
        or similar combination
Drain vegetables, reserving broth.
In saucepan combine:
    5 T. flour

½ c. light cream or milk
2½ c. chicken and vegetable broth
1 t. salt
⅛ t. pepper

Cook over medium heat, stirring constantly, until thickened. Stir in vegetables. Place ⅓ of vegetable mixture in 2 qt. casserole. Add chicken meat, then remaining vegetable mixture. Bake at 400° until bubbly, about 20 minutes.

Meanwhile, prepare 1 recipe biscuits **see p. 34**. Cut with doughnut cutter, if desired. Top casserole with biscuits and return to oven for 10-15 minutes until biscuits are golden.

Option:

Substitute canned tuna or leftover cooked beef for chicken. Use bouillon cubes to replace broth.

Arnetta Kaufman, Fonda, Iowa
Anna K. Hersh, Glenshaw, Pa.

Chicken Potpie

A traditional Pennsylvania Dutch dish, sometimes seasoned with saffron.

Serves 6-8

Cook in large kettle until tender:
1 large chicken fryer or
    stewing hen, cut in pieces
2-3 qt. water
salt and pepper

Cook until tender. Remove chicken pieces, cool, and remove meat from bones.
Prepare vegetables:
2-3 potatoes, cubed
1 onion, chopped
2 stalks celery, chopped
¼ c. parsley, chopped

Prepare potpie dough:
Combine:
2 c. flour
¼ t. salt
Cut in:
1 T. lard or shortening

Add:
¼ c. water
1 large egg, slightly beaten

Mix to form a ball. Cover bowl and let stand 15 minutes.
Add vegetables and chicken meat to broth. Cook just until vegetables are tender. On a floured surface, roll out potpie dough as thin as possible, cut into 1½" squares, and drop into broth. Cook 5-10 minutes and serve.

Rhoda King, Cochranville, Pa.

Chicken–Pineapple Skillet

T·S

Serves 6

Bone and skin:
2 or 3 chicken breasts
    (cook bones and skin for broth
    to use in another dish)
Cut each breast half into 10-12 strips.
Assemble:
1 onion, halved and sliced
1 c. celery, sliced diagonally
1 green pepper, cut in strips
2 c. pineapple chunks, drained
    (reserve juice)
Combine in bowl:
pineapple juice
2 t. cornstarch
½ t. cinnamon
1½ t. soy sauce
Heat in large skillet:
2 T. margarine or oil

Over high heat sauté strips of chicken. Sprinkle with salt and stir constantly for 3 minutes. Add onion, celery and green pepper and continue to cook, stirring constantly 2 minutes. Add pineapple, then juice mixture. Stir and bring to a boil. Reduce heat and cook just until clear. Serve over hot rice.

Option:

Use leftover cooked chicken; add to sautéed vegetables just before adding juice mixture.

Rhoda Ehst, New York, N.Y.
Marjorie Ropp, Montreal, Que.

Chicken Strata

Contributor suggests freezing leftover turkey in 2-c. containers for use in this recipe.

Serves 6
325°
50 min.

Prepare:
8 slices day-old bread
Butter 2 slices bread, cut in ½" cubes and set aside. Cut remaining bread in 1" cubes and place half in bottom of 8x8x2" baking dish.
Combine in a bowl:
**2 c. diced cooked chicken or turkey
½ c. chopped onion
½ c. chopped green pepper (optional)
½ c. finely chopped celery
½ c. mayonnaise
¾ t. salt
dash pepper**
Spoon over bread cubes. Sprinkle remaining unbuttered bread cubes over chicken mixture.
Combine in bowl:
**2 slightly beaten eggs
1½ c. milk**
Pour over all. Cover and chill 1 hour or overnight.
Preheat oven to 325°.
Spoon on top:
**1¼ c. white sauce made with mushrooms or chicken broth (*see p. 70*)
OR 1 can cream of mushroom soup**
Sprinkle with buttered cubes. Bake 50 minutes, or until set.

Janice Wenger, Ephrata, Pa.

Chicken Pilau I

Contributor says, "My grandmother brought this recipe when she came with other Mennonites from Russia to the United States. They stopped for some time in Turkey where they learned to make pilau."

Serves 8-10

Cook until tender:
**1 stewing hen
5-6 c. water
salt and pepper**
Remove chicken pieces and skim broth.
Combine in large saucepan:
**4 c. broth
2 c. rice
¼ c. finely diced carrot
½ c. raisins
1-2 t. salt
dash pepper**
Bring to boil, stir briefly, cover and cook without stirring on very low heat until rice is almost done. Place chicken pieces on top and finish cooking.

Option:

For a spicier pilau, add onion, garlic, and curry.

Elsie Epp, Marion, S.D.

Chicken Pilau II

Serves 8

Combine in large kettle:
   1 3-4 lb. frying chicken, cut up
   2 qts. water
   1 clove garlic
   1 t. salt
Sauté in small skillet:
   3 T. oil
   2 onions, minced
Add to chicken and bring to a boil. Cover and simmer 20 minutes.
Add:
   2½ c. brown rice
Cover and simmer 40 minutes, or until chicken and rice are done.
Remove chicken to a platter.
Stir into rice:
   1½ c. raisins
   1½ T. curry powder
   1 t. salt
   1 T. honey
   2 T. lime or lemon juice
Mound rice around chicken and garnish with:
   ½ c. slivered almonds (optional)
   ¼ c. chopped parsley

Cleta Gingerich, Colorado Springs, Colo.

Chicken or Turkey Loaf

Serves 6
325°
1 hr.

Preheat oven to 325°.
Combine in large bowl:
   1 c. chicken broth
   2 slightly beaten eggs
   1 c. soft bread crumbs
   2 T. chicken fat or margarine
   3 c. cooked chicken or turkey, ground or finely chopped
   ½ c. finely chopped celery
   3 T. finely chopped onion
   2 t. crushed sage
   1 t. salt
   ¼ t. pepper
Mix thoroughly and place in greased loaf pan. Bake 1 hour, or until firm.

Chicken Wings Hawaiian

Sometimes chicken wings are available cheaply by the pound—or you can slowly accumulate a bagful in the freezer.

Serves 5-6
350°
45 min.

Cut off tips from:
   2 lbs. chicken wings
Cook tips in 1½ c. salted water to make broth. Reserve for sauce below.
Cut remaining pieces in two. Arrange side by side in shallow baking pan.
Combine in saucepan:
   ½ c. soy sauce
   1 clove garlic, crushed
   ½ c. finely chopped green onions (or 1 onion)
   ¼ c. sugar
   1 t. dry mustard
   1 t. ground ginger
   ¼ c. margarine
   ¼ c. water
Bring to boil and cool. Pour over chicken, refrigerate, and marinate several hours. Turn pieces, then place in 350° oven without removing sauce. Bake uncovered 45 minutes, turning pieces after 30 minutes.

Cook rice. Lift out chicken pieces and arrange like spokes of a wheel on platter of hot cooked rice. Garnish with parsley.

Skim fat from remaining sauce if necessary and heat quickly with 1 c. chicken broth. Thicken with:
   2 t. cornstarch
   2 T. water
Pass sauce.

Author's Recipe

Oyako Domburi (Japanese Parent–Child Dish)

The chicken is the parent; the egg, the child, in this very standard Japanese meal. Serve with salty pickles and green tea.

Serves 4

Cook rice for 4 persons (**see p. 76**)
Cut into small servings:
  **½ lb. raw chicken cut from bone
    (use 1 large breast)
  OR chicken leftovers**
Beat in a bowl:
  5 eggs
Dust chicken pieces with flour, dip in beaten egg (reserve extra), and fry on both sides in hot oil until brown.
Combine in saucepan:
  **1 c. water
  3 dried mushrooms**
Simmer 10 minutes, remove mushrooms, and cut fine.
Drain any excess oil from skillet. Add to skillet:
  **mushrooms and liquid
  ¼ c. sugar
  ⅓ c. Japanese-type soy sauce**
Simmer 15 minutes. Add:
  **2 scallions, cut diagonally,
  OR 1 onion, sliced**
Simmer 10 more minutes. Add:
  2 c. chopped fresh spinach
While spinach is still bright green, add reserved beaten eggs to skillet and cover. Cook briefly, just until set. Ladle over individual rice servings in bowls and top with chopped parsley.

Mary Alene Miller, Obihiro, Japan

Indian Chicken

Serves 6
350°
1 hr.

Heat in large skillet:
  **2 T. margarine
  2 T. vegetable oil**
Flour and fry until browned:
  1 3-lb. fryer, cut up
Remove from skillet and place in casserole.
Preheat oven to 350°.
In remaining fat, sauté until golden:
  2 medium onions, chopped
Combine and add to onions; stirring to blend well:
  **3 T. flour
  2 T. curry powder
  1 t. ground ginger
  2 t. salt**
Combine and add to onion mixture:
  **⅓ c. honey
  ¼ c. soy sauce
  3 c. chicken broth or bouillon**
Cook over high heat, stirring, until sauce thickens. Pour sauce over chicken and bake, covered, about 1 hour.

Options:
Add 3-4 c. cooked drained chick-peas (garbonzos) to casserole before adding sauce.
Serve with rice.

Helen Peifer, Akron, Pa.

Creamed Chicken Over Confetti Rice Squares

Serves 8
325°
40 min.

Rice Squares:
Preheat oven to 325°.
Combine:
  **3 c. cooked rice
  1 c. shredded cheese**

½ c. chopped parsley
⅓ c. chopped onion
⅓ c. chopped pimento or
   sweet red pepper
1 t. salt
Add:
   3 eggs, beaten
   1½ c. milk
Turn into 1½ qt. buttered baking dish.
Bake 40 minutes or until knife inserted
near center comes out clean. Cut into
squares and serve with creamed
chicken.

Gladys Longacre, Susquehanna, Pa.

Creamed Chicken

Serves 6

Heat in skillet or heavy saucepan:
   ¼ c. margarine or chicken fat
      skimmed from broth
Add and sauté just until soft:
   1 onion, chopped
   ½ green pepper, chopped
      (optional)
Add, stir, and cook until bubbly:
   ¼ c. flour
Add:
   2 c. chicken broth
   1 c. milk
   salt and pepper to taste
Cook, stirring constantly, until smooth
and thickened.
Add:
   2-3 c. diced cooked chicken
   1 T. chopped parsley
Heat through and serve over rice,
noodles, mashed potatoes, waffles, or
with one of the following recipes:
   Confetti Rice Squares
   Cornbread Dressing
   Potpie Crackers

Option:

Add 1 c. cooked or frozen peas.

Author's Recipe

Creamed Chicken With Potpie Crackers

*Tiny crisp crackers turn creamed
chicken into special fare.*

Serves 6-8
375°
10 min.

Combine in large bowl:
   3 c. flour
   ½ t. salt
Cut in:
   ½ c. shortening or margarine
Add:
   2 eggs, slightly beaten
   ¼ c. milk
Stir lightly with fork and form into ball.
Divide dough into three parts. Roll each
part out a little thinner than for pie dough.
Lay rolled out dough on greased cookie
sheets and cut into ½-1" squares. Bake at
375° for 10 minutes or until crackers are
lightly browned. Makes 2 qt. crackers.

Make creamed chicken seasoned
lightly with saffron. Place crackers in
serving dish and pour creamed chicken
over, or arrange on individual serving
plates. Garnish with parsley.

Crackers keep well in tightly covered
container and can be made in advance.

Option:

Dough may be used for patty shells; cut
into 5" circles, fit over upside-down
muffin tins, prick with fork, and bake until
golden.

Doris Brubaker, Mt. Joy, Pa.

Creamed Chicken With Corn Bread Dressing

Tester called it "absolutely the most delicious dressing I've ever eaten." But don't bake corn bread just for this—plan ahead and serve meaty chicken pieces on Monday, baked beans and hot corn bread (double recipe) on Tuesday, and this finale on Wednesday.

Serves 6
325°
40 min.

Combine in saucepan:
About 2 lbs. giblets and bony chicken pieces
1 qt. water
seasonings as desired
Cook 1 hour or until meat is tender. Remove chicken and take meat from bones. Reserve meat and broth.

Dressing:
Combine in large bowl:
4 c. corn bread, crumbled
1¾ c. croutons (see p. 44)
Melt in skillet:
¼ c. margarine
Add:
4 stalks celery, sliced
1 large onion, chopped
⅓ c. chopped walnuts (optional)
1 t. celery seed
¼ c. minced parsley (optional)
2 t. poultry seasoning
salt and pepper
Sauté until tender and add to bread mixture.
Brown in skillet:
3 oz. pork sausage
Add to bread mixture along with 1 c. reserved chicken broth. Combine and turn into greased casserole. Sprinkle with sausage drippings. Bake at 325° for 40 minutes.
Use reserved chicken meat and broth to make creamed chicken. Serve over dressing.

Linda Albert, Visalia, Calif.

Baked Fish

T·S

Serves 6
350°
35 min.

Preheat oven to 350°.
Place in shallow greased baking dish:
1½ lbs. fish fillets, cut in serving pieces
Sprinkle with:
¼ t. salt
dash pepper
1 T. lemon juice
Make 1¼ c. white sauce, adding 2 t. dry mustard (*see p. 71*).
Pour over fish.
Sprinkle with:
⅓ c. buttered bread crumbs
1 T. minced parsley
Bake 35 minutes.

Options:
Add ½ c. grated cheese to white sauce.
TS
Easy, low-calorie baked fish: Simply place whole cleaned or filleted fish on greased pan; sprinkle with lemon juice and seasonings. Bake at 350° about 25 minutes for 1 lb., 35-40 minutes for 2 lbs. Thin people may add melted margarine.

Karen Rix, Fonda, Iowa
Anna K. Hersh, Glenshaw, Pa.

Fish Cakes

Serves 6-8

Combine in mixing bowl:
**2 c. shredded, cooked, salt codfish
OR 1 lb. canned mackerel
(use half of liquid)
2 c. mashed potatoes
⅛ t. pepper
1 beaten egg
1 onion, chopped (optional)**
Mash all ingredients together. Salt to taste if using unsalted fish. Shape into cakes and fry slowly in small amount hot fat.
Good served with tomato or cheese sauce.

*Laura Dyck, Winkler, Man.
Ruth Weaver, Reading, Pa.*

Scalloped Mackerel

Serves 8
375°
40 min.

Preheat oven to 375°.
Place alternate layers into casserole or 9x5x3" loaf pan:
**1 lb. canned mackerel, flaked
2 c. cracker crumbs**
Combine in a bowl:
**2 eggs, beaten
2 c. hot milk
1 t. salt
dash pepper
poultry seasoning
¼ c. melted butter**
Pour over contents of casserole. Sprinkle with parsley or paprika.
Bake 40 minutes.

Option:
Substitute 6 oz. flaked tuna, or cooked salmon if available at low price.

*Carolyn Yoder, Grantsville, Md.
Marian Zuercher, Wooster, Ohio*

Chinese Fish And Vegetables

Serves 6

Clean and bone:
1 2-lb. fish
Cut against grain into steaks. Wipe dry; dredge lightly in cornstarch.
Heat 2-3 T. oil in skillet and brown fish quickly on both sides.
While fish browns, prepare:
**3 c. sliced vegetables—celery,
cabbage, carrots (slice thinly),
onions, mushrooms**
Mince finely:
**1 clove garlic
2 slices fresh ginger root (optional)
2 scallions**
Combine in bowl:
**1 c. broth or stock
2 T. soy sauce
1 T. cooking sherry (optional)
1½ t. brown sugar
½ t. salt
2 t. cornstarch**
Remove fish from skillet. Add 1 T. oil and heat. Add minced vegetables, then sliced vegetables and stir-fry about 1 minute. Add liquid and bring to boil. Return fish to skillet. Simmer, covered, about 5 minutes until fish is done and vegetables crisp-tender. Serve over hot rice.

Options:
Use frozen fish fillets.
Sweet-sour dish: add 2 T. vinegar to liquids and increase brown sugar to 3 T.

Louise Lehman, Wapakoneta, Ohio

San Francisco Fish Stew

T·S

Serves 5-6

Sauté in Dutch oven or large saucepan:
- **1 T. oil**
- **1 clove garlic, chopped**
- **½ c. chopped onion**
- **⅓ c. chopped green pepper**

Add:
- **¼ lb. mushrooms, sliced (optional)**
- **2 c. cooked tomatoes**
- **¾ c. tomato paste**
- **1 c. chicken broth**
- **1 T. lemon juice**
- **1 small bay leaf**
- **½ t. dried oregano**
- **1 t. sugar**
- **¾ t. salt**
- **⅛ t. pepper**

Cook uncovered 20 minutes. Add:
- **1-1½ lbs. flounder or other white fish, cut into large pieces**

Cook 10-15 minutes, or until fish flakes easily. Serve over rice or spaghetti.

Catherine Kornweibel, Easton, Pa

Mock Lobster

T·S

Serves 3-4

Bring to a boil in a saucepan:
- **2 c. water**
- **1 t. vinegar**
- **1 t. seafood seasoning**

Add:
- **1 lb. haddock or other white fish, left in large pieces**

Reduce heat, cover, and simmer about 10 minutes or just until fish is cooked. Cut or break into bite-sized pieces. Serve with melted margarine blended with lemon juice if desired.

Bonnie Zook, Leola, Pa.

Tuna Souffle Sandwiches

Tuna, eggs, milk, and cheese yield a very high protein dish. Omit meat the rest of the day.

T·S

Serves 4
375°
45 min.

TS—a make-ahead dish

Place in greased 9x13" baking pan:
- **4 slices bread, spread with mayonnaise**

Combine in bowl:
- **1 7-oz. can tuna, flaked**
- **¼ c. chopped celery**
- **¼ c. chopped onion**
- **1 t. salt**
- **½ t. paprika**

Spread tuna mixture over bread slices
Add:
- **4 slices Swiss cheese**

Top with:
- **4 slices bread**

Combine in bowl:
- **3 eggs**
- **1½ c. milk**

Pour over sandwiches. Refrigerate 2-12 hours.
Bake at 375° for 45 minutes

Option:
Use salmon, mackerel, or other canned fish.

Lena Hoover, Leola, Pa
Carolyn Weaver, Lancaster, Pa

Poor Man's Lobster Thermidor

Serves 4
425°
6-10 min.

Preheat oven to 425°.
Sauté:
    2 T. chopped onion
    ½ c. sliced mushrooms (optional)
    2 T. margarine
Stir in:
    2 T. flour
    ½ t. salt
    dash pepper
    dash paprika
Cook until bubbly. Add:
    ½ c. milk
    ½ c. chicken broth
    ½ t. Worcestershire sauce
Cook and stir until thickened. Add:
    1 egg yolk
    1 T. sherry flavoring or 2 T. white cooking wine (optional)
Add:
    2 c. cooked white fish pieces (halibut, perch, flounder etc.)
Place in shallow casserole or individual baking dishes.
Top with:
    buttered bread crumbs and/or grated cheese
Bake 6–10 minutes.
    Loretta Leatherman, Akron, Pa.

Clam Whiffle

"A whiffle is a soufflé that any fool can make."—Peg Bracken

Serves 6
350°
40-45 min.

Preheat oven to 350°
Combine in bowl:
    1 c. milk
    1¼ c. crumbled soda crackers
Let soak 5 minutes. Add:
    ¼ c. melted margarine
    1 can (8 oz.) minced clams, drained and rinsed
    2 T. finely chopped onion
    4 T. finely chopped green pepper
    ¼ t. salt
    dash pepper
    dash Worcestershire sauce
    2 eggs, well beaten
Pour into greased casserole and bake 40-45 minutes until puffy and golden. Serve at once.

    Evelyn Kreider, Goshen, Ind.

Lentil Burgers

Among mock meats this recipe received highest ratings from our testers.

Serves 6

Combine in a bowl:
    2 c. cooked, cooled lentils, drained
    1 egg
    ½ c. cracker crumbs
    1 small onion, minced
    tomato juice
    salt and pepper
Mix all ingredients together using just enough tomato juice to hold mixture in shape when pattied. Fry like hamburgers in small amount hot oil, shortening or bacon fat.

    Carolyn Yoder, Grantsville, Md.

Bacalaitos

Maria serves these to in-and-out guests on Christmas evening. In Puerto Rico bacalaitos are sold at small food stands along the beach and at baseball games.

Serves 4-6

Bone and cut in small pieces:
½ lb. codfish
If using salted fish, wash and soak in cold water to remove extra salt.
Combine in mixing bowl:
2 c. flour
½ t. baking powder
½ t. salt (omit if using salted fish)
Add:
cut up codfish
2 garlic cloves, minced, or
¼ t. garlic powder
white pepper to taste
Mix well. Add:
1½ c. cold water
Set aside 10-15 minutes.
Heat oil for deep frying to 275°. Drop the mixture by tablespoonfuls into hot oil. Turn once or twice and fry until golden brown. Serve hot.

Maria Luisa Rivera de Snyder, Hesston, Kan.

Grits Croquettes

Serves 6

Combine in a bowl:
2 c. cooked hominy grits
2 c. ground cooked chicken or flaked fish
2 T. chopped onion
1 t. salt
dash pepper
1 t. Worcestershire sauce
½ c. bread or cracker crumbs
1 egg, beaten
Chill, then shape into 12 croquettes. Roll in additional crumbs; dip in egg and roll again. Pan-fry until golden brown.

Rhoda Sauder, Spring Grove, Pa.

Fancy Flounder Roll-Ups

Serves 8
350°
20 min./15-20 min.

Cook and drain:
1¼ lbs. fresh or frozen broccoli spears
Place broccoli on:
8 fillet of flounder (2 lbs.)
Preheat oven to 350°.
Roll up; secure with toothpicks. Arrange in 12x8x2" baking dish. Bake 20 minutes.

Combine:
1¼ c. white sauce with celery (see p. 70)
OR 1 can cream of celery soup
¼ c. mayonnaise
1 T. lemon juice
Pour over fish, stirring in liquid around the sides. Bake 15-20 minutes.
Arrange roll-ups on a platter; stir sauce and pour over.

Danita Laskowski, Goshen, Ind.

Pia-Pia (Indonesian Shrimp Fritters)

Serves 4

Combine:
1 c. flour
1 egg, beaten
½ c. bean sprouts, fresh or canned, drained
¼ c. chopped celery
¼ c. finely chopped onion
1 clove garlic, pressed
½ t. salt
pepper
2 T. water
½ c. small shrimp
Heat in wok or small heavy saucepan:
2 c. oil
Drop a soup spoonful of the mixture into hot oil, holding it down until it takes on a rounded shape. Turn and fry until golden. Several may be fried at once. Serve with rice and a mixture of sweet soy sauce and hot peppers for dipping.

Armini Djojodihardjo, Pati, Indonesia

Gather Up the Fragments

1.
Include skin when grinding cooked chicken for croquettes or sandwich spread.

2.
Save pieces of chicken fat in container in freezer. When enough is accumulated, melt down and return to refrigerator. Use in baking. (Or melt down immediately when cooking chickens.)

3.
Use fat from chicken, pork, or bacon in baking bread.

4.
Trim excess fat from meat, dice finely, and melt in skillet instead of using oil or shortening to fry the meat.

5.
Make a sandwich spread by mashing one or two cooked chicken livers and combining with chopped hard-cooked eggs and a little mayonnaise.

6.
Save all bones and meat scraps for making soup. See Soups.

7.
Chop and freeze leftover ham in small packages for adding to soups, salads, and casseroles.

8.
Sprinkle a chunk of leftover roast beef with a little water. Wrap tightly in foil and bake one hour at 250-300°. Slice and serve. Tastes like just-roasted beef.

9.
Recipes using leftover meats:

Beef and other meats
Vietnam Fried Rice, *p. 79*
Kay's Japanese Rice, *p. 79*
Mandarin Rice Bake, *p. 81*
Easy Curry, *p. 84*
Garden Supper Casserole, *p. 86*
Empanadas, *p. 93*
Meat-Potato Quiche, *p. 102*
Basic Burger Mix, *p. 110*
West African Groundnut Stew, *p. 114*
Zucchini Skillet Supper, *p. 163*

Chicken and Turkey
Chicken-Cheese Casserole, *p. 75*
Turkey-Apple Casserole, *p. 88*
Chicken Soufflé, *p. 100*
Chicken Pineapple Skillet, *p. 121*
Chicken Strata, *p. 122*
Chicken or Turkey Loaf, *p. 123*
Creamed Chicken, *p. 125*
Summer Night Salad, *p. 177*
Chinese Chicken-Cucumber Salad,
  p. 180

Ham Bones and Ham
Calico Baked Beans, *p. 56*
Easy Lentil Stew, *p. 61*
Newfoundland Boiled Dinner, *p. 88*
Quiche Lorraine, *p. 101*
Meat-Potato Quiche, *p. 102*
Bean Soup, *p. 141*
Blackbean Soup, *p. 42*
Hambone Dinner, *p. 146*
Hunter's Stew, *p. 148*
Summer Night Salad, *p. 177*

Soups

"Gather Up the Fragments" fits better at the beginning of this chapter than at the end. Soup making is collecting the odds and ends—cleaning out the refrigerator, going through the cupboards, finishing off the garden. Leftover soup is generally no problem. It is reheated next day for two at lunch, served as a first course at dinner, or poured into someone's thermos. Most soups freeze well and many actually improve with reheating.

A Way with Bits, Bones, and Broths

I save all bones from poultry and meat in my freezer until I have enough for my largest kettle. This is my method: Crack the largest bones (with a cloth-covered hammer) to allow the marrow to escape. Barely cover the bones with water adding ¼ c. vinegar and 2 t. salt for each 2 qt. water. This aids dissolving calcium out of the bones into the stock. Cover the kettle and simmer 3 to 4 hours—or cook 30 minutes in a pressure cooker. (I have a wood range so use the slower method.) Add chopped parings and vegetable leftovers, 4 peppercorns, and 1 crumbled bay leaf, and simmer it slowly.

Strain broth through colander, cool, and chill overnight. Discard bones and parings (but let the dog pass inspection on them first!). Remove the chilled fat on top and use stock as a base for delicious soups.
—Norma Fairfield,
Singers Glen, Va.

A variation of Norma's method was unappetizingly called Garbage Soup by one newspaper clipping, but the results can surpass any canned consommé. You identify one kettle as the ongoing soup pot and fill it half full with water. Keep it in the refrigerator, but get it out every evening and place on the stove to cook for an hour or so while making and cleaning up from dinner. Into it go all bones (long cooking kills germs from dinner plates), clean vegetable parings, vegetable liquid, leftover vegetable salads (rinse away dressing), bits of gravy, and other odd things too small to save. If you cook meat but don't make gravy, add a little water to cooking pan, heat and swish, then pour into soup pot. Allow the kettle to cool until bedtime, then return it to the refrigerator. After a week or so strain out solids and broth is ready to use. Start over.

> *Although the butcher looks at me very strangely, I always ask to have all the bones saved when we have a quarter of beef cut and wrapped. I take them home, put them in my canner, cover with water, and boil 3 to 4 hours. I strain the broth and can it. It's ready anytime to start off a wonderful soup, or to take to sick people.*
> *—Evelyn Fisher, Akron, Pa.*

> *Get "dog-bones" free and trimmed bones cheap. Cook into broth, then feed bones to the dog.*
> *—Carol Ann Maust, Upland, Calif.*

> *Broth sometimes spoiled before I used it all. Now I take fresh broth and freeze in ice-cube trays. Store cubes in plastic bag in freezer. One cube is about ¼ cup. It's easy to take out the number you need for any recipe.*
> *—Linda Albert, Visalia, Calif.*

Reserved Leftovers

Some people let leftovers die in the back of the refrigerator in lovely Tupperware caskets. Here's a better way:

> *I keep a large plastic container in the freezing compartment of our refrigerator. Into it go leftovers — vegetables, noodles, broth, meat — anything which might be good in a vegetable soup. When the container is full, I add water, perhaps more broth and seasonings and cook everything together. We have had some delicious soups made this way and since each is just a little different, it is always a surprise (not another rerun of Standard-Brand Vegetable-Beef). Some advantages; we seldom have to eat leftovers and I rarely have to throw food away which sat too long in a corner of the refrigerator.*
> *—Helen Peifer, Akron, Pa.*
> *—Joann Smith, Goshen, Ind.*

Grains, Legumes, and Vegetables on Tap

You have the broth and leftover vegetables from gathering fragments. Now the soup needs thickening and enriching if it's going to hit the empty spot. Keep a row of jars, maybe on top of the cupboard, with rice, barley, dried peas, lentils, and beans in them. Of these, the first four need no presoaking. Toss in a handful early in the process and they will simmer to tenderness while you're chopping vegetables and herbs. Or base the soup entirely on one of the legumes. A bean or lentil soup eaten with whole-grain bread provides cheap high-quality protein. (see p. 12 on complementary proteins.)

Blenders are a great aid to soup

making. Almost any leftover vegetable, blended with a little milk, forms the base of a cream soup. Simply add more milk, heat, season, and soup is ready. The blended vegetable usually provides enough thickening. If not, stir in a bit of white sauce mix (*p. 71*).

The same trick can be used with leftover casseroles. Whirl up a cup of leftover chicken-noodle mixture and you have a good stand-in for cream of chicken soup. Leftover macaroni and cheese blended makes a thick, mild cheese sauce. Leftover baked beans go into bean soup.

A Back-Door Herb Garden

My mother planted parsley around the outside water faucet. Spills and drips kept the plants a luscious green through scorching Kansas summers. But most herbs grow fairly well in dry, poor soil. To the parsley add a clump of chives, some dill, and as space allows, a variety that can bring gourmet taste to the plainest soup. Dry herbs for the winter. Many of these plants fit windowsill pots if no outdoor space is available.

Dry celery leaves in a napkin-lined basket in a warm spot in the kitchen. When dry, crumble into a jar and keep on hand for soups.

Using the Recipes

For quick method for soaking and other information on beans, *see p. 52.* Precooked frozen or canned beans may also be used in bean soup recipes.

Whenever a recipe calls for broth, use home-cooked broth or stock, or substitute 1 c. water plus 1 bouillon cube (1 t. powdered bouillon) for each cup required. Commercially canned broths are expensive and waste containers.

Cream of Tomato Soup

T·S

Serves 3-4

Sauté:
   2 T. margarine
   2 T. onion, chopped
Blend in:
   3 T. flour
   2 t. sugar
   1 t. salt
   ⅛ t. pepper
   dash of garlic salt, basil, oregano, thyme
Remove from heat. Gradually stir in:
   2 c. tomato juice
Bring to a boil, stirring constantly. Boil 1 min.
Stir hot tomato mixture into:
   2 c. cold milk
Heat almost to boiling and serve.

Option:

Thicken the soup with doodles:
Combine:
2 eggs, beaten
2 T. water
1 t. salt
flour to make very thick batter
Drop by teaspoonfuls into boiling soup, coating spoon with hot soup each time. Turn off heat and cover until serving time.

Ann Burkholder, Orrville, Ohio
Esther Lehman, Lowville, N.Y.

Good Friday Vegetable Soup

T·S

Serves 4-5

Heat in heavy kettle:
3 T. vegetable oil
Add:
3 medium carrots, sliced
2 medium onions, sliced
1 or 2 stalks celery, sliced
1 to 2 c. shredded cabbage
¼ c. chopped parsley
¼ t. salt
Cook over medium heat about 15 min.,
stirring occasionally.
Add:
4 c. chicken broth
2 c. fresh or frozen French-cut green beans
¼-½ t. caraway seed
Heat to boiling. Reduce heat to low,
cover, and simmer 15 min. or until
vegetables are tender.
Dice into soup bowls:
¼ lb. cheese
Ladle hot soup directly onto cheese to
melt it slightly.

Rosemary Moyer, North Newton, Kan.

Kidney Bean Soup

Serves 6

Combine in large kettle:
1 lb. dry kidney beans
2 qts. water
Soak overnight or by quick·method.
Add:
1 c. sliced celery
2 c. sliced carrots
½ c. chopped onion
1 T. Worcestershire sauce
1 T. salt
1 bay leaf
⅛ t. ground cloves
Over high heat, bring to boil. Reduce
heat and simmer 1½ hours, stirring often.

Vegetable Chowder

T·S

Serves 6

Combine in kettle:
½ c. rice, uncooked
3 chicken bouillon cubes
5 c. water
½ c. diced carrots
1 c. diced potatoes
1 minced onion
½ c. finely cut celery
1 c. canned tomatoes
2 t. salt
⅛ t. pepper
Bring to boil and simmer 45 minutes.
Add when ready to serve:
1 c. milk
Heat almost to boiling and serve
immediately.

Mildred Langs, Cambridge-Preston, Ont.

Quick Corn Soup

T·S

Serves 4

Puree in blender:
2 c. corn, whole kernel or cream-style
1 c. milk
Pour into saucepan. Add:
2 c. milk
½ t. salt
pepper
celery and onion salt to taste
Heat through. Pureed corn serves as
thickening.

Option:
Any leftover cooked vegetable may
substitute for corn.

Sara Claassen, Beatrice, Neb.

German Potato Soup

T·S

Serves 4-6

Combine in saucepan:
    **4 medium potatoes, peeled and
        diced**
    1 onion, sliced
    1 t. salt
    dash pepper
    3½ c. water
Cook until potatoes are tender.
Heat in second saucepan:
    1 T. butter
    1 T. flour
Allow butter and flour to brown, stirring
constantly.
Add:
    3 c. liquid drained from potatoes
Cook and stir until smooth. Add potatoes
and onions and heat through. Sprinkle
with parsley.

Martha Roggie, Lowville, N.Y.

Golden Potato Soup

T·S

Serves 4

Sauté slowly in saucepan until yellow:
    2 T. oil or shortening
    ⅓ c. finely cut onion
Blend in:
    1 T. flour
    1 t. salt
    dash pepper
Add:
    1 c. water
Boil 2 min., stirring constantly. Add:
    **1 c. (or more) leftover mashed
        potatoes**
    2½ c. milk
    ½ c. grated cheese
Heat slowly until cheese melts. Do not
boil. Garnish with parsley or croutons.

Ruth Sommers, Kokomo, Ind.

Green Bean Soup

*Susan serves the soup with
traditional Roll Kuchen (see p. 76),
for a favorite summer supper.*

T·S

Serves 6

Sauté in heavy kettle until golden:
    3 T. butter
    1 large onion, diced
Add:
    6 c. water or stock
    1 c. carrots, shredded
    1 c. potatoes, diced
    **4 c. fresh or frozen green beans,
        cut up**
    fresh parsley, chopped
    **1 bunch summer savory, tied for
        easy removal**
Cook until vegetables are tender. Just
before serving, remove summer savory.
Add:
    **½ c. cream or evaporated milk
    salt and pepper**
Heat through and ladle into bowls.
Sprinkle over each serving:
    diced hard-cooked eggs

Susan Duerksen, Killarney, Man.

Cream of Pea Soup

T·S

Serves 4

Combine in blender:
- 1½ c. frozen green peas, thawed
- 2 chicken bouillon cubes
- 1 thin slice onion
- 2 T. flour
- 3 c. milk
- dash pepper
- dash mace

Whirl until smooth. Pour into saucepan and heat slowly, stirring constantly. Additional milk may be added.

Option:

Leftover cooked vegetables may replace frozen peas.

Loretta Leatherman, Akron, Pa

Corn and Bean Chowder

Serves 6-8

In a large soup pot, sauté:
- ¼ c. oil
- 2 c. sliced onions
- 2 cloves garlic, minced

Add:
- 3 c. corn (fresh or frozen)
- 4 c. stock or broth
- ¼ t. nutmeg

Bring mixture to a boil. Simmer until corn is tender.

Puree in a blender:
- 1 additional c. corn

Add to soup:
- pureed corn
- ½ c. dry milk solids
- 1½ c. cooked kidney beans
- ½ t. salt

Bring soup almost to boiling, lower heat, and simmer a few minutes.

Option:

To make a thicker soup increase dry milk to 1 c. and add 1-2 cooked potatoes.

Cheese and Corn Chowder

T·S

Serves 4

Combine in saucepan:
- ½ c. water
- 2 c. diced potatoes
- 1 c. sliced carrots
- 1 c. chopped celery
- 1 t. salt
- ¼ t. pepper

Cover and simmer 10 minutes. Add:
- 2 c. cream-style corn

Simmer 5 minutes. Add:
- 1½ c. milk
- ⅔ c. grated cheese

Stir until cheese melts and chowder is heated through. Do not boil.

Option:

Use leftover whole kernel corn pureed in blender.

Jean Horst, Lancaster, Pa.
Elvera Goering, Salina, Kan.

Ham-Green Bean Soup

Serves 6-8

Combine in 6 qt. saucepan:
- 2 lb. meaty ham bone
- 2 qt. water

Cook 1½ hrs. Remove meat from bone and cut in chunks. Add to soup stock, along with:
- 4 c. cut-up green beans
- 3 c. cubed potatoes
- 2 medium onions, sliced
- ¼ c. chopped parsley
- 4 sprigs summer savory, chopped
- OR 1 t. dried savory
- 1 t. salt
- ¼ t. pepper

Bring to boil; reduce heat and simmer, covered, 20 min., or until vegetables are tender. Skim off excess fat. Just before serving, stir in:
- 1 c. light cream or milk

Timeless Vegetable-Beef Soup

Serves 8-10

Combine in a large kettle:

2-3 lbs. beef soup bones
3 qts. water or stock
1½ t. salt
¼ t. pepper
1 bay leaf

Cover and simmer 2-3 hours. Remove bones and skim fat if necessary. Cut off, chop, and reserve meat.
Add:

½ c. barley

Continue cooking about ½ hour.
Add:

1 c. diced carrots
1 c. diced potatoes
1 c. peas or green beans
1 c. diced celery and leaves
½ c. chopped onion
2 c. shredded cabbage
2 c. cooked tomatoes
herbs and seasonings to taste
reserved meat

Cook just until vegetables are tender. Add any leftover vegetables available. Heat through.

Options:

Add chili sauce or chili powder to taste
Stir in ½ c. sour cream just before serving.

Mary Ella Weaver, Lititz, Pa.
Helena Pauls, Inman, Kan.

Fresh Asparagus Soup

Serves 4

Cook in covered saucepan:

1 lb. fresh asparagus, chopped
¼ c. chopped onion
1 c. chicken broth

When asparagus is just tender, if desired, press through food mill or blend until smooth.
Heat in saucepan:

2 T. margarine
2 T. flour
½ t. salt
dash pepper

Stir in:

1 additional cup chicken broth

Cook over medium heat, stirring constantly, until mixture reaches boiling point.
Stir in:

asparagus puree
1 c. milk

Stir a little hot mixture into:

½ c. sour cream or plain yogurt

Stir into hot mixture. Add:

1 t. fresh lemon juice

Heat just to serving temperature, stirring frequently. Sprinkle with fresh chives.

Option:

Tough ends of asparagus may be included if blender or food mill is used.

Rosemary Moyer, North Newton, Kan.

Barley–Cabbage Soup

Serves 6

Combine in kettle:

¼ c. pearl barley
4 c. meat or vegetable broth
(may use bouillon)

Simmer, covered, for 2 hours.
Sauté in skillet:

3 T. oil
2 medium onions, chopped

3-4 c. green cabbage, finely chopped
¼ c. parsley, chopped
Cook until soft, but do not brown.
Make a white sauce with:
4 T. vegetable oil
4 T. flour
4 c. milk
4 chicken bouillon cubes
½ t. celery salt
Add white sauce to barley and broth. Stir in sautéed cabbage and onion.
Check seasonings. Serve sprinkled with bacon bits, chopped ham, or croutons.

Rosemary Moyer, North Newton, Kan.
Joann Smith, Goshen, Ind.

Cream of Carrot–Cheddar Soup

Marcia calls this "wonderful for Christmas Eve-type supper."

Serves 6

Sauté in large kettle:
2 T. butter or margarine
½ c. finely chopped onion
Add and simmer until vegetables are tender:
1 lb. carrots (8-10), shredded
1 lb. potatoes (3-5), shredded
6 c. chicken broth
½ t. dried thyme
1 bay leaf
⅛ t. Tabasco sauce (or more to taste)
½ t. Worcestershire sauce
½ t. sugar
salt and pepper to taste
Add, stirring until cheese is melted:
1½ c. milk (may use part cream)
1-2 c. cheddar cheese, shredded
Discard bay leaf. Serve hot with parsley sprinkled over.

Marcia Beachy, DeKalb, Ill.
Janet Landes, Phoenix, Ariz.

French Onion Soup

Serves 6

Combine in skillet:
¼ c. margarine
3 c. thinly sliced onions
Cover and cook slowly about 15 minutes.
Blend in:
1½ t. salt
2 T. flour
Add:
4 c. beef broth or stock
Heat to boiling. Reduce heat and simmer about 1 hour.

Options:

Toast slices of French bread in slow oven until dry and crisp. Put one slice in each soup bowl. Sprinkle toast with grated cheese and ladle hot soup over.

Pour soup into casserole. Float enough toasted French bread on top to cover. Sprinkle liberally with grated Swiss cheese; finish with dash of Parmesan. Heat in 425° oven 10 minutes, or until cheese bubbles. Serve from casserole.

Annie Lind, Windsor, Vt.

Spinach Soup

T·S

Serves 6

Fry in deep skillet:
   4 slices bacon
Remove slices, drain, and reserve.
Add to bacon fat:
   **2 large leeks, thinly sliced
      (or green onions)**
   **6 medium unpeeled potatoes,
      diced**
   1 t. salt
   3 c. boiling water
Cover and simmer 15 min.
Melt in separate saucepan:
   2 T. butter
Blend in:
   3 T. flour
   1 t. vegetable broth powder
Add:
   **1½ c. dry milk solids, mixed with
      3 c. water**
Cook and stir until thick. Then add to
cooked vegetables and heat.
Add:
   1½ c. finely shredded spinach
Simmer 5 minutes. Sprinkle on dash of
pepper, nutmeg, and crumbled bacon.

Marian Franz, Washington, D.C.

Buzz and Don's Leek Soup

Serves 6-8

Bring to boil:
   3 qts. water and
   **4 chicken bouillon cubes
      OR 3 qts. chicken stock**
Chop and add:
   **1½ lbs. fresh leeks, including
      green tops**
   1½ lbs. potatoes
   1½ lbs. carrots
   1 stalk celery
Simmer 1-2 hours or until vegetables are
soft.
Add:
   ½ t. summer savory
   ½ t. marjoram
   pinch of rosemary
   1 T. parsley, chopped
   salt to taste
Simmer another half hour. Puree in
blender or put through a fine sieve or
food mill. Reheat before serving.

Don Ziegler, Lancaster, Pa.

Pumpkin Soup

T·S

Serves 6

Melt in large heavy kettle:
   2 T. margarine
Add:
   ¼ c. chopped green pepper
   1 small onion, finely chopped
Sauté until vegetables are soft but not
brown.
Blend in:
   2 T. flour
   1 t. salt
Add:
   2 c. chicken stock or broth
   2 c. pumpkin puree
   2 c. milk
   ⅛ t. thyme
   ¼ t. nutmeg
   1 t. chopped parsley

Cook, stirring constantly, until slightly thickened.

Option:

Add 1 c. cooked tomatoes.

Elvesta Hochstedler, Kalona, Iowa

Cream of Cauliflower Soup

Serves 6-8

Cook in salted water until soft:
1 medium head cauliflower, chopped
Sauté in large saucepan until yellow:
4 T. butter or margarine
¼ c. chopped onion
Blend in:
¼ c. flour
Add:
3 c. chicken broth
2 c. milk
1 t. Worcestershire sauce
cauliflower and cooking water
Cook until mixture thickens slightly. Add:
1 c. shredded cheese
Stir to melt cheese and serve sprinkled with herbs.

Option:

Zucchini (use 2-3 medium) substitutes well for cauliflower. May be whirled in blender after cooking.

Miriam Witmer Manheim, Pa.

Bean Soup

Serve with corn bread or graham muffins to complement legume protein.

Serves 8

Soak overnight or by quick method:
2 c. navy or marrow (pea) beans
2 qts. water
Add:
1 ham bone or several pork hocks (optional)
1 onion, chopped
3 stalks celery with leaves, chopped
3 carrots, sliced
1 qt. tomato juice or stewed tomatoes
salt and pepper to taste
Simmer 2 hours or more until beans are tender. Add more liquid if necessary. Remove meat from bones, chop, and return to soup.

Ruth Ressler, Sterling, Ohio
Marcia Beachy, DeKalb, Ill.

Minute Minestrone

Serves 6

Stir together in saucepan:
3 c. boiling water
1 envelope dry tomato-vegetable or similar soup mix
Add:
1 medium onion, chopped
2 c. cooked kidney beans
2 c. cooked or frozen corn
1 c. tomato sauce
1 t. salt
⅛ t. pepper
Cook 10 minutes. Add:
¼ c. chopped parsley

Option:

Hot broth plus extra vegetables and herbs could substitute for water and soup mix.

Russian Borsch

Huge pots of mutton borsch traditionally served Russian Mennonite weddings. The given combination of herbs is a must in real borsch.

Serves 8-10

Combine in large kettle:
   2 lbs. mutton neck or lamb bones
   2 qt. water
   2 t. salt
   1 T. vinegar
Simmer 2-3 hours. Remove bones from broth and set aside. Set kettle in cold place to harden fat. Remove fat. Measure out and return to soup kettle:
   6 c. mutton broth
Add:
   1 large onion, chopped
   1 qt. cabbage, coarsely chopped
   5 c. potatoes, diced
   1 c. tomato sauce or 2 c. cooked tomatoes
   2 sprigs parsley or parsley root
Secure in bag or tea strainer:
   5 peppercorns
   3 sprigs dill
   1 dried red pepper
   1 bay leaf
Drop spice bag into soup. Simmer until vegetables are tender. Cut meat from bones and add to soup. Simmer a few minutes longer to blend flavors. Remove spice bag before serving and add salt and pepper if needed.

Options:

Use beef or chicken.

Add beets or beet tops.

Add 1 c. sweet or sour cream just before serving, or pass cream.

   Martha B. Nafziger, LaCrete, Alta.
   Selma Martin, Corn, Okla.

Blackbean Soup

Serves 8

Soak overnight, or by quick method:
   1 lb. dried black beans in water to cover
Drain and add water to make 6 c. liquid. Add:
   1 c. chopped onion
   1 c. chopped green pepper
   1 minced clove garlic
   1 smoked ham bone
   2 bay leaves
   2 t. salt
   ¼ t. pepper
Cover and cook slowly for 2 or 3 hours, or until beans begin to fall apart, adding more water if necessary. Remove ham bone, dice meat, and return to soup. Add:
   ¼ c. wine vinegar or 2 T. cider vinegar
Ladle soup over a mound of rice in each bowl and sprinkle with chopped parsley. Pass lemon slices, chopped hard-cooked eggs, and chopped onions.

   Ruth Ressler, Sterling, Ohio

Minestrone Soup

Serves 8

Soak overnight or by quick method:
8 oz. pea or navy beans
Cover and cook 1½ hours. Drain,
reserving liquid.
Place in large heavy pan:
**8 oz. salt pork, skinned and
diced, or other diced pork**
Cover and sauté in its own fat until brown.
Drain off some fat.
Add:
1 onion, chopped
2 cloves garlic, minced
Sauté until soft. Add:
**10 c. liquid (reserved bean liquid
plus water)**
4 beef bouillon cubes
2 carrots, thinly sliced
2 stalks celery, chopped
¼ cabbage, thinly shredded
**2 tomatoes, peeled and chopped
(or ¾ c. cooked tomatoes)**
salt and pepper
Cover, bring to a boil, reduce heat and
simmer soup for 1½ hours.
Add:
2 c. frozen peas or green beans
½ c. elbow macaroni
Simmer for another 20 minutes.
Just before serving stir in:
3 T. chopped parsley
Serve hot, sprinkled with Parmesan
cheese.

Kay Gusler, Wise, Va.

Quick
Soybean Soup

T·S

Serves 4

TS—using precooked beans

Fry in large heavy saucepan:
3 strips bacon, chopped
Pour off excess drippings if necessary,
leaving about 2 T.
Add and sauté briefly:
1 onion, chopped
1-2 cloves garlic, mashed
2 stalks celery, chopped
Add:
**1 qt. cooked tomatoes or
tomato juice**
**1 c. water, vegetable stock,
or bean liquid**
2 c. cooked soybeans
1½ t. chili powder
1 t. salt
½ t. pepper
½ t. basil
**additional herbs and seasonings
to taste**
Bring to a boil, reduce heat, cover, and
simmer 15-30 minutes to blend flavors.

Options:

Any cooked beans may replace
soybeans.

Slow-simmered soup: Double recipe,
using 1 lb. soaked uncooked soybeans.
Cook slowly 3 hours. Add more liquid if
necessary. Add sautéed bacon ½ hour
before serving.

Louise Leatherman, Akron, Pa.

Savory Grain and Bean Pot

Serves 8-10

Heat in large kettle:
  2 T. olive oil or other oil
Add and sauté:
  1 c. chopped onions
  2 c. chopped vegetables (carrots, mushrooms, celery)
Add:
  1 c. cooked soybeans
  1 c. cooked tomatoes
  2-3 peppercorns
  pinch cayenne
  ¼ t. *each* **basil, tarragon, oregano, celery seed, summer savory**
  pinch *each* **thyme, rosemary, marjoram, sage**
  2 T. soy sauce
  ½ c. brown rice
  ⅓ c. bulgar or cracked wheat
  6-8 c. vegetable stock or broth
Bring soup to a boil. Reduce heat and simmer 1-2 hours until grains are tender. or pressure cook 10-15 minutes.

Option:

Soup may be further enriched with 3 T. soy grits if available. Combine grits with a little liquid and add to soup with grains

Elvera Goering, Salina, Kan.

Basic Lentil Soup

T·S

Serves 6

Combine in kettle:
  ½ lb. lentils
  6 c. water
Cook 30 minutes or until lentils are tender.
Add:
  2 carrots, chopped or sliced
  ½ c. sliced green onions
  1 clove garlic, crushed
  1½ c. tomato juice

  ½ c. minced parsley
  1 T. margarine
  1½ t. salt
  dash pepper
  ½ t. dried oregano
Bring to boil, reduce heat, and simmer just until carrots are tender.
Check seasonings and serve.

Options:

Add diced bacon or ham cubes.

Stir in 1 T. wine vinegar just before serving soup.

Use the whole pound of lentils in a double recipe and freeze half.

Twila Strickler
Alice Lapp, Goshen, Ind.

Hearty Lentil–Sausage Soup

Serves 8

Brown in 5 qt. kettle:
  1 lb. pork sausage, broken into chunks
Remove meat and pour off all but ¼ c. drippings.
Add:
  2 medium onions, chopped
  1 garlic clove, minced
  4 medium parsnips, cut in chunks (optional)
Cook 5 minutes or until onions and garlic are tender
Add:
  2 c. lentils
  1 T. salt
  ½ t. marjoram
  2 c. cooked tomatoes or juice
  2 qt. water
  browned sausage
Simmer 30 minutes or until tender.
Cut in diagonal slices:
  1 loaf Italian bread
To serve, place a bread slice in each soup bowl and spoon soup over bread. Pass Tabasco sauce.

Mabel Eshleman, Lancaster, Pa.

Middle Eastern Lentil Soup

T·S

Serves 4-6

Combine in soup kettle:

1 c. lentils
4 c. water
½ t. cumin

Cook until lentils are soft (30-45 minutes), adding water if necessary for good soup consistency.
Heat in skillet:

1 T. olive oil

Add and sauté just until yellow:

1 onion, chopped
1 clove garlic, minced

Blend in:

1 T. flour

Cook a few minutes. Then add sautéed ingredients to lentils and bring soup to boiling point, stirring occasionally. After soup boils, remove from heat and stir in:

2 T. lemon juice
salt and pepper to taste

Option:

Olive oil is expensive but worth the price to some who recognize Middle Eastern flavors. Others may substitute vegetable oil or margarine.

Louise Claassen, Eikhart, Ind.
Carolyn Yoder, Cairo, Egypt

Spicy Split Pea Soup

Serves 6

Combine in large saucepan:

5 c. chicken broth or bouillon
5 c. water
1 lb. dried split peas or lentils

Heat to boiling, turn off heat, cover, and let stand for 1 hour. (Omit this step if using lentils.) Reheat, and simmer over low heat for 45 minutes.
Sauté in skillet over medium heat:

2 T. butter or margarine

½ c. chopped onion
1 clove garlic, finely chopped
1 T. curry powder
1 t. crushed coriander seeds
¼ t. crushed red peppers
1 t. salt

Stir-fry about 7 minutes. Stir spice mixture into split peas, cover, and cook over low heat for 20 minutes. Cool slightly. Puree 2 c. of the soup in covered blender, holding lid partially ajar to let steam escape. Repeat until all has been pureed.
Stir in:

½ c. light cream or milk

Heat to serving temperature. If soup is too thick, thin with small amount of water or milk.

Option:

Soup can be served without blending. Substitute ¾ t. ground coriander for coriander seeds, and cayenne pepper for crushed peppers.

Evelyn Bauer, Goshen, Ind

Poor Man's Soup

Serves 8

Combine in large kettle:

1 c. dried marrow or pea beans
3 qts. water

Soak overnight or by quick method. Simmer beans 45 minutes.
Add:

2 c. tomato juice or cooked tomatoes
1 c. diced celery
1 carrot, cubed
1 potato, cubed
¼ c. uncooked rice
⅓ c. chopped onion
1 beef bouillon cube
1 T. salt
¼ t. pepper
pinch basil

Brown in skillet:

½ lb. ground beef

Bring soup to boil, add meat, cover and simmer 1 hour.

Spicy Chicken Gumbo

Gumbo is a favorite company meal with both contributors. "Make it with just the backs, wings, and ribs," says Francis.

Serves 8

Sauté in large, heavy kettle:
  ¼ c. oil or margarine
  2 onions, sliced
  2 cloves garlic, minced
  1 green pepper, diced
Blend in:
  2 T. flour
Cook and stir over low heat until vegetables are tender.
Add:
  2½ c. cooked tomatoes
  2 c. cooked okra, or 1½ c. frozen whole okra
  ⅔ c. tomato paste
  3 c. broth or stock
  1½ T. salt
  ¼ t. pepper
  1½ T. Worcestershire sauce
  ⅛ t. ground cloves
  ½ t. chili powder
  pinch dried basil
  1 bay leaf
Simmer 1 hour. Prepare cooked rice (*see p. 76*).
Chop and reserve:
  ⅓ c. parsley
Add to gumbo:
  2-3 c. cooked chicken, diced
Simmer briefly. To serve, combine hot cooked rice with chopped parsley and mound rice in center of soup bowls, using ice-cream dipper or large spoon. Pour hot gumbo around.

Options:

Omit okra.

Add 1 T. gumbo filé, if available.

Substitute cooked clams for chicken.

*Pearl Zehr, New Wilmington, Pa.
Francis Griffin, Ft. Worth, Tex.*

Ham Bone Dinner

Serves 6-8

Combine in large kettle:
  2 c. dried yellow or green split peas
  4 peppercorns
  1 ham bone
  salt to taste
  water to cover
Bring to boil, then simmer 2-3 hours until peas are done, adding water if necessary. Remove ham bone, cut off meat and chop finely.
Add to soup:
  ham bits
  6 carrots, sliced
  1 green pepper, chopped
  2 onions, diced
Cook until carrots are done, about 30 min. Check seasonings and serve.

Options:

Substitute chopped bacon or salt pork for the ham bone, or omit meat entirely and flavor with herbs.

Just before serving add several chopped hard-cooked eggs.

Add dumplings:
Combine:
  2 c. flour
  ½ t. salt
  4 t. baking powder
Rub in:
  1 T. margarine
Gradually add:
  1 c. water
Place on top of simmering soup in large spoonfuls. Cover and cook without peeking 15 min. Use dumplings when all the soup can be eaten at once—they do not reheat well.

*Martha B. Nafziger, LaCrete, Alta.
Laura Dyck, Winkler, Man.*

Greek Egg–Lemon Soup

Simple but elegant version of chicken-rice soup.

Serves 4

Cook together:
Bony pieces from 1 chicken
5 c. water
1 bay leaf
1 t. salt
dash pepper
When chicken is tender, remove meat and discard bay leaf. Take meat from bones
Add to broth and cook until tender:
⅓ c. rice
Return meat to soup. Adjust seasonings. Heat soup to boiling, then remove from heat.

In small bowl, beat until light:
1 egg
Stir into egg:
several tablespoons hot soup
juice of ½ lemon
Stir egg mixture into soup. Serve immediately with parsley sprinkle.

Louise Claassen, Elkhart, Ind.

Meatball Soup

Meatball Soup (Sauer Klops) is a traditional dish still found on the table in North American Mennonite homes of Prussian ancestry. Broth has a distinctive spicy-sour flavor.

Serves 4

Combine in mixing bowl:
½ lb. lean ground beef
½ c. finely rolled cracker or bread crumbs
½ c. evaporated or whole milk
½ t. salt
dash pepper
Form into balls 1½" in diameter, and set aside.
Combine in 3 qt. saucepan:
2 c. cubed potatoes
1 small onion cut in half
7 kernels allspice
chopped parsley
1 carrot, sliced
2 c. water
1 t. salt
dash pepper
Bring ingredients to boiling point, then add meatballs. Cook 6 minutes in pressure pan, or 20-30 minutes by regular method.
Add:
½ c. milk or cream
2 t. vinegar
Skim fat off top, if necessary, before serving

Options:

Add 1 c. fresh or frozen peas shortly before removing from heat.

Omit potatoes in soup. Boil unpeeled new potatoes separately and serve along with soup.

Thicken soup slightly with flour, if desired.

Elsie Epp, Marion, S.D.

Martin Stew

Martin Stew was named by a youth group who were often served this by Elizabeth Martin, who says she was never sure what they would arrive. It can be made ahead of time and holds well.

T·S

Serves 6-8

Bring to boil in large kettle:
1½ qts. water
Add:
2½ c. macaroni
Meanwhile, brown in skillet:
1½ lbs. ground beef
1 onion, chopped
When redness is gone, add meat to macaroni kettle.
Add:
1 qt. tomato juice
1 T. salt
pepper
Simmer ½ hour. Just before serving, add:
2 c. frozen peas
Cook a few more minutes and serve in soup bowls.

Elizabeth S. Martin, New Holland, Pa.

Hunter's Stew

Combine in large kettle:
1 ham bone with leftover meat
5 c. water
Boil until meat is very tender (1-2 hours). Remove bone, chop meat, and return to broth.
Add:
1 c. fresh, frozen, or canned lima beans
1 c. spaghetti, broken into pieces
2 c. canned, frozen or fresh corn
1 large onion, chopped
1 qt. tomato juice
salt and pepper to taste
Simmer 20-30 minutes to finish cooking and blend flavors.

Elsie Mann, Fairbault, Minn.

Pot-Of-Gold Peanut Soup

Serves 6

Combine in large saucepan:
1 oz. dried mushrooms (optional)
8 c. water
Soak about 5 minutes or until mushrooms are rehydrated; remove and reserve mushrooms. Add to water:
3 T. instant chicken bouillon
1 dried red chili pepper
OR ¼ t. dried crushed red pepper
Bring to boil. Stir in:
⅓ c. pearl barley
Cover and simmer 1 hour or until barley is tender. Remove saucepan from heat and blend in:
1 c. chunky peanut butter
Stir with wire whip until smooth. Return to heat and continue stirring until soup is thickened. Stir in:
2 c. frozen chopped broccoli, thawed and drained
reserved mushrooms
Simmer 3-5 minutes. Remove from heat and add:
2 T. fresh lemon juice
2 T. chopped parsley

Option:

When omitting dried mushrooms, begin by cooking barley in water and bouillon (or broth). Fresh mushrooms may be sautéed briefly and added with broccoli.

Elma Esau, Akron, Pa.

Peanut Soup

Serves 3-4

Sauté in heavy saucepan:
  2 T. margarine
  1 medium onion, chopped
When onion is yellow, stir in:
  1 T. flour
Mix in a small bowl:
  ½ c. chunky peanut butter
  1 c. hot water
Add to onions, cooking over low heat and
stirring until smooth.
Add:
  1 chicken bouillon cube
  3 c. milk
Heat slowly, stirring often, until bouillon
dissolves and soup is hot.
Serve with croutons and garnish with
parsley.

Option:
Chicken broth may replace the hot water
and bouillon cube, plus part of the milk if
desired.

Beth Fry, Conestoga, Pa.
Helen and Adam Mueller,
* Cape Girardeau, Mo.*

Quick Beet
Borsch

T·S

Serves 4

Combine in saucepan:
  1 c. cabbage, finely chopped
  1 onion, finely chopped
  2 c. water
Cook 10 min. Add:
  2 c. stock or broth
  2 medium beets, cooked and
  ** chopped**
  ½ c. beet juice
  ½ t. salt
  dash pepper
  1 T. lemon juice
Bring to a boil. Pour into soup bowls and

top each serving with:
  2 T. whipped sour cream
Serve with toasted rye bread.

Options:
Add diced carrots with cabbage.
Add tomatoes.

Mabel Hertzler, Mechanicsburg, Pa.
Ruth Ressler, Sterling, Ohio

Vietnamese-Style
Chicken Noodle Soup

*Janet learned to make this soup from
Vietnamese students attending
Goshen College, Goshen, Ind. While
it originates in a tropical climate, the
peppery broth is equally good for
warming up on cold nights. Make
nothing else and eat two bowlfuls.*

Serves 6-8

In large kettle, cook until tender:
  1 chicken, or 2-3 lbs. bony pieces
  2½ qt. water
  ½ t. monosodium glutamate
  1-2 cloves garlic, crushed
  salt and pepper
Remove chicken; skin and bone it.
Return meat to broth and keep at simmer.
Cook separately until tender:
  1½ lbs. thin spaghetti
Drain.
To serve, fill individual soup bowls with
spaghetti. Pour over hot broth with
chicken. Sprinkle over each bowl:
  1-2 T. chopped scallions
Each person may add, to taste:
  chopped red pepper or Tabasco
  soy sauce
  freshly ground black pepper
Eat with chopsticks and soup spoon.

Janet Friesen, Seattle, Wash.

Vegetables

Possibilities for eating plants are vast. yet many cooks dish up the same dull round of boiled carrots. corn. and green beans every week. Eating vegetables is for adventuresome people—people who look at a new food the same way they look at a book that hasn't been read or a hill that wants climbing.

Menus can be full of new experiences with vegetables for very little money. Consider what happened to two teachers in Zambia:

> *I'm impressed with what Zambians eat that North Americans throw away. Mostly this pertains to vegetables and the lungs and intestines of chickens. Mark and I haven't taken to intestines yet, but we've learned to throw away less vegetable matter. We're eating beet tops, bean, broccoli, and pumpkin leaves. Wash the leaves, chop, and boil with salt and a handful of finely chopped peanuts. It makes a lovely vegetable in peanut gravy.*
> *—Darlene Keller,*
> *Lusaka, Zambia*

> *Our neighbor's cauliflower would not produce a head, and since they had no other vegetables, they decided to eat the leaves. The interesting thing is, the leaves taste like cauliflower.*
> *—Ruth Martin, Katete, Zambia*

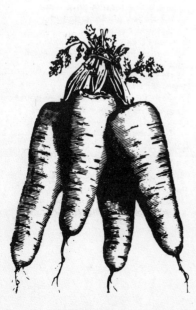

No book can say which vegetables are cheapest for those who don't garden. Every locale has its specialties. In most of North America, potatoes, carrots and cabbage are still the cheapest high-nutrient vegetables. Potatoes contain helpful amounts of vitamins and minerals. Baking potatoes in the skin preserves more nutrients than any other cooking method. Home-cooked and mashed potatoes, though not as good as baked, have twice the vitamins and minerals of the instant mashed variety. Carrots provide carotene which our bodies use to make Vitamin A. Cabbage, especially raw, is an excellent source of Vitamin C.

Iceberg lettuce, now standard salad fare on many tables year-round, is not usually a valuable buy for the nutrients it yields. There is no magic in the fact that iceberg lettuce is raw and crunchy. Its pale color gives away all but the outer leaves as a relatively poor source of vitamins. Grow your own greens in summer. Let the family chew carrots and cabbage in winter. Any of the following contain more vitamins for the money than iceberg lettuce: leafy, dark-green lettuce such as romaine; raw or cooked greens like endive, spinach, chard, collard greens; dark yellow-orange vegetables like carrots, yellow squash, or sweet potatoes.

Most vegetables should be cooked briefly in small amounts of water. Vegetable steamers, which fit inside ordinary saucepans, are available in some department stores. These steamers do a lovely job of preserving taste and nutrients.

Another fast, tasty, and vitamin-saving way to prepare vegetables is to stir-fry Chinese-style. Cut the raw vegetables, often a combination, into attractive uniform shapes. Set aside, grouping each kind of vegetable separately. If the recipe calls for a sauce, combine those ingredients in a small bowl and set aside. Have everything ready. Heat a skillet, add one or two tablespoons of oil, and when quite hot, add garlic if specified, and then vegetables, longest-cooking varieties first. With a wooden spoon or chopsticks, stir almost constantly over medium-high heat. As vegetables turn bright in color and begin to tenderize a bit, add other faster-cooking vegetables. When vegetables are still partly crisp (crisp-tender is the word used in recipes), add sauce mixture all at once, cook just until sauce clears and coats vegetables, and serve immediately. If no sauce is used, season while frying. The cooking itself may only take three to five minutes. A little practice lets you know just how crisp you should leave it. A little practice will also have you forgetting recipes as you invent new combinations from what is on hand.

The attractive color and delicious flavor of stir-fried vegetables has to be experienced. Somehow, half-cooked vegetables taste bad when done in water, but absolutely wonderful when stir-fried. Their fresh crunchiness makes salads unnecessary. Cutting and chopping can be done well in advance, but once the dish is hot and sauced, making it wait means sacrificing the perfect texture.

Sometimes I forget other details of the meal because it's so much fun to get right into assembling the stir-fry dish. Then my frantic alarm cries out to the rest of the family to finish setting the table because I can't leave the stove. But it's only the last five minutes that are hectic. The rewards are great. See Stir-fried Green Beans (*p. 153*, Zucchini (*p. 162*), and Broccoli (*p. 155*).

Vegetables Au Gratin

This old favorite still dresses up any vegetable and can serve as main dish (milk-chese protein) if you make plenty. Add salad and hot bread. Nice for a buffet.

Serves 6-8
350°
20 min.

Preheat oven to 350°
Prepare:
1½ lbs. or about 4 c. cooked vegetables (especially good are sliced carrots, cabbage, green beans, zucchini, broccoli, cauliflower, small onions, or a combination)
Toss together:
½ c. crushed cornflakes
1 T. oil or margarine
Set aside for topping.
Sauté in saucepan over low heat:
3 T. oil or margarine
⅓ c. (or more) chopped onion
Stir in:
3 T. flour
1 t. salt
⅛ t. pepper
Cook, stirring, until bubbly. Add:
1½ c. milk (use vegetable stock and powdered milk)
Cook and stir until smooth. Add:
1 c. (4 oz.) grated cheese
Stir until melted; remove from heat. Add:
cooked vegetables
1 T. dried or fresh snipped parsley
Spread mixture in shallow 1½-qt. baking pan. Sprinkle crumb mixture evenly over top. Bake 20 minutes or until sauce is heated and bubbly. Let stand 3-5 minutes before serving.

Options:

Omit cheese.

Substitute bread crumbs for cornflakes.

Use leftover vegetables in combination.

Prepare ahead of time and refrigerate until ready to bake.

Add 1 c. slivered ham for main-dish special.

Basic Cooked Greens

Contributor says, "We eat greens this way 'most every day and they are nutritious and easily digested—good for people who can't eat lots of raw cold salad."

Serves 3

Prepare 1 qt. washed finely chopped greens:
celery with leaves
lettuce
dandelion
turnip greens
kale
beet greens
spinach
cabbage
sauerkraut
endive
Swiss chard
Place in covered saucepan. Add chopped onions if desired. Water clinging to leaves from washing is usually sufficient. Cook just enough to wilt.
Beat together:
1 c. milk
2 T. flour
1 egg
seasoning to taste—salt, pepper, vinegar, mustard, sugar
Pour over hot greens and cook, stirring, until mixture thickens. Serve at once.

Option:

Add chopped cooked meat or hard-cooked eggs.

Naomi Coffman, Harrisonburg, Va.

Stir-Fried
Green Beans

Paper-thin slices are easy to cut from partially frozen meat. Freeze some meat in ¼ lb. packages for quick stir-fried dinners, which can usually be prepared in the 25 minutes it takes to cook rice.

T·S

Serves 4

Combine in small bowl and set aside:
    ½ t. salt
    1 t. sugar
    1 t. cornstarch
    1 T. soy sauce
    ½ c. water or soup stock
Heat in skillet:
    2 T. cooking oil
Add:
    ¼ lb. raw beef chuck, thinly sliced
        in bite-sized pieces
    2 cloves garlic, minced
    ½ c. onion, diced
Stir-fry over high heat until beef begins to change color. Remove beef, onions, and garlic from skillet and set aside. If necessary, add more oil and reheat skillet. Add:
    1 lb. fresh French-cut green beans
Stir until beans become bright green. At once add reserved soy sauce mixture and cook, stirring, until clear. Cover skillet and cook over medium heat until beans are just crisp-tender. Return beef to skillet, stir well and remove from heat. Serve immediately with rice. Add salad or light soup to complete the menu.

Options:

Use 1 chicken breast or ¼ lb. pork in place of beef.

Frozen green beans may be used but will not have the tender-crisp texture of fresh beans. Increase cornstarch to 1 T.

Pat Hostetter Martin, Quang Ngai, Vietnam

Puffy
Green Bean–Cheese Bake

Serves 4
350°
50-60 min.

Preheat oven to 350°.
Grease a 1½-qt. casserole. Break in:
    2 large or 3 medium eggs
Beat with rotary beater. Add:
    1 c. milk
    ¼ t. salt
    ½ c. fine cracker crumbs
    1 T. finely chopped onion
    1 c. cheddar cheese cubes
Stir well. Arrange on top:
    1¼ c. fresh green beans, cut in
        small pieces or equal amount
        frozen or canned beans
Drizzle over:
    1 T. melted margarine
Bake, uncovered, 50-60 minutes.
May be prepared in advance except for adding melted margarine.

Vera R. Buehler, Conestoga, On.

Stir-Fried
Bean Sprouts

Serves 4

Heat in wok or skillet until very hot:
    2 T. oil
Add and stir-fry 2 minutes:
    1 lb. fresh bean sprouts
    2 green onions, cut in 1½" lengths
    1½ t. salt
    dash soy sauce
Serve with rice.

Jessie Hostetler, Portland, Ore.

Egyptian
Tabikh

Prepare for cooking:
Green beans
Zucchini squash
OR a vegetable mixture
Instead of cooking in water, cook in tomato juice.
Thicken the juice with tomato paste, if desired.
Add sautéed onion and seasonings, as desired.
Serve over rice.

Option:

Cook small pieces of meat in the tomato juice until tender. Add vegetables during last 15-20 minutes.

Carolyn Yoder, Cairo, Egypt

Sweet–Sour
Beets

T·S

Serves 4-6

Grate finely:
1 large or 2 medium raw beets,
peeled
Melt in saucepan:
2 T. margarine
Add grated beets. Cover and cook slowly until beets are tender, stirring occasionally.
Add:

salt and pepper
1 T. vinegar
3 T. sugar
2 t. cornstarch dissolved in
¼ c. water
Cook stirring, until sauce clears. Serve hot.

Options:

Add 2 T. orange juice with water.

Simply add salt and pepper to sautéed beets and serve without sauce.

Minnie O. Good, Denver, Pa.

Fresh Broccoli
With Mock Hollandaise

Serves 4-6

Note: Cooking sulfur-containing vegetables such as broccoli, brussel sprouts, cauliflower, or cabbage, in larger quantities of boiling water shortens cooking time and lessens the formation of undesirable sulfur compounds. Any of these vegetables can be used in the following recipe.

Bring to boil in a large saucepan:
enough water to cover broccoli
2 t. salt for each quart water
Wash 1 head broccoli. Split large stem into fourths, but do not cut through head. Submerge broccoli in boiling water. Over high heat, quickly return to boiling. Reduce heat and cook gently, uncovered, just until stems are tender (7-10 min.) Remove from hot water immediately. Cut into serving pieces and arrange in oblong dish with heads at each end and stems in the center. Pour mock hollandaise over stems.

Mock Hollandaise
Melt in saucepan:
2 T. margarine
Blend in:
2 T. flour
1 T. sugar
¼ t. salt
Stir in:
1 c. water
2 T. vinegar
Cook until thickened. Cool slightly. Add:
2 egg yolks, beaten or
1 whole egg, beaten
Blend. Heat briefly before pouring over vegetables, but do not boil.

Olive Wyse, Goshen, Ind.

Broccoli–Celery Hollandaise

A good way to make broccoli stems acceptable and to use celery not in first-class condition for serving raw.

Serves 4-6

Wash and prepare:
1 lb. fresh broccoli
Remove heads and set aside. Slice stems diagonally into ½" pieces. Slice diagonally in ½" pieces:
2-3 stalks celery
Bring to boil in large saucepan:
2 qts. water (approx.)
4 t. salt
Add celery and broccoli stems. Boil, uncovered, about 8 minutes. Add broccoli heads. Cover until water returns to boiling. Uncover and cook gently for 5 min. Using some of the cooking water, prepare Mock Hollandaise sauce (**see p. 154**). Drain vegetables well and arrange broccoli heads in circle in serving dish. Add broccoli stems and celery to sauce. Combine thoroughly. Pour sauce in center of serving bowl.

Olive Wyse, Goshen, Ind.

Stir-Fried Broccoli

Cut broccoli heads in flowerets and slice stems diagonally.

T·S

Serves 4-5

Combine and set aside:
½ c. chicken broth
1 t. cornstarch
2 T. soy sauce
1 t. sugar
Heat in skillet:
3 T. oil
Add:
½ medium onion, diced
Fry until golden.
Add:
1 lb. broccoli,
  cut in small pieces
Stir-fry for three minutes. Add sauce ingredients. Stir-fry for 1 minute until sauce clears.

Option:

May be used for cauliflower cut into thin fan-shaped slices or broccoli-cauliflower combination (lovely color contrast!).

Olive Wyse, Goshen, Ind.

Plan more oven meals that cook vegetables and dessert at same time and temperature as main dish. Cook frozen vegetables in a tightly covered casserole at 350° for 40 to 45 minutes for small pieces and 50 to 60 minutes for larger pieces.
—Gertie Martens,
   Killarney, Man.

Broccoli Stuffing Bake

Serves 6-8
325°
45 min.

Preheat oven to 325°
Heat and stir in saucepan until blended:
  2 c. milk
  1 c. (4 oz.) shredded sharp cheese
Beat in mixing bowl:
  4 eggs
Gradually stir hot mixture into eggs.
Add:
  2½ c. herb-seasoned croutons
    (see p. 44)
  2 c. frozen chopped broccoli,
    thawed
  ¼ t. salt
Mix well. Turn into greased 1½-qt. casserole. Bake 45 minutes.

Lois Beck, West Liberty, Ohio

Formosan Fried Cabbage

Anna's not sure the dish is recognized in Taiwan, but it's been a family favorite with this name.

T·S

Serves 4

Brown together in heavy saucepan or large skillet:
  4 strips bacon or ½ lb. sausage,
    chopped
  ½ medium onion, chopped
Drain off some of the fat. Add:
  ½ medium cabbage, coarsely
    chopped
Stir-fry over low heat until cabbage is tender. Add:
  1 T. soy sauce
Serve over rice and pass additional soy sauce.

Anna Juhnke, North Newton, Kan.

Skillet Cabbage

T·S

Serves 4

Heat in large skillet:
  2 T. butter or margarine
Add:
  ⅔ c. chopped onions
  1 clove garlic, minced
Stir-fry briefly. Add:
  3-4 c. finely sliced cabbage
  ½ c. coarsely shredded carrots
Stir-fry about 5 minutes over medium heat, until vegetables are crisp-tender. Add:
  ⅛ t. paprika
  1 t. salt
  dash freshly ground pepper
  2 t. soy sauce (optional)
Stir until thoroughly blended and serve immediately.

Options:

Indonesian—When vegetables are crisp-tender, season well and pour over 2 eggs, beaten. Cook a few more minutes over low heat, stirring just enough to allow eggs to become cooked. Serve as a main dish with rice.

Vietnamese—Top with a generous sprinkling of chopped roasted peanuts, serve with rice, and pass soy sauce. Slivers of meat may be added at the beginning with onions.

Dorothy Liechty, Berne, Ind.

Potato Filling

Potato filling isn't filled into anything but hungry Pennsylvania Dutch stomachs. It's simply a tasty make-ahead version of mashed potatoes.

Serves 4-6
350°
1 hr.

Preheat oven to 350°.
Sauté in skillet:
- **¼ c. margarine**
- **1 c. chopped celery**
- **1 c. chopped onions**

Pare and boil in salted water:
- **4 medium-sized potatoes**

When done, mash but do not add milk.
Mix into potatoes:
- **1 egg, slightly beaten**
- **2 slices bread, torn in small pieces**
- **onions and celery**

Season with salt and pepper to taste. Put into greased baking dish. Bake for 1 hour. Cover for first half hour, uncover for remaining time.

Mabel Stoltzfus, Harrington, Del.
Edna Longacre, Barto, Pa.

Carrot–Cheddar Casserole

Mash drained carrots easily by whirling in blender with eggs and milk.

Serves 8
350°
30 min.

Preheat oven to 350°.
Combine in mixing bowl:
- **3 c. cooked, mashed carrots (about 1½ lb.)**
- **3 beaten eggs**
- **2 c. milk**
- **1⅓ c. shredded cheddar cheese**
- **1⅓ c. crushed crackers (reserve ¼ c. for topping)**
- **2-3 T. softened butter**
- **1½ t. salt**
- **dash pepper**
- **1 T. chopped parsley**

Mix well. Turn into greased casserole and sprinkle with reserved crumbs. Bake 30 minutes, or until knife inserted in center comes out clean.

Mary Lou Houser, Lancaster, Pa.

Ginger-Glazed Carrots

Serves 4

Boil in small amount of water:
- **8 small carrots (or equivalent carrot sticks)**

When almost tender, drain well. (Reserve liquid for soup making.)
Heat in heavy skillet:
- **1½ T. margarine**
- **¼ t. ground ginger**
- **1 T. honey or sugar**

Add carrots and stir carefully to coat. Cook over low heat until glazed, turning frequently.

Option:

Omit ginger. Add 1 T. prepared mustard. Sprinkle with chopped chives, mint, or parsley.

Jean Edmonds, Sparta, Tenn.
Winifred Paul, Scottdale, Pa.

Golden Eggplant Casserole

Serves 4-6
350°
45 min.

Preheat oven to 350°
Combine in a bowl:
- **15 soda crackers, crumbled**
- **2 T. melted margarine**

Toss. Take out and reserve ¼ c. for topping.
Add to remaining crumbs:
- **3 c. cubed eggplant (¾" cubes)**
- **½ c. shredded sharp cheese**
- **¼ c. chopped celery**
- **½ t. salt**
- **¼ t. pepper**
- **1 c. evaporated milk**

Turn into greased casserole. Top with reserved crumbs. Bake 45 minutes.

Author's Recipe

Eggplant Supreme

T·S

Serves 4

Prepare:
1 eggplant, peeled and sliced
¼" thick
1 onion, finely chopped
1 large green pepper, thinly sliced
Heat in 10" skillet:
1 T. margarine
Place 4 slices eggplant symmetrically in
skillet. Add some onion and green
pepper in spaces between eggplant.
Sprinkle with:
chili powder
salt
In bowl, beat until foamy:
4-5 eggs
When eggplant softens, pour into skillet
some of beaten egg, just enough to cover
eggplant. Fry over low heat, without
stirring, until egg is cooked. Turn
"pancake" and brown other side.
Remove to platter and hold in warm oven.
Repeat, adding more margarine to
skillet, until eggplant and eggs are used.
One "pancake" serves one person as a
main dish.

Option:

Add chopped tomatoes.

Ed Peters, Choma, Zambia

Eggplant Parmesan

*Lots of fuss but yields a really elegant
meatless casserole.*

Serves 6
375°
10-15 min.

Preheat oven to 375°.
Cut in ½" slices:
1 medium eggplant
Cover with hot water and let stand 5 min.
Dry slices. Fry in ⅓ c. oil until lightly
browned. Sprinkle with salt and pepper.
Put in bottom of 9 x 13" baking pan.
Mix together and sprinkle over the
eggplant:
1 c. bread crumbs
½ c. Parmesan cheese
2 T. chopped parsley
1 t. salt
⅛ t. pepper
1 t. oregano
Combine in saucepan:
6 tomatoes, chopped
2 green peppers, chopped
2 onions, chopped
2 T. oil
1 clove garlic, minced
2 T. tomato paste (or thicken
sauce with 1 T. flour)
Simmer uncovered about 20 minutes,
then spread on top of crumb mixture. Top
with:
1-2 c. grated Swiss cheese
¼ c. additional Parmesan
Bake 10-15 minutes. Can be made
ahead and refrigerated.

Options:

Broil eggplant instead of frying as in
Easy Moussaka, *p. 86*

Substitute zucchini for eggplant

Zona Galle, Madison, Wis.

Corn Cheese Bake

Serves 6
350°
40-45 min.

Preheat oven to 350°.
Combine and mix well:
   2 c. cooked corn, drained
   ⅔ c. milk
   2 eggs, beaten
   ½ t. salt
   dash pepper
   1 c. shredded cheese (4 oz.)
   2 T. minced onion (optional)
   2 T. minced green pepper
      (optional)
Pour into greased 1½-qt. casserole. Top with:
   ½ c. cracker crumbs
   2 T. melted margarine
Bake 40-45 minutes.

Jocele Meyer, Brooklyn, Ohio

Sweet Potatoes Recife

Serves 8
400°
30 min.

Preheat oven to 400°.
Combine in mixing bowl:
   4 c. cooked mashed sweet
      potatoes
   2 c. cooked crushed pineapple,
      drained
   6 T. margarine, melted
   1 t. salt
   3 T. brown sugar
   ¼ t. ground cloves
Turn into ungreased casserole. Sprinkle on:
   ½ c. bread crumbs
Bake 30 minutes.

Josefa Soares, Recife, Brazil

Mashed Potato Casserole

Serves 6-8
400°
20 min.

Preheat oven to 400°.
Cook and mash:
   3-4 large potatoes
Add:
   ⅓ c. sour cream or yogurt
   1 t. salt
   dash pepper
   ½ t. sugar
   ¼ c. margarine
Add just enough milk to bring to proper consistency and beat until fluffy. Add:
   ⅛ t. dill seed
   2 t. chives, chopped
   1 c. cooked spinach,
      well drained and chopped
Place in greased casserole and top with:
   ½ c. grated cheddar cheese
Bake 20 minutes.
May be made a day or two ahead and refrigerated, or make a double recipe and freeze half to add to future oven meal.

Helen June Martin, Ephrata, Pa.

Creamy Cabbage

T·S

Serves 6

Cook about 7 minutes, just until crisp-tender:
   6 c. shredded cabbage
   ¼ c. onion, chopped
   ⅓ c. water
   ⅛ t. salt
Drain. Add and toss lightly while hot:
   3 oz. cream cheese, cubed
   ½ t. celery seed
   2 T. butter or margarine
   paprika

Zona Galle, Madison, Wis.

Golden Potato Bake

Tester reported leftovers made extra delicious potato cakes.

Serves 8
350°
25 min.

Cook together in salted water until tender:
   2 lbs. potatoes (about 6 medium), peeled
   2 c. thinly sliced carrots
When done, preheat oven to 350°.
Drain vegetables, reserving liquid. Mash with mixer on low speed.
Add: enough vegetable liquid for mashed potato consistency.
   ½ c. dry milk powder
Beat until mixture is fluffy. Stir in:
   1 T. margarine
   salt and pepper to taste
Turn into 2-qt. greased casserole.
Dot with additional margarine if desired.
Bake 25 minutes.

Option:
For main dish, stir in 1 c. shredded cheese before baking.

Miriam LeFever, East Petersburg, Pa.

MCC-Brussels French Fries

Serves 4

Scrub but do not peel:
   4-6 medium potatoes
Cut into lengthwise strips ¼ x ¼".
Fill deep fryer half full of oil or lard. (Lard is preferred for flavor.) Heat to 375°. Fill wire basket ¼ full of potato strips and immerse in hot oil. If bubbles spill over, raise basket several times till they subside.
As strips fry, stir gently with long fork to keep them from sticking together. Fry 5 minutes or until strips soften and bend under fork without breaking. Remove from oil, let drip, and spill out onto clean newspaper to absorb excess oil. Repeat with all strips.
Now shake strips all together. Fill basket half full. Fry again about 5 minutes or until golden brown, slightly soft inside and crispy outside.
Remove, let drip, and drain French fries onto dry newspaper. Agitate to dry excess oil. Repeat with remaining strips. Salt lightly. Serve hot.

Don Ziegler, Lancaster, Pa.

German Potato Noodles

A traditional dish used specifically for leftover mashed potatoes.

Serves 6

Combine in a bowl:
   2 c. mashed potatoes
   1 egg, beaten
   ¾ c. flour
   1 t. salt
Mix to form a dough. On lightly floured board, roll out pieces into long strips ¼" thick, and cut into strips 1" wide. In skillet, heat fat (½" deep) and fry until brown. Serve hot.

Skillet Eggplant

T·S

Serves 4

Heat in a skillet:
2 T. margarine
Add:
2 c. diced unpeeled eggplant
**1 c. thinly sliced scallions,
green tops included**
**1 large green pepper, cut in
thin strips**
1 large tomato, diced
¼ c. water
½ t. salt
¼ t. ground allspice
1 t. sugar (optional)
Mix well. Simmer, covered, until eggplant is tender, about 20 minutes. Add additional water if necessary

Option:

Substitute ½-1 c. tomato sauce for fresh tomato and water

Rosemary Moyer, North Newton, Kan.

Brown Tomato Gravy

Serves 3

Peel and slice:
2-3 firm, ripe tomatoes
Heat in skillet:
2 T. margarine or shortening
Roll tomato slices in flour and brown quickly on both sides.
Reduce heat.
Add to skillet:
2 T. sugar
1 t. salt
1 c. water
Simmer 30 minutes, stirring occasionally and breaking up tomato chunks. Serve with potatoes, rice, noodles, or on toast.

Edna Mast, Cochranville, Pa.

Potato Pancakes

Serves 4

Combine in a bowl:
**2½ c. grated raw potato
(about 3 medium)**
1 t. salt
dash pepper
2 eggs
2 T. flour
1 T. finely chopped onion
Drop by spoonfuls into a lightly oiled hot skillet. Fry until brown on one side, then turn and brown on other side. Good served with syrup, ketchup, or cheese sauce.

Option:

Add 1 cup finely chopped cooked turkey, chicken, or ham. Good with cranberry sauce.

Anna Ediger, Drake, Sask.
Elvera Goering, Salina, Kan.
Nell Peters, Choma, Zambia

Spinach Loaf

Serves 4-6
350°
35-40 min.

Preheat oven to 350°.
Cook briefly and drain well:
   2 c. frozen chopped spinach
   OR
   2 qt.-saucepan fresh spinach,
      heaping full
Make a white sauce:
   2 T. margarine
   3 T. flour
   ⅛ t. pepper
   1 t. salt
   1 c. milk
Combine:
   spinach
   white sauce
   2 eggs, slightly beaten
Pour into buttered casserole. Bake 35-40 minutes, until knife inserted comes out clean.

Options:
Sauté 1 onion, chopped, in margarine when making white sauce.

Add ¾ c. grated cheese to white sauce.

Mary Lou Houser, Lancaster, Pa.
Elvera Goering, Salina, Kan.

Corn–Squash Bake

Serves 6
350°
40 min.

Preheat oven to 350°.
Cut in 1" rounds:
   3-4 medium zucchini or other
      summer squash, unpeeled
Cook in small amount of boiling salted water until tender. Drain and mash with fork.

Sauté:
   1 T. margarine
   1 small onion, chopped
Combine:
   mashed zucchini
   sautéed onion
   2 c. corn, fresh cut, cooked or
      frozen (thawed)
   1 c. shredded Swiss cheese
   ½ t. salt
   2 beaten eggs
Turn into 1-qt. greased casserole.
Combine and sprinkle on top:
   ¼ c. dry bread crumbs
   2 T. grated Parmesan cheese
   1 T. melted margarine
Place casserole on baking sheet; bake for 40 minutes, or until set. Let stand 5-10 minutes before serving.

Linda Grasse, Chambersburg, Pa.

Stir-Fry Zucchini

T·S

Serves 4

Heat in large skillet over medium heat:
   3 T. salad oil
Add:
   1 lb. zucchini, cut into
      strips about 3" long
   1 c. onion, cut in large pieces
Cook uncovered, stirring frequently, until crisp-tender (about 5-8 minutes). Stir in:
   2 T. sesame seeds
   1 T. soy sauce
   ½ t. salt
   dash pepper

Option:
Cut zucchini and onion in rounds.

Evelyn Liechty, Berne, Ind.

Cook overripe peas and add to cooked rice with onions, garlic, and curry seasonings.
—Kamala Misra,
Bhubaneswar, India

Skillet Italian Zucchini

T·S

Serves 4

Slice diagonally, ½" thick:
8 small zucchini, unpeeled
Heat in skillet:
2 T. butter or margarine
Add and sauté about 5 minutes:
½ onion, chopped
sliced zucchini
Add:
2 c. spaghetti sauce, tomato sauce, or canned tomatoes
2 T. grated Parmesan cheese (optional)
1 t. salt
½ t. leaf thyme
½ t. oregano
½ t. basil
dash pepper
Cover and simmer just until crisp-tender.

Linda Grasse, Chambersburg, Pa.

Baked Italian Zucchini

Serves 6
350°
45 min./10 min.

Preheat oven to 350°.
Place in casserole, adding seasoning to each layer:
2 medium or 3-4 small unpeeled zucchini, sliced ½" thick
1 onion, sliced
1 whole tomato, sliced (optional)
1 t. oregano
½ t. basil
salt and pepper
Pour over:
1-2 c. tomato sauce, enough to barely cover vegetables
Cover and bake 45 minutes.

Uncover and add:
1 c. cubed buttered bread or ½ c. bread crumbs
½ c. grated cheese
Bake an additional 10 minutes, uncovered.

Option:
Use frozen sliced zucchini, but increase first baking time to 1 hour.

Author's Recipe

Zucchini Skillet Supper

Tester reported: "Husband HATES zucchini but liked this and never knew what he was eating until told."

Serves 4-5

Sauté in skillet in small amount hot fat:
4 c. zucchini, thinly sliced
1 onion, sliced
Add:
2 c. canned tomatoes with juice
¾ c. canned mushrooms, drained (optional)
salt, pepper, and oregano to taste
cubes of cooked chicken, beef, ham, or browned ground beef
Simmer just until heated through. Serve in soup bowls and sprinkle with Parmesan cheese.

Options:
Use fresh sliced mushrooms and sauté with zucchini.

Use fresh tomatoes in season. Add tomato juice for liquid.

Omit meat and serve as vegetable.

Eat over noodles or rice.

Ruth Sherman, Goshen, Ind.

Zucchini Omelet

T·S

Serves 4-5
350°
25-30 min.

Preheat oven to 350°.
Heat in skillet:
   2 T. margarine
Sauté gently until fork-tender, 5-7
minutes:
   1 medium onion, sliced thinly
   1 clove garlic, minced
   **2 lbs. zucchini squash, coarsely
      grated**
Add:
   1½ t. salt
   ¼ t. pepper
Put squash in baking dish.
Meanwhile, combine:
   2 eggs
   ½ c. milk
   3 T. flour
   **½ c. grated Parmesan or other
      cheese**
Pour over squash. Bake 25-30 minutes,
or until firm.

Option:
Add 2 beaten eggs and seasonings
directly to sautéed vegetables. Cook and
stir until eggs are set.

Barbara Longenecker, New Holland, Pa.

Zucchini And Eggs

T·S

Serves 3

Prepare:
   4 small zucchini, unpeeled
Cut squash in half, then split each half
into 4 pieces. Heat in skillet:
   2 T. margarine
   2 T. oil
Flour squash lightly and fry until brown.

Sprinkle with salt and pepper. Arrange
zucchini evenly in skillet. Combine and
pour over top:
   2 eggs, lightly beaten
   1 T. milk
Cook slowly until set. Sprinkle with:
   grated Parmesan cheese

Option:
Sauté onion with zucchini and season
with garlic salt, parsley, and oregano.

Olive Wyse, Goshen, Ind.
Linda Grasse, Chambersburg, Pa

Zucchini Egg Foo Yung

Serves 4

Grate coarsely:
   4 medium unpeeled zucchini
Mix in:
   3 eggs, beaten
   ¼ c. flour or ½ c. wheat germ
   ¼ t. garlic powder (optional)
   1 t. salt
   1 onion, grated
Fry by tablespoonfuls in hot oiled skillet,
turning once when golden brown.
Arrange on platter and top with sauce:
Combine in saucepan:
   1 c. chicken broth
   2 T. soy sauce
   1 T. cornstarch
Cook and stir over low heat until
thickened. Serve with rice.

Options:
Add fresh bean sprouts with grated
zucchini.
Switch from Chinese to Italian meal by
topping with tomato sauce and
Parmesan cheese sprinkle. Serve with
spaghetti.

Evelyn Liechty, Berne, Ind.
Eleanor Hiebert, Elkins Park, Pa.

Tomatoes
Stuffed with Spinach

Serves 6
375°
20 min.

Preheat oven to 375°.
Prepare for stuffing:
   6 firm tomatoes
Cut off tops and scoop out centers.
Combine:
   2 c. cooked spinach
   1 T. melted butter
   ½ t. salt
   ½ onion, minced
Pack into tomato shells. Place in greased casserole and bake about 20 minutes. Serve with creamed hard-cooked eggs as a main dish.

   Grace Horning, Ephrata, Pa.

Salsify-Carrot
Casserole

Salsify is a white root vegetable. The all-salsify version of this dish is called "mock oyster scallop" in Pennsylvania Dutch country.

Serves 6
350°
35-40 min.

Preheat oven to 350°.
Combine:
   3 c. cooked mashed carrots
      and salsify
   1 c. cracker crumbs
   2 c. milk
   2 T. grated onion
   3 T. melted margarine
   3 eggs, slightly beaten
   salt and pepper
Bake in casserole 35-40 min.

   Option:
All carrots or all salsify may be used, but the combination is delicious.

   Ann Huber, Lancaster, Pa.

Prussian
Kale

T·S

Serves 3

Prepare:
   1 qt. fresh kale, finely chopped
Cover with cold water and bring to a boil. After boiling 2 minutes, drain off water and discard.
Add:
   1 c. fresh water
   ½ t. salt
   dash pepper
   ¼ c. oatmeal
   one of the following to flavor:
      piece of boiled fresh pork
      ham bits
      several strips crisp bacon,
         crumbled
      2 T. bacon fat or margarine
Simmer about 10 min.

   Option:
Use other greens such as Swiss chard, turnip or beet greens, collards, spinach. Parboiling results in some loss of vitamins but is necessary with kale to remove bitterness. Other greens may not require this step.

   Helene Janzen, Elbing, Kan.

Fried Squash Blossoms

Squash flowers are a delicacy in many parts of the world when blossoms are plentiful enough to predict an ample harvest. Hopi, Pueblo, and Zuni Indians enjoyed their crisp, light texture.

Serves 6

Wash carefully and drain:
12 large squash blossoms (pick when blossoms are just ready to open)
Make batter:
**2 eggs, beaten
1 c. flour (may use ⅓ or more soy flour)
1 c. water
1 t. salt
¼ t. cayenne
½ t. tumeric**
Heat in heavy saucepan:
½-1 c. oil
Dip blossoms in batter until well coated, then fry in hot fat (375°) until golden brown. (Takes less than a minute for each.) Drain on absorbent paper and serve warm.

LaVonne Platt, Newton, Kan.

Gado Gado (Indonesian vegetable platter)

Vegetables may be cooked an hour or two in advance and need not be kept hot. In Indonesia the dish is served at room temperature.

Serves 8

Vegetables:
Cook or steam each vegetable separately just until crisp-tender:
**½ small head cabbage, cut up
½ lb. fresh green beans, cut or French-style
1 small head cauliflower, cut into flowerets
1 can or 2 c. fresh bean sprouts
4 carrots, cut in small strips
other vegetables may be added or substituted**
Drain vegetables, reserving stock for peanut sauce.
Peel and quarter:
4 hard-cooked eggs
Slice:
**2 cucumbers
6-10 radishes**

Peanut Sauce
Sauté in heavy saucepan:
**3 T. oil
½ c. finely chopped onions
2 cloves garlic, minced**
Stir-fry until onions are soft and transparent, not brown.
Add:
**3½ c. hot water or vegetable stock
1 c. peanut butter (an additional 2 T. if chunky peanut butter is used)
2 t. fresh chopped hot peppers, or Tabasco sauce to taste
2 bay leaves
1 t. scraped, finely grated fresh ginger root
2 t. lemon juice
grated rind of one lemon
1 t. salt**
Reduce heat and simmer for 15 minutes. Taste for seasoning and set pan aside.

Group vegetables attractively on a large platter or two, with a bowl of peanut sauce in the center. Garnish platter with eggs, radishes, and cucumbers. Serve with hot rice.

Jean Miller, Akron, Pa.

Ratatouille

T·S

Serves 6-8

Combine in large saucepan:

> **1 medium eggplant, pared, cubed**
> **2 small zucchini, cubed**
> **1 c. finely chopped green pepper**
> **1 medium onion, finely chopped, about ½ c.**
> **4 medium tomatoes, peeled and quartered**
> **¼ c. salad oil**
> **1 clove garlic, crushed**
> **2 t. salt**
> **¼ t. pepper**

Cook and stir ingredients until heated through. Cover, cook over medium heat, stirring occasionally, about 10 minutes, or until vegetables are crisp-tender.

Mary Alderfer, Scottdale, Pa.
Kathleen Kurtz, Richmond, Va.

Mahsi (Middle Eastern Stuffed Vegetables)

Mahsi recipe came with raves (especially for the grape leaves) from all around the Mediterranean.

Serves 6
325°
1½ hrs.

Preheat oven to 325°.
Prepare a variety of vegetables for stuffing:

> **Tomatoes, bell peppers, zucchini, small eggplant—**

Cut off tops, reserving lids. Clean out center seedy portions, reserving tomato pulp.

Leafy vegetables—
Cabbage and green grape leaves
Parboil 3 minutes to soften. Use newer grape leaves—old ones are tough.
Four-inch size is needed to stuff easily.
Prepare *stuffing:*
Brown in a skillet

> **½-1 lb. ground beef, pork, or lamb**
> **1 large onion, finely chopped**
> **3 cloves garlic, minced (optional)**

Add:

> **½ c. minced parsley**
> **1 c. uncooked rice**
> **3 T. margarine or olive oil**
> **1 t. salt**
> **dash pepper**
> **2 c. tomato sauce plus any reserved tomato pulp**
> **fresh chopped mint and/or dill to taste**

Taste to check seasonings. Fill hollowed-out vegetables ⅔ full with rice mixture, replacing "lids."
For leaf vegetables, place 1 T. stuffing mix on each. Roll up loosely so rice can expand, folding in sides. May be fastened with toothpicks.
Place vegetables in baking dish, add water to ¼" depth, and bake 1½ hours.

Options:

To cook on top of stove, place vegetables in a well-buttered skillet, add 2 c. boiling water or thin tomato juice, 2 T. lemon juice, and cover with a light-fitting lid. Bring to boiling and reduce heat to simmer. Cook 1 hour or until rice is tender.

Omit meat and increase rice and tomato sauce amounts.

Carolyn Yoder, Cairo, Egypt
Louise Claassen, Elkhart, Ind. (Crete)
Esther Samuel Geladah, Atbara, Sudan
Gwen Peachey, Amman, Jordan

Gemüse Eintopf (one-dish vegetable meal)

Developed in Algeria to use oversupply of pumpkin.

TS

Serves 8

Combine in large kettle:
**2 lbs. potatoes, cut up
2 lbs. turnips or carrots, cut up
OR 1 lb. cooked pumpkin, mashed
2 onions, chopped
2 stalks celery, chopped
3 T. fresh or dried parsley
2 cloves garlic, minced
salt and pepper to taste**
Add:
**small amount of water
¼ c. margarine or other fat**
Cook slowly until vegetables are tender.
When almost done, add:
1 T. powder bouillon or 3 cubes (dissolve in ¼ c. hot water)
Serve as is, or put through food mill to form a thick puree.

Irene L. Bishop, Perkasie, Pa.

Barbecued Potatoes And Carrots

Serves 7-8
375°
1¼ hrs./15 min.

Preheat oven to 375°
Combine in a bowl:
**4 c. thinly sliced potatoes (may scrub and leave unpared)
1 c. bias-sliced carrots
½ c. chopped celery
½ c. chopped onion
½ c. (2 oz.) shredded sharp cheese**
Add to vegetables, tossing to coat:
**3 T. all-purpose flour
1 t. salt
dash pepper**
Turn into casserole. Blend together in a bowl:

**½ c. ketchup
⅛-¼ t. cayenne (optional)
1 t. Worcestershire sauce
½ t. garlic salt
2 c. milk**
Pour over vegetables. Cover; bake 1¼ hours. Stir; bake, uncovered, 15 minutes more. Garnish with parsley.

Lucy Weber, Mohnton, Pa.

Gather Up the Fragments

1.
Collect bits of cooked vegetables in container in freezer, along with juices from cooking. Use to make soup.
2.
Whirl leftovers in blender and add to cream soup, gravy, stew, casseroles.
3.
Pour oil and vinegar dressing over cooked green beans, beets, carrots, broccoli, cauliflower, asparagus. Marinate in refrigerator and serve on lettuce or add to tossed salad.
4.
Heat leftover pickle juice and pour over leftover vegetables; chill and serve on pickle tray. *see p. 179*
5.
Reheat several vegetables with onion, garlic, and tomato sauce. Add curry seasonings and serve on rice. Curry powder masks any leftover taste.
6.
Leftover corn does not reheat with much flavor; stir it into corn fritters, corn bread (*p. 32*), or one of the corn soups (*pp. 135-137*).
7.
Using scorched vegetables: Remove from heat. Place in another saucepan. Add small amount of liquid, place slice of bread or toast on top to absorb burned taste from vegetable and resume cooking.
—Mae Holty, Roxbury, Pa.
8.
Recipes that take well to vegetable leftovers:
Vegetables Au Gratin, *p. 152*
German Potato Noodles, *p. 155*
Corn-Cheese Bake, *p. 159*
Corn-Squash Bake, *p. 162*
Puffy Green Bean-Cheese Bake, *p. 153*
Vietnam Fried Rice, *p. 79*
Many soup recipes

Salads

Good cooks don't need many salad recipes. The best salads are simple collections of raw vegetables with only a light touch of dressing. Once you know how to put together the vegetables at hand, keep them crisp, and stir up an easy dressing, you can almost go on to the next chapter.

Too many salad recipes read like dessert: 2 boxes flavored sugared gelatin, sweetened canned fruit, marshmallows, nuts, and a whipped topping folded in. The first economy move would be to omit nuts; actually they are the single nutritious ingredient listed. Name these concoctions for what they are—expensive sweets. Serve them as desserts if at all.

Raw vegetable salads are more nutritious. But people still manage to go wrong by drowning their greens in sugary, orange stuff called French dressing. (Reportedly the French never allow it across their borders.)

Bottled salad dressings are expensive and high in fats and sugars. They contain enough preservatives to last forever in the

door of your refrigerator. The glass bottles that go to waste may be worth more than their contents.

Homemade dressings are cheaper. With imaginative use of herbs and seasonings, they taste better than anything you can buy.

But beware the salad dressing recipe with ½ to 1 cup of sugar. These formulas are everywhere, teaching people to expect a foretaste of dessert on their greens. Develop gradually your household's taste for herbs, lemon, garlic, and the natural flavors of crisp raw vegetables.

Raw Vegetable Salads

1. If you raise nothing else edible, plant at least a salad garden. A double-bed-sized plot of scallions, herbs, greens, and tomato vines can keep salad on the table May through October.

2. Iceberg lettuce has few vitamins. Use other greens or mix it with endive, romaine, Boston Bibb, or raw spinach.

3. Wash greens, drain well, pat dry with a clean towel, and refrigerate in plastic bag or closed container. Excess water clinging to the leaves makes dressing turn watery and tasteless.

4. Tear greens into a salad bowl instead of cutting them. You can then make salad hours ahead of time, cover it with plastic, and refrigerate. Torn edges do not wilt and darken quickly.

5. Shake together a little oil and vinegar dressing (*p. 172*).

6. Just before serving, add dressing, toss, and serve. Garnish salads with croutons, sliced hard-cooked eggs, sliced radishes or scallions, chopped parsley, peanuts, or toasted sunflower seeds. Use these touches rather than sweet dressing by the cupful to make salads appealing.

Blender Mayonnaise

Depending on cost of oil and eggs, this can run as high as commercial mayonnaise. Check prices.

Makes 1 pint

Whirl in blender:
 2 eggs
 1½ t. salt
 1 t. dry mustard
 ½ t. paprika
Clean down sides. Add
 2 T. lemon juice
Start blender, remove cover, and *very* slowly pour in:
 ½ c. salad oil
Add:
 2 T. vinegar
Slowly, with blender running, add:
 1½ c. salad oil

Esther Hostetter, Akron, Pa
Sharal Phinney, Elkton, Va

Low-Cal Mock Mayonnaise

Makes about 1 cup

Shake in covered jar until smooth:
 ¾ c. skim milk
 2 T. flour
 3 T. sugar
 ½ t. salt
 ½ t. dry mustard
Pour into saucepan and cook until thickened, stirring constantly. Add:
 ¼ c. vinegar
Use hot or cold as a substitute for mayonnaise. Just before using, stir in finely chopped onion and/or other herbs and seasonings to taste.
Makes 1¼ c

Mary Slabaugh, Harrisonburg, Va

Cooked Mayonnaise

Costs about two thirds as much as commercial mayonnaise.

Makes 3 cups

Combine in saucepan:
  ⅓ c. flour
  ½ c. sugar
  1 t. salt
Add:
  ¾ c. water
  ½ c. vinegar
Cook over low heat, stirring until thickened. Remove from heat and pour into small mixing bowl or blender. While beating, add:
  1 clove minced garlic (optional)
  2 whole eggs or 4 yolks
Continue beating and slowly add:
  ⅔ c. salad oil
Chill before serving.

  Katie Swartzendruber, Wellman, Iowa

Cooked Salad Dressing

Makes 2 cups

Combine in saucepan:
  ¼ c. sugar
  ¼ c. flour
  2 t. salt
  2 t. dry mustard
Add:
  1½ c. milk
  ½ c. mild vinegar or lemon juice
Cook over low heat, stirring until thickened.
Stir at least half of the mixture into:
  1 beaten egg
Return egg mixture to saucepan and bring to boil. Boil 1 minute. Remove from heat. Stir in:
  1 T. butter or margarine
Cool.

  Bonnie Zook, Leola, Pa.

Salad Dressings With Mayonnaise Base

Thousand Island
Combine:
  1 c. mayonnaise
  ¼ c. chili sauce or ketchup
  2 hard-cooked eggs, chopped
  2 T. each finely chopped green pepper and onion
  2 T. pickle relish (optional)
  1 t. paprika
  ½ t. salt

Green Goddess
Combine:
  ½ c. mayonnaise
  ¼ c. sour cream or yogurt
  2 T. lemon juice or vinegar
  2 T. snipped chives
  2 T. snipped parsley
  ¼ t. salt
  freshly ground pepper

Blue Cheese
Combine:
  1 c. mayonnaise
  ¼ c. crumbled blue cheese
  2 T. milk
  dash cayenne pepper

Honey–Lemon Dressing

Tangy sweet-sour flavor without being sugary. Use on tossed salads.

Makes almost 1 cup

Shake together:
  2 T. honey
  ¼ c. lemon juice
  ½ c. oil
  salt, pepper and herbs to taste

  Twila Strickler

Fresh Fruit Salad Dressing

Makes about 1½ cups

Beat well:
2 eggs
Pour into saucepan. Add:
½ c. sugar
⅔ c. pineapple juice
1½ T. lemon juice
Cook over low heat, stirring constantly, until thick. Chill.

Marian Franz, Washington, D.C.

Parsley Dressing

Makes 2 cups

Whirl in blender:
½ c. parsley, packed into cup
⅓ c. salad oil
¼ c. water
¼ c. honey
¼ c. lemon juice
2 t. basil
salt
½ c. chopped avocado (optional)
Use on greens or Chop Salad, *p. 175*

Twila Strickler

Basic Oil and Vinegar Dressing

The simplest of all salad dressings—make it anywhere, anytime by remembering equal parts oil and vinegar.

Serves 6-8 on green salad

Shake together or combine in bottom of salad bowl:
2 T. salad oil
2 T. vinegar or lemon juice or combination
½ t. salt
dash each freshly ground pepper, dry mustard
Add to taste:

pressed garlic	**poppy seeds**
minced onion	**celery seeds**
oregano	**ketchup**
basil	**honey**
chopped parsley	
chopped chives	

Winifred Paul, Scottdale, Pa.

French Dressing

Contributor says, "I haven't bought any bottled dressing since I found this recipe."

Makes 1⅓ cups

Shake, beat, or whirl in blender:
1 T. grated onion
1 t. salt
2 T. sugar
2 T. vinegar
½ c. salad oil
½ c. ketchup
2 T. lemon juice
1 t. paprika
Keeps well in refrigerator.

Esther Hostetter, Akron, Pa.
Grace Whitehead, Kokomo, Ind.

French-Style Lettuce Salad

So simple and just right with almost any main dish.

Serves 4-6

Wash. drain, and dry thoroughly:
½-1 head lettuce
Rub salad bowl with:
1 clove garlic, sliced
Add directly to salad bowl:
2 T. salad oil
1 T. wine vinegar
¼ t. salt
freshly ground pepper to taste
1-2 T. minced parsley
1 t. lemon juice (optional)
Mix well with salad spoon. Criscross salad fork and spoon in salad bowl to keep lettuce from dressing until ready to serve. With hands, tear lettuce leaves and place over top of salad fork and spoon Just before serving, toss thoroughly.

Cathy Bowman. Kotabumi, Sumatra

Garden Salad

Serves 6

Combine in salad bowl:
½ c. shredded carrots
1 c. diced cauliflower
1 c. frozen peas, thawed
     OR 1 c. cooked chick-peas, drained ·
1 c. chopped celery
3 c. tomatoes, chopped
1 c. cucumbers, chopped
1 c. lettuce, chopped
½ c. roasted sunflower seeds
Toss and serve with Honey-Lemon Dressing, *p. 171*

Twila Strickler

Greens With Croutons

Serves 6

Sauté lightly or brown in the oven:
1½ c. cubed bread
2 T. oil or margarine
Set aside.
Add to the bottom of salad bowl:
2 cloves garlic, minced
½ t. salt
½ t. dry mustard
freshly ground pepper to taste
2 T. wine vinegar
¼ c. salad oil
Stir with back of spoon. Set bowl aside.
When ready to serve, add:
5-6 c. fresh torn greens, using
     spinach, endive, leaf lettuce,
     romaine, or others as available
toasted croutons
Toss and serve. Reserve a few croutons for topping, and add a sprinkle of Parmesan cheese if desired.

Eleanor Hiebert, Elkins Park, Pa.

Corn and Cabbage Slaw

Serves 6

Combine in salad bowl:
4 c. shredded cabbage
½ c. chopped onion
1-1½ c. cooked corn
½ c. diced sharp cheese
2 T. sliced black olives (optional)
2 T. chopped parsley (optional)
Combine for dressing:
⅓ c. cooked salad dressing or mayonnaise
2 t. prepared mustard
¼ t. celery salt
Pour dressing over salad and toss.

Eleanor Kaufman, Newton, Kan.

Cucumber Salad

T·S

Serves 4

Place in a bowl:

1 large cucumber, thinly sliced
1-2 T. finely cut fresh dill (use feathery leaves, not seeds)

Combine in small bowl:

2 T. mayonnaise or sour cream
1 T. vinegar
2 T. oil
1 t. salt
dash pepper

Mix and pour over cucumber slices. Chill and serve.

Irmgard Hildenbrand,
Rusinga Island, Kenya

Sprouts Salad

Serves 6

Place in dry skillet:

½ c. sunflower seeds

Toast by stirring over medium heat for about 3 minutes.

Combine in large salad bowl:

1 c. alfalfa or bean sprouts, loosely packed
3-4 c. salad greens, torn into bite-size pieces
6 or 8 radishes, sliced
½ cucumber, sliced
toasted sunflower seeds

Shake together for dressing:

¼ c. salad oil
2 T. vinegar
⅛ t. salt
freshly ground pepper
⅛ t. garlic powder

Pour over salad and toss. Garnish with:

1 or 2 hard-boiled eggs, sliced

Eleanor Hiebert, Elkins Park, Pa.

Fresh Spinach Salad

Guaranteed to tempt spinach-haters, old and young.

Serves 6

Combine in large salad bowl:

1 qt. chopped fresh spinach
½ c. chopped celery
1 onion or 3 scallions, chopped
¾ c. small Swiss cheese cubes
3 hard-cooked eggs, chopped

Combine in small bowl:

½ c. mayonnaise
2 T. vinegar
½ t. salt
½ t. horseradish
½ t. Tabasco, or dash cayenne pepper

Just before serving, pour mayonnaise mixture over salad bowl and toss.

Carolyn Blosser, Akron, Pa.

Dandelion Salad

Good served with boiled potatoes in the jacket and apple crisp for dessert.

Serves 4-6

Gather dandelion very early in spring before buds develop. At this time of year other greens are expensive, so take advantage of it as a first fruit. With a small sharp knife gather entire plants; cut off leaves, wash carefully, drain, and chop into a bowl. Proceed as follows:

Hard-cook:

2 eggs

Cool and shell.

Fry in skillet until crisp:

2 slices chopped bacon

Remove bacon and drain. Leave 2 T. drippings in skillet.

Combine and add to skillet:
- **4 T. flour**
- **1 t. salt**
- **3 T. sugar**
- **3 T. vinegar**
- **1½ c. water or milk**

Cook, stirring constantly, until sauce is smooth and thick. Pour sauce over:
- **4 c. chopped dandelion greens**

Stir lightly to coat greens. Garnish with sliced hard-cooked eggs and bacon bits.

Options:

Add 1 egg, beaten, to dressing mixture before pouring into skillet. Increase liquid to 2 cups.

Replace dandelion with other chopped greens such as endive, spinach, oak-leaf lettuce.

Martha Nafziger, LaCrete, Alta.
Ruth Eitzen, Barto, Pa.

Chop Salad

Serves 6-8

Combine in bowl:
- **1 c. finely chopped celery**
- **1 c. chopped green pepper**
- **½ c. sliced scallions or chopped onions**
- **1-2 c. diced tomatoes**
- **1 c. chopped cucumbers**
- **chopped chives (optional)**
- **chopped parsley (optional)**
- **2-3 T. vinegar or lemon juice**
- **1 t. sugar**
- **½ t. salt**
- **dash freshly ground pepper**

Stir thoroughly and chill. Serve as salad or as relish (chutney) with rice and curry.

Options:

Omit celery, green pepper, or cucumber if unavailable.

Omit last 4 ingredients and use Parsley Dressing. *p. 172*

Twila Strickler

Refrigerator Coleslaw

Here is an easy way to preserve cabbage when heads begin to split in the garden. A large quantity provides instant salad for weeks.

Makes about 3 qts.

Chop in blender, or shred and cut finely:
- **2 large or 3 medium heads cabbage**
- **2 stalks celery**
- **3-4 carrots**
- **1 onion**

Sprinkle generously with salt and set aside while making dressing. Before adding dressing, squeeze dry.

Dressing:
Combine in saucepan:
- **2 c. sugar**
- **1 t. salt**
- **1 c. vinegar**
- **⅛ t. pepper**
- **1-2 t. celery seed**

Bring to a boil. Remove from heat. When cool, add to cabbage. Mix well.

Can be made in large amounts and stored in refrigerator or freezer. Keeps in refrigerator several months. Store in tightly covered containers.

Loretta Leatherman, Akron, Pa.

Deluxe Coleslaw

Serves 10

About 1½ hours before serving or early in day, remove and reserve 4-5 outer leaves from:

1 medium head cabbage

Shred remaining cabbage to make 8 cups.

In large bowl toss gently:

**shredded cabbage
1 green pepper, thinly sliced
⅔ c. diced celery
⅔ c. finely shredded carrots
½ c. sliced radishes
2 T. minced onion**

Combine for dressing:

**1 c. mayonnaise or cooked
  salad dressing
2 T. milk
2 T. vinegar or lemon juice
1 t. sugar
¾ t. salt
¼ t. paprika
¼ t. pepper**

Mix well. Pour over vegetables and toss gently. Cover and chill. When ready to serve, arrange coleslaw on reserved cabbage leaves.

Anne Weaver, Blue Ball, Pa.

Company Chicken Salad

Serves 12

Combine in large bowl:

**4 c. cooked, diced chicken
4 c. grated carrots
4 c. finely chopped celery
1 medium onion, chopped**

Toss with:

3 c. salad dressing or mayonnaise

Chill. Just before serving, stir in:

**2-3 c. shoestring potatoes
  (optional)**

Dorothy Yoder, Hartsville, Ohio

Cauliflower Salad

Serves 6

Combine in bowl:

**2 c. diced raw cauliflower
½ c. sliced scallions
1 carrot, sliced
¼ c. salad oil
1½ T. lemon juice
1½ T. wine vinegar
1 t. salt
½ t. sugar
dash pepper**

Mix well. Chill before serving.

Option:

Add ¼ c. sliced black olives.

Esther Yoder, Topeka, Ind.

Israeli Supper

T·S

Put on the table in a bowl:

**cucumbers
tomatoes
onions
green peppers
hard-cooked eggs**

Give each person:

**salad bowl
scrap bowl
sharp knife**

Each person peels and chops his own cucumber, tomato, and adds a bit of onion and green pepper, then peels and chops his hard-cooked egg over it. Add a bit of salad oil, salt and pepper, and stir it up. Eat with good homemade bread, butter and jam, and hot tea. White cheese and/or yogurt may also be served.

Elizabeth Yoder, Bluffton, Ohio

Taco Salad

Serves 6

Brown together in skillet:
- **1 lb. ground beef**
- **1 onion, chopped**

Remove from heat and stir in:
- **2 c. cooked kidney beans, drained**
- **1 t. salt**
- **½ t. pepper**

Combine in large salad bowl:
- **1 head lettuce, torn up**
- **2 large tomatoes, chopped**
- **3-4 tortillas, fried crisp and broken up**
- **meat-bean mixture**

Toss together. Serve with Chili-Tomato Sauce, as a dressing.

Options:

Omit meat. Add raw chopped onion and 1-2 c. grated cheese.

Arrange ingredients separately in bowls. Each person assembles their own salad.

A 5 oz. package corn or tortilla chips may be substituted for fried tortillas but will make the dish more expensive.

Esther Kniss, Arcadia, Fa.
Bonnie Zook, Leola, Pa.

Beet and Apple Salad

Serves 6

Mix together:
- **2 c. cooked beets, diced**
- **2 c. raw apple, diced**
- **2 hard-boiled eggs, diced**

Add:
- **½ c. cooked salad dressing or mayonnaise**
- **¼ c. nuts**

Toss lightly. Serve on lettuce and garnish with chopped nuts and parsley.

Lena Brown, Grantham, Pa.

Green Bean And Sprout Salad

Serves 6

Cook just until crisp-tender:
- **3 c. fresh French-cut green beans**

Drain and cool. Add:
- **1-2 c. fresh bean sprouts**
- **⅓ c. green onions, sliced**
- **½ c. celery, thinly sliced**
- **1 sweet red pepper, sliced**

Toss to mix. Combine separately:
- **¼ c. vegetable oil**
- **2 T. vinegar**
- **salt, sugar, pepper, and herbs to taste**

Pour over vegetables, toss and chill 1-2 hours. Serve on lettuce, garnished with tomato wedges.

Author's Recipe

Summer Night Salad

Contributor suggests using any of the following: cooked broccoli, cauliflower, asparagus, corn, peas, green beans, and lima beans.

Dressing serves 6

Combine in bowl:
- **variety of leftover cooked vegetables**
- **small amounts fresh garden vegetables, cooked separately just until crisp-tender**
- **cooked diced chicken or ham and/or diced cheese**
- **1 hard-cooked egg per person, diced**
- **½ c. pecans, chopped**

Use favorite salad dressing or the following:
- **¼ c. mayonnaise**
- **¼ c. cream**
- **1 T. vinegar**
- **1 t. salt**
- **1 t. sugar**

Toss all ingredients lightly with dressing and chill several hours. Serve on lettuce garnished with colorful raw vegetables.

Lettuce–Tomato with Beef

T·S

Serves 4-6

Stir together and set aside:
  **¼ lb. beef, sliced paper thin
    (use chuck or round steak)
  ½ medium onion, grated or
    crushed
  2 cloves garlic, crushed
  ¼ t. salt
  dash pepper
  ½ t. sugar
  ¼ t. monosodium glutamate**
Arrange on platter:
  **1 head Boston Bibb lettuce leaves
  2 tomatoes, sliced
  1 cucumber, sliced**
Place tomatoes and cucumbers on lettuce leaves, leaving well in the center for meat.
Combine dressing in bowl and set aside:
  **½ onion, chopped
  3 T. vinegar
  3 T. oil
  ½ t. salt
  dash pepper
  1½ T. sugar**
Heat in skillet over high heat:
  1 T. oil
Add marinated beef and stir-fry quickly just until beef loses red color (about 1 min.). Put beef in "well" on salad platter. Add 1 T. water to skillet, swish, and pour into dressing. Stir and pour over meat and vegetables. Serve with rice.

Mary Martin, Saigon, Vietnam

Cabbage and Pork Salad

Vietnamese cooks cut beautiful cabbage salads without a grater. Here's how: remove leaves from head one by one. Lay several together and roll up tightly. Lay roll on board and slice across as thinly as possible with very sharp knife. Surprisingly fast, and yields a dish completely different from the usual shredded affair.

Serves 4

Mix together in large bowl:
  **½ head cabbage, cut in long,
    slender pieces (see above)
  2 carrots, grated**
Add:
  **¼-½ lb. pork, boiled and thinly
    sliced
  several sprigs fresh dill and
    mint, chopped**
Mix thoroughly.
Combine in small bowl:
  **1 T. soy sauce
  3 T. sugar
  3-4 T. vinegar
  2 t. lemon or lime juice**
Pour over salad mixture and toss well. Just before serving, sprinkle over the top of the salad:
  **¾ c. roasted peanuts, salted and
    chopped**
  Eat with hot rice or as a salad accompaniment to soup or stew.

Option:

To serve as main dish with rice, garnish with hard-cooked egg and tomato wedges.

Tran thi Kim Trinh, Quang Ngãi, Vietnam

Dilled Carrot Sticks

If dill pickles disappear at your house, so will these interesting additions to a relish tray.

Makes 2 cups

Simmer until not quite tender:
  **6-8 carrots, cut in sticks
  small amount salted water**
Drain carrots. Pour over:
  **leftover brine from 1 qt. dill
    pickles**
Heat just to boiling. Cool. Keeps in refrigerator several weeks.

Iona Weaver, Collegeville, Pa.

Dilled Onions

Makes 2 cups

Place in bowl:
   **6 white onions, sliced into
      thin rings**
Combine in saucepan and heat:
   **½ c. sugar
   2 t. salt
   ¾ t. dill seed
   ½ c. white vinegar
   ¼ c. water**
Bring mixture to a rolling boil. Remove
from heat and pour over onions. Let stand
until cool. Store in refrigerator.

Miriam E. Shenk, Migori, Kenya

Greens, Peas'n' Cheese Salad

*Complete the meal with a light soup
and whole grain bread.*

T·S

Serves 5-6

Have ready:
   **4-6 c. bite-size greens (lettuce,
      spinach, endive)
   1 small onion, thinly sliced
   2 c. cooked peas
   4 oz. Swiss cheese, julienne strips
   6 T. cooked salad dressing or
      mayonnaise
   2 t. sugar
   2 slices bacon, fried crisp and
      crumbled OR equivalent
      soybean-based bacon
      substitute**
In large salad bowl, place half the
greens, onions, peas, cheese; sprinkle
with 1 t. sugar. Dot with 3 T. mayonnaise.
Repeat layers. Cover and refrigerate 2
hours. Add bacon and toss just before
serving.

Mary Lou Houser, Lancaster, Pa.

Dried Apple–Cranberry Relish

Makes 6 cups

Combine in saucepan:
   **8 oz. dried apple slices
   2½ c. water**
Bring to boil, reduce heat, and simmer
covered 10 minutes. Pour into bowl.
Combine in same saucepan:
   **2 c. fresh cranberries
   ¾ c. light brown sugar or honey
   1¼ c. water**
Bring to boil and cook until cranberries
have popped. Add cooked apples and
simmer 10 minutes, stirring
occasionally. Chill.

Catherine Mack, Ardmore, Pa.

Tangy Carrot–Pineapple Mold

Serves 6

Drain, reserving juice:
   1 c. crushed pineapple
Dissolve and chill until slightly
thickened:
   **1 3-oz. pkg. lemon gelatin
   1 c. boiling water (include
      reserved pineapple juice)**
Fold in:
   **1 c. plain yogurt
   crushed pineapple
   1 c. grated carrots
   1 t. lemon juice**
Pour into mold and chill until firm.
Unmold and serve on bed of lettuce.

Option:

Replace orange gelatin with lime;
replace pineapple and carrots with
canned grapefruit sections.

Rosemary Moyer, North Newton, Kan

Green Bean Salad

Serves 6-8

Combine in salad bowl:
    **3 c. cooked green beans, cut in
        1" pieces**
    4 hard-cooked eggs, chopped
    1 medium onion, diced
    1 large dill pickle, chopped
Combine and pour over:
    2 T. vinegar
    1 t. salt
    **⅔ c. mayonnaise or cooked
        salad dressing**
Stir gently, chill and serve.

Anna Petersheim, Kinzers, Pa.

Basic Three-Bean Salad

Serves 10-12

Use 2 c. *each* of three kinds of cooked, drained beans. Choose an attractive color combination.
    cut green beans
    cut yellow wax beans
    soy beans
    red kidney beans
    green lima beans
    great northern or navy beans
    chick-peas or garbanzos
In large bowl, toss beans with:
    1 medium onion, finely chopped
    1 medium green pepper, chopped
Combine and pour over
    ½ c. salad oil
    ½ c. vinegar
    ½ c. sugar
    1 t. salt
    ¼ t. pepper
Chill before serving. Improves with marinating overnight or longer.

Gladys Sweigart, Lancaster, Pa.
Karen Harvey, Leola, Pa.

Chinese Chicken–Cucumber Salad

Goes well as one of several dishes in a Chinese dinner menu. Add a stir-fried vegetable-meat dish, soup, and rice.

T·S

Serves 4-6

Cut or shred:
    1 c. cooked chicken
Peel:
    2 cucumbers
Cut in half lengthwise and scoop out seeds; cut in strips.
Arrange cucumber strips on flat plate; top with chicken. Cover and chill until mealtime.
Combine and pour over chicken:
    ½ t. dry mustard
    ½ t. salt
    2 T. vinegar

Louise Lehman, Wapakoneta, Ohio

Tabouleh (Middle East)

Serves 6-8

Pour 4 c. boiling water over:
    **1¼ c. raw bulgur wheat or
        cracked wheat**
Let stand 2 hours, or until wheat is fluffy. Drain well. Mix with:
    **1 c. cooked chick-peas
        (garbanzos), drained**
    1¼ c. minced parsley
    ¾ c. minced mint
    **¾ c. minced scallions, or 1 onion,
        finely chopped**
    3 tomatoes, chopped
    ¾ c. lemon juice
    ⅓ c. oil (preferably olive oil)
    1 t. salt
Chill at least 1 hour. Serve on lettuce.

Alice and Willard Roth, Elkhart, Ind.
Helen King Stork, Ventura, Calif.

Main-Dish Tuna Salad

Serves 6-8

Cook and drain as directed on package:
  7 oz. noodles, spaghetti rings,
  or macaroni
Cook, drain, and cool noodles or
spaghetti.
Combine in large mixing bowl:
  cooked pasta
  1 7-oz. can chunk tuna
  1 c. chopped celery
  ½ c. finely chopped scallions
  with greens
  ½ c. chopped sweet pickles
  3 hard-boiled eggs, chopped
  ½ c. mayonnaise
  2 T. sweet pickle juice
  1 T. prepared mustard
  ½ t. salt
  dash pepper
Chill and serve on lettuce leaves.
Sprinkle with paprika.

Rosemary Moyer, North Newton, Kan.

Soybean Salad Special

Serves 5

Combine in salad bowl:
  ½ head lettuce, torn in bite-size
  pieces
  1½ c. cooked soybeans, drained
  1 fresh orange, peeled and diced
  2 T. chopped onion or scallion
Combine in a jar and shake:
  ¼ c. oil
  1 T. lemon juice
  1 T. vinegar
  ¼ t. dry mustard
  1 T. honey
  1 T. orange juice
  ½ t. sugar
  ¼ t. salt
  ½ t. paprika
Pour dressing over salad ingredients
and toss lightly.

Option:

Mix dressing in advance and pour over
soybeans. Marinate several hours or
overnight. Then add lettuce, orange and
onion; toss and serve.

Mary Lou Houser, Lancaster, Pa.

Salade Nicoise

*A gorgeous summertime salad—bring
with crusty fresh bread to an
outdoor table.*

Serves 5-6

Prepare in advance and chill in separate
containers:
  3 c. potato salad (omit
  hard-cooked eggs)
  3 c. fresh green beans, cooked
  exactly 5 minutes and drained
  3-4 tomatoes, quartered
  1 head Boston or other leaf lettuce,
  separated, washed and
  drained
  3 hard-cooked eggs, peeled and
  quartered
  1 c. Basic Oil and Vinegar dressing
  with herbs and garlic
  2-3 T. minced fresh herbs such as
  chives, parsley and dill
Also chill:
  1 7-oz. can tuna
Shortly before serving:
—Season green beans and tomatoes
with 2 T. each of prepared dressing.
—In salad bowl, toss lettuce with 2 T.
dressing, then arrange leaves around
bottom and outside of bowl.
—Place potato salad in bottom of the
bowl on lettuce. Arrange green beans,
tomatoes, eggs, and drained tuna in an
attractive design on top of potato salad.
Pour remaining dressing over all,
sprinkle with herbs, and serve
immediately.

Author's Recipe

Gazpacho

Serves 4

Combine in bowl:
  **1 c. peeled tomatoes,
    finely chopped
  ½ c. finely chopped green pepper
  ½ c. chopped celery
  ½ c. chopped cucumber
  ¼ c. chopped onion
  2 t. snipped parsley
  1 t. snipped chives
  1 small clove garlic, minced
  3 T. wine vinegar
  2 T. salad oil
  1 t. salt
  ¼ t. freshly ground pepper
  ½ t. Worcestershire sauce
  3 c. tomato juice**
Chill. Serve as an appetizer or cold soup.

Option:
Gazpacho relish: omit tomato juice.

Marian Franz, Washington, D.C.
Beverly Ehst, Ambler, Pa.

Soybean Salad

Serves 4

Combine in bowl:
  **1½ c. cooked soybeans, drained
  ½ c. diced celery
  ½ c. diced carrots
  1 t. minced onion
  ½ c. diced cheese
  2 hard-cooked eggs, diced
  ¼ c. chopped sweet pickles**
Cover and chill thoroughly.
Combine by stirring French dressing slowly into mayonnaise:
  **½ c. French dressing (see p. 172)
  1 T. mayonnaise**
Pour over salad, toss, and chill 1 more hour or longer.

Clara Breneman, Waynesfield, Ohio

Blender Cranberry Salad

Use frozen cranberries and the salad will congeal quickly.

T·S

Serves 6

Combine in small saucepan:
  **1 envelope unflavored gelatin
  1 c. cold water**
Warm over low heat until gelatin dissolves.
Combine in blender container:
  **2 c. cranberries
  1 unpeeled orange, seeded and
    quartered
  1 apple, cored and quartered
  ½-¾ c. sugar or honey**
Pour dissolved gelatin into blender. Blend only until orange peels are well chopped. Add:
  ¼ c. nuts (optional)
Chill until firm.

Options:
Omit gelatin and water and serve as a relish.
Use food grinder in place of blender to chop fruits.

Patricia Franke, Welcottville, Ind.

Rhubarb Salad

Serves 8

Cook together:
  **3 c. finely cut rhubarb
  ½ c. sugar
  ¼ t. salt
  ⅓ c. water**
Add:
  **2 3-oz. pkgs. strawberry gelatin
  1 c. finely chopped celery
  2¼ c. water
  1 T. lemon juice
  ½ c. chopped nuts**
Chill until firm.

Virginia Ebersole, Landisville, Pa.
Mona Sauder, Wauseon, Ohio

Desserts, cakes, and cookies

Traveling in India we could toss banana peels out of the bus window without concern for littering. Momentarily a goat or a cow would wander past and dispose of the peel in a single gulp.

One day two small children retrieved the banana peels our family discarded. The girl, about eight years old, wore a ragged saree. Her little brother of four or five was clad only in an oversize shirt. They were not beggars but watched for banana peels because they saw me coming from the fruit stand. As four peelings landed on the dusty road the children pounced.

The girl brushed dirt from the peels. She handed all the peelings to her brother, pulled a grimy square cloth from the folds of her saree and smoothed it out carefully beside the road. She and the boy sat down.

Meticulously, the girl pulled the soft portion of each banana peel away from the outer skin and placed it on the cloth. The outer tough portions she tossed aside. She gave half to her brother. They began to eat.

Whoever says that hungry people eat like animals when they have the chance did not see that Indian girl serve banana peels to her brother.
—LaVonne Platt, Newton, Kan.

Our biggest area of doing with less is desserts—we have them only occasionally.
—Janet Landes, Phoenix, Ariz.

I use less sugar in my cookies and coffee cakes than the recipes call for. I cut the amount of sugar by ¼ to ½. My children don't even notice the change. Cookies don't last any longer.
—Marianne Miller,
Topeka, Kan.

I have been using ⅓ less sugar in all ice cream, cookies, brownies, pudding, and pie recipes and haven't ruined anything yet.
—Pauline Wyse,
Mt. Pleasant, Iowa

Sugar never was good for us. This fact seems to be rediscovered whenever the price goes up. We've long been aware of sugar's role in tooth decay, diabetes, and obesity. Recent research adds that excessive use of sugar can lead to premature atherosclerosis.

Much land now devoted to sugar should be used for other crops yielding proteins, vitamins, and minerals. Eating less sugar is one way of conserving world food resources.

A dessert is (almost by definition) a food containing sugar. But before getting into dessert recipes, let's remind ourselves that not all meals require a sweet ending. The daily dessert habit is firmly entrenched in North America, but not with most other peoples. In many countries sweets are used for celebrations only, not to top off everyday meals.

Mary Alene Miller, Obihiro, Japan, writes, "We usually eat fresh fruit after the evening meal. About once a week we have desserts—when guests are here or for other special occasions." Ann Zook, Americus, Ga., says, "I have grown to appreciate a much simpler way of cooking and have reached a point of preparing a guest meal without a dessert."

Fruit, with its natural sweetener, is the perfect dessert. People protest that fresh fruit is too expensive. This is true in certain seasons and localities. But if good oranges, for example, are a dollar a dozen, it will cost fifty cents to serve six people an orange each for dessert. You can hardly bake a cake or buy ice cream for six for that price. Any dessert concocted of gelatin, whipped topping, fruit, and graham cracker crumbs will run closer to a dollar. Add up the cost of a favorite snack or dessert recipe before concluding that fresh fruit is out of reach.

What is an economical dessert?

I read somewhere that economical cooking means nutritious cooking. Therefore fresh fruit or a dessert with milk and eggs is most economical since it provides the most nutrition.
—Elsie Epp, Marion, S.D.

What will this food do for us? is the question to ask. If dessert only adds more calories, better to be old-fashioned and tell everyone to have another slice of bread. It's cheaper and more nutritious.

Use milk, egg, and cheese desserts to good advantage with low-protein meals. For example, vegetable soup made with a bone or two doesn't really have much protein. Finish the meal with cheesecake, a rich dessert high in complete protein that goes well with a light meal. But you don't need cheesecake after roast beef, gravy, mashed potatoes, and corn.

Puddings, traditional fruit moos, cobblers, and crisps are good to round out light lunches and suppers. Yogurt and fruit is a perfect high-nutrient, low-calorie dessert. Made at home, yogurt is also economical.

What about the mixes?

Cake mixes are usually as cheap as home-baked cakes, unless you get your staples in quantity at a good price. If a cake-mix type cake is what you like, costwise they're acceptable. At our house we prefer not to have cake very often. With some patience my husband has convinced me that mix-made cakes are dusty—his description—and fairly worthless as a food. When we have cake we enjoy a moist, home-baked product that includes applesauce, dates, nuts, rolled oats, carrots, coconut, or some other texture and flavor in addition to just sweetness.

Most other dessert mixes are grossly overpriced. Stick to simple desserts and stir up your own.

Honey, corn syrup, and molasses

Honey is the only natural sweetener not refined with chemicals. It is high in calories, but doesn't yield most of the other harmful effects associated with refined sugar. The problem with honey is that it is too expensive to replace a heavy sugar habit unless you keep bees yourself. Better economy is cutting down on all sweets.

Keep some honey on hand for subtle sweetening on cereal, breakfast toast, or in salad dressings. Use it in desserts such as custards or cheesecakes which call for small quantities of sweetener. Baking cakes or cookies with honey, however, becomes very expensive. Since these products depend on sugar for structural qualities, you need specially developed recipes or the results will be heavy.

Cup for cup, corn syrup and molasses will not yield as sweet a product as honey. Corn syrup has little nutritional advantage over sugar. Dark molasses contributes usable amounts of iron and calcium. Too often molasses is more expensive than sugar, when actually the reverse ought to be true because molasses takes less refining than sugar.

More with less sugar

Use less sugar and you will notice subtle sweetening qualities in other foods. Last Christmas I discovered that the filling in date bars needs no added sugar—flavor is enhanced without it! Canned and frozen fruits need some sugar for texture and preservation, but cut down on the amounts and learn to enjoy the tart fruit flavor. Unsweetened canned pineapple is now on grocery shelves and is a taste delight compared to the typical syrupy canned fruits we have come to expect.

Be forwarned! The recipes in this chapter are not very sweet. Many came in with reduced sugar amounts and some we reduced further. But our testers still gave them good ratings. Typical comment was, "Recipe calls for ¾ cup sugar. I made it a second time with only ⅔ cup and it still disappeared quickly. Half a cup would be enough." With sugar, when half a cup is enough, you get more with less.

Making Yogurt

Yogurt is simply milk jelled to a pudding consistency by certain acid-forming bacteria growing in it.

Yogurt is made from sweet milk, not sour, but has a characteristic sour taste that blends lusciously with the natural sugar of fruit. Mary Kathryn Stucky, a yogurt enthusiast who makes a gallon at a time for a family of four, writes, "Yogurt is something a person has to learn to like. Once you develop the taste for it, you will hate to be without." Yogurt is for people who enjoy tart flavors.

Yogurt is a dairy dessert without the added fats, sugars, and calories of ice cream. Essentially it contains the same calories, proteins, minerals, and other nutrients as milk. It may be made from whole or skim milk. Yogurt bacteria is friendly to the digestive tract, and leaves you with a good feeling of having eaten something light, tasty, and satisfying.

Yogurt is almost as cheap as milk if you make your own, but more expensive than ice cream if you buy it. Since it's easy to make, the advantages are all with home production.

Here is a method:

1. *Scald utensils* to be used with boiling water.

2. *Prepare the milk*. Start with 1 quart. Use raw, pasteurized-homogenized, dry, or evaporated milk, or follow recipe on page 264. Fresh milk should be brought up to 180°. Use a candy thermometer and watch closely so it doesn't boil over. Cool milk to 110°. If using dry or evaporated milk, reconstitute with warm water. If using skim or nonfat dry milk, add at least a little whole milk for a thicker culture.

3. *Add the starter*. Buy one container of plain commercial yogurt. Stir ¼ to ⅓ cup yogurt into 1 cup prepared milk, then add this to remaining warm milk and stir or shake briskly. Or buy yogurt starter at a health food store and follow directions. Pour milk into scalded jars and fasten lids loosely.

4. *Incubate the mixture* at 110-120° by any of these methods:
—Use a yogurt maker.
—Set jars into styrofoam ice chest. Fill chest with warm water (110-120°) to top of jars; cover. Add warm water as needed within next few hours to keep temperature up.
—Set jars into warm oven and turn off heat. Leaving oven light on may be exactly the right temperature. Check with thermometer.

—Set jars on rack in large pan of warm water on the stove; occasionally turn heat on briefly. Or set pan over pilot light.

—Set jars in pan of warm water, cover, and wrap all in a blanket.

—Set jar under tea cozy near radiator or heater.

5. *Check consistency.* Yogurt should not be moved while it is setting. Check in 2 to 3 hours, and every half hour after that. Usually 3 to 6 hours is needed for junket-like consistency. Refrigerate. Save ¼ cup to start next batch. Yogurt stays tasty in the refrigerator 1 to 2 weeks.

6. Serve yogurt

—with any fresh, frozen or canned fruits

—blended with frozen orange, grape, or pineapple concentrate (see Yogurt Popsicles, *p. 225*)

—with honey or molasses

—sprinkled with wheat germ or granola

—as a low-calorie sour cream substitute in salads, salad dressings, casseroles, or on baked potatoes

—accompanying hot, spicy dishes, especially curries

Always add fruit, sugar, or honey to yogurt with a folding motion. Stirring or beating breaks down the gel.

When introducing yogurt for the first time, be a little generous with the sweetener. Once people have acquired a taste for it, they will enjoy the tangy flavor for its own sake.

When you spoon yogurt out of its container, there is often some watery separation. This does not affect the taste, but to avoid it entirely, stir one envelope unflavored gelatin into ¼ c. cold water, warm to dissolve, and stir well into 1 qt. yogurt. Chill. Use this method to salvage a batch that won't thicken properly.

Yogurt

See p. 186 for detailed method.

Makes 2 qts.

Combine in large bowl:
   3 c. powdered milk
   6 c. warm water
Stir well. Add:
   1 can evaporated milk OR
      1⅔ c. scalded whole milk
Combine separately:
   ¼-½ c. yogurt
   1 c. milk from the bowl
Blend until smooth and return to remaining milk. Mix well. Pour into clean jars. Incubate at 110-120° until set. Refrigerate.

Mary Lou Houser, Lancaster, Pa.
Mary Kathryn Stucky, Burrton, Kan.
Marcia Beachy, DeKalb, Ill.

Quick Chocolate Pudding

T·S

Serves 4-6

Combine in heavy saucepan:
   ⅓ c. sugar or honey
   2 T. cornstarch
   2 T. cocoa
   2 c. milk
Cook over low heat until thickened, stirring constantly.
Add:
   1 t. vanilla
   1 T. margarine (optional)
Serve warm or cold.

Option:

Stir in ¼ c. peanut butter. Omit margarine.

Grace Whitehead, Kokomo, Ind.

Fluffy
Vanilla Pudding

T·S

Serves 4-6

Combine in heavy saucepan:
⅔ c. dry milk solids
¼ c. water
Add:
1½ c. hot water
Place saucepan over low heat.
In small bowl, beat together with fork or wire whisk:
¼ c. sugar
2½ T. cornstarch
¼ t. salt
2 egg yolks (reserve whites)
¼ c. water
Pour egg mixture into hot milk, stirring constantly until thickened. Cook 2 minutes over low heat. Remove from heat and add:
1 t. vanilla
1 T. margarine (optional)
Cool pudding 10 minutes.
Fold in:
2 stiffly beaten egg whites

Options:

Use 5 T. flour to replace cornstarch.

Make pudding in double boiler; takes longer but doesn't require constant stirring.

Serve with fruit.

Use for cream pies; instead of folding in egg whites, reserve for meringue.

Serve with waffles and fruit.

Layer into serving dish with graham cracker crumbs and sliced bananas.

Add 3 T. cocoa to egg yolk mixture; increase sugar to ⅓ c.

Margot Fieguth, Mississauga, Ont.
Mary Kathryn Yoder, Garden City, Mo.
Carol Smith, Mechanicsburg, Pa.

Orange Yogurt: Mash frozen orange juice concentrate in a bowl to soften, then fold in yogurt. Serve garnished with orange sections, if desired.
—Joanne Janzen, Newton, Kan.

Company
Pudding

Serves 6-8
425°
10 min.

Prepare one recipe Fluffy Vanilla Pudding, increasing cornstarch to 3 T. Preheat oven to 425°.
Crumble together in a bowl:
⅓ c. brown sugar
½ c. whole wheat or white flour
½ c. rolled oats
½ t. cinnamon
⅓ c. soft margarine
Press two thirds of the mixture into a 7x11" baking pan. Place remaining crumbs on a pie pan. Bake both pans 5-10 minutes, or until brown. Cool.
On top of crust in 7x11" pan, spread thin layer of *one* of these:
applesauce
chopped dates cooked in small
amount water until thick
drained peaches
sliced bananas
Top with pudding. Sprinkle over remaining toasted crumbs.
Chill at least 3 hours before serving.

Margot Fieguth, Mississauga, Ont.

Cream of Wheat
Pudding

The humble breakfast cereal makes a lovely dessert. Grandmother unmolded this pudding into a shallow serving bowl and surrounded it with cooked raspberries or homemade grape juice.

Serves 6

Bring to boil in heavy saucepan:
2 c. milk
Add slowly, stirring constantly:
⅓-½ c. cream of wheat
Cook until thickened, about 5 minutes.

Combine and beat until light:

2 egg yolks (reserve whites)
⅓ c. sugar
pinch salt

Add slowly to cream of wheat, stirring constantly. Cook 2 minutes. Remove from heat and add flavoring:

1 t. vanilla, vanilla and lemon
extract blended, or almond
and lemon

Beat until stiff:

2 egg whites

Fold into pudding. Pour into serving bowl or mold. Chill thoroughly. Serve with strawberries or raspberries.

Helen E. Regier, Newton, Kan.

Baked Custard

Serves 4
325°
50 min.

Preheat oven to 325°
Mix together:

⅔ c. dry milk solids
¼ c. sugar or honey (add honey
after dry milk and water
are combined)
few grains salt

Add slowly and stir until smooth:

2 c. water

Mix in:

2 eggs, slightly beaten
1 t. vanilla

Pour into 4 custard cups. Sprinkle with nutmeg. Set in flat pan containing 1" hot water. Bake 50 minutes or until knife inserted near edge of custard comes out clean.

Options:

Add 1½-2 c. cooked rice and ½ c. raisins before baking. Serves 6-8.

Add ⅔ c. coconut before baking.

Miriam LeFever, East Petersburg, Pa.

Fruit Moos

Traditionally, moos is served with fried ham and potatoes, or as a dessert; it also makes a good light meal accompanied simply by fresh bread and butter.

Serves 6

Moos, a Russian Mennonite dish, is a fruit soup made from fresh, canned, frozen, or dried fruits. Traditional *plume moos* uses raisins and prunes. Tart, flavorful fruits are best; try fresh or canned sour cherries, apricots, peaches, rhubarb, apple-blackberry, or gooseberry. Dried fruits should be covered with boiling water and allowed to soak overnight.

Heat in heavy kettle:

1 qt. fruit in syrup
3 c. additional water and/or milk
(if available, use 1 c. cream)
½ c. honey or sugar

Cook slowly until fruit is soft. Combine in small bowl:

4-5 T. flour
additional honey or sugar if
needed (check sweetness
of fruit)
1 c. milk or cream

Mix to a smooth paste. Dip out some hot fruit and stir into the paste; then slowly pour mixture back into the fruit, stirring constantly. Continue cooking over low heat until thickened. Serve warm or cold. For large quantity, use ½ c. flour to 1 gal. liquid.

Stein Goering, Gillingham, Wis.

Indian Dessert Yogurt: Add sugar to taste when preparing yogurt. Chill, then fold in and garnish with sliced bananas. Serve after curry meal.
—Herta Janzen, Calcutta, India

Pumpkin Custard

Serves 4-6
350°
45 min.

Preheat oven to 350°.
Combine in mixing bowl:
  1½ c. cooked, strained pumpkin
  ⅔ c. brown sugar
  3 eggs, beaten
  1½ c. scalded milk
  1 T. cornstarch
  1 t. cinnamon
  ½ t. ginger
  ¼ t. *each* ground cloves and nutmeg
Pour into buttered baking dish. Bake 45 minutes.

Nora Bohn, Goshen, Ind.
Linda Yoder, Hartville, Ohio

Rice Pudding

Serves 6
275°
2-2½ hrs.

Preheat oven to 275°.
Combine in buttered baking dish:
  4 c. milk, scalded
  ⅓ c. rice
  ⅓ c. sugar
  ¼ t. salt
  dash nutmeg, cinnamon, or dried orange peel
Bake 2-2½ hours, until rice is tender and milk is creamy. Stir occasionally during first half of baking time. Pudding thickens as it cools. Serve warm or cold.

Option:
One-half hour before removing from oven, add ⅓ c. raisins.

Edna Longacre, Barto, Pa.
Florence Ressler, Dalton, Ohio
Ella May Miller, Harrisonburg, Va.

Creamy Rice Pudding

Serves 6

Combine in top of double boiler:
  ¼ c. rice
  2 c. milk
Cook uncovered 45 minutes or until rice is tender.
Beat together:
  2 egg yolks (reserve whites)
  ¼ c. sugar
  ¼ t. salt
Stir some of rice mixture into beaten yolks; add yolks to hot rice mixture and cook 3-4 minutes, stirring constantly. Remove from heat and add:
  1 t. vanilla
Beat until frothy:
  2 egg whites
Add:
  2 T. sugar
Beat until stiff. Fold egg whites into pudding. Chill and serve.

Options:
Place pudding in a baking dish. Spread beaten whites on top and brown delicately in the oven.

Add ½ c. raisins to pudding.

Special orange pudding: Add whites along with egg yolks. Stir in 1 t. grated orange rind. When chilled, blend in ½ c. cottage cheese.

Carolyn Yoder, Grantsville, Md., in
Mennonite Community Cookbook

In Africa we seldom saw brown sugar. Missionaries gave me this recipe: To each cup of white granulated sugar, add 2 T. old-fashioned molasses. Stir well and store in airtight container. Excellent flavor in cookies or cake toppings, or on oatmeal. I make it since we're back because it's much cheaper and we like the flavor better.
—Evelyn Fisher, Akron, Pa.

Applesauce Bread Pudding

Serves 8
350°
55-60 min.

Preheat oven to 350°.
Arrange in bottom of greased 9" square pan:
  4 slices dry bread
Combine:
  2 c. applesauce
  ½ c. raisins
  ¼ c. brown sugar
  ½ t. ground cinnamon
Spread over bread. Top with:
  4 additional slices dry bread
Beat together:
  2 eggs
  2 c. milk
  ½ c. brown sugar
  ½ t. vanilla
  ¼ t. salt
  dash ground nutmeg
Pour over bread. Top with:
  ½ c. applesauce
  sprinkle of cinnamon-sugar
Bake 55-60 minutes. Serve warm or cold.

Miriam LeFever, East Petersburg, Pa.

Lemonade Sherbet

Serves 6

Pour into a freezer tray:
  1 can (1⅔ c.) evaporated milk
Freeze until ice crystals form around the edges.
While milk is in freezer, chill mixing bowl and rotary beater.
Pour chilled milk into bowl. Add:
  1 (7 oz.) can frozen lemonade, thawed
Beat until fluffy. While beating, add gradually:
  3-4 T. sugar
Pour into freezer tray and freeze 2 hours, or until firm. Serve within 24 hours.

Jamaican Baked Bananas

Serves 4-6
350°
25-30 min.

Preheat oven to 350°.
Peel and arrange in casserole:
  4-6 bananas, sliced if desired
In saucepan, combine:
  2 T. margarine
  2 T. sugar
  1 c. orange juice
Cook and stir about 1 minute. Combine:
  2 T. cornstarch
  ¼ c. cold orange juice
Add to hot mixture and cook until clear and thickened.
If desired, add:
  ¼-½ c. raisins
Pour over bananas. Top with grated coconut. Bake 25-30 minutes at 350°.
Serve warm with custard sauce.

Option:

Simple baked bananas: Place 4 bananas in shallow buttered casserole. Drizzle over: 2 T. melted margarine, 2 T. honey, and ⅓ c. apple or orange juice. Sprinkle with cinnamon-sugar. Bake 20 min. at 350°. Serve warm.

Sarah Eby, Akron, Pa.

Scalloped Rhubarb: Combine 3 c. cubed stale bread, ½ c. melted margarine, 2 c. diced rhubarb, and 1 c. sugar. Put 1 T. water in each corner of baking dish. Bake at 325° for 45 min.
—Judy Classen, Akron, Pa.

Banana Special: Peel a banana and cut in half lengthwise. Spread with peanut butter and press together. Place in dessert dish, sprinkle with cinnamon, and pour over slightly beaten evaporated milk.
—Adele Mowere, Phoenixville, Pa.

Fruit Dumplings

Serves 8
350°
45 min.

Prepare 2-3 c. finely chopped fresh fruit. Use apples, peaches, rhubarb, etc. Set aside.
Preheat oven to 350°.
Prepare 1 recipe biscuit dough, *p. 34*
Roll dough into large rectangle on floured board. Cover thickly with fruit. Sprinkle with cinnamon. Roll up like jelly roll and cut into 1" rings. Place in greased 9x13" baking pan.
Combine in saucepan:

1 c. sugar
1 T. flour
1 c. cold water

Let come to a boil and pour over dumplings. Bake 45 minutes. Serve warm with milk.

Phoebe Coffman, Dayton, Va.

Fruit Crumble

Serves 6
375°
25 min.

Preheat oven to 375°.
Place in buttered 8x8" baking dish:

2½ c. fruit—cherries, or pared and sliced apples or peaches

Combine in bowl and mix to form crumbs:

1 c. flour
1 egg
dash salt
½ t. cinnamon
½ c. sugar
1 t. baking powder

Sprinkle over fruit. Drizzle over:

¼ c. melted margarine

Bake 25 minutes.

Adele Mowere, Phoenixville, Pa.

Apple Crisp

Serves 6
375°
35 min.

Preheat oven to 375°.
Combine and put in greased casserole:

3 c. sliced or chopped apples
1 T. flour
¼ c. sugar
1 t. cinnamon
⅛ t. salt
1 T. water

Cut together with pastry blender:

½ c. rolled oats
¼ t. salt
¼ c. margarine
⅓ c. brown sugar

Sprinkle on top of casserole mixture. Bake 35 minutes.

Option:

Add ¼ c. peanut butter to rolled oats mixture. Reduce margarine to 2 T.

Verna Wagler, Baden, Ont.
Ruth Weaver, Reading, Pa.

Granola Apple Crisp

Serves 6
350°
25-30 min.

Preheat oven to 350°.
Place in greased 9" square baking pan:

5 medium cooking apples, peeled and sliced

Combine:

⅓ c. flour
1 t. cinnamon
½ c. firmly packed brown sugar
1½ c. granola
⅓ c. margarine, melted

Sprinkle granola mixture over apples. Bake 25-30 minutes. Serve warm or cold with milk.

Option:

Peach Crisp: Substitute 4 c. fresh or canned (drained) peach slices for apples.

Author's Recipe

Essie's Cobbler

Serves 6-8
350°
45-50 min.

Preheat oven to 350°.
Cream together in bowl:
  ¼ c. soft shortening
  ½ c. sugar
Combine separately.
  1 c. flour
  2 t. baking powder
  ¼ t. salt
  ½ t. cinnamon (optional)
Add dry ingredients to creamed mixture alternately with:
  ½ c. milk
Mix until smooth. Pour batter into greased 10x5" or 9x9" baking pan.
Spoon over:
  2 c. drained fruit (reserve juice) use peaches, berries, or cherries
Sprinkle with:
  2-4 T. sugar
Pour over:
  1 c. fruit juice
Bake 45-50 minutes. Serve warm with cold milk, whipped topping, or ice cream.

Esther Hostetter, Akron, Pa.

Baked Apples: Fill centers of cored apples with raisins or dates. Drizzle with honey and sprinkle with cinnamon and nutmeg. Add ½ inch water. Bake until tender, basting occasionally. To save fuel, cover and cook slowly on top of stove.
—F. Mabel Hensel, Harrisburg, Pa.

Applesauce Crunch

Serves 4-6
375°
15/30 min.

Preheat oven to 375°.
Mix together:
  2 c. applesauce
  ⅓ c. brown sugar
  ¼ c. raisins
  ½ t. cinnamon
Pour into 9x9" baking pan. Heat in oven 15 minutes.
Combine:
  1 c. biscuit mix (*see p. 32*)
  ¼ c. sugar
Cut in:
  3 T. cold solid margarine
Add:
  ¼ c. chopped nuts
Sprinkle over applesauce mixture and bake until nicely browned.

Sharol Phinney, Elkton, Va.

Quick Fruit Cobbler

Crust begins on the bottom, and ends on top. Consistency of cobbler varies depending on variety of fruit and amount of juice, but still tastes delicious.

Serves 6
350°
40 min.

Preheat oven to 350°.
Combine in bowl:
  ½ c. sugar
  ½ c. flour
  ½ c. milk
  1 t. baking powder
  ¼ t. salt
Pour into 9x9" greased baking pan.
Add:
  2 c. fruit—fresh, frozen, or canned
Bake for 40 minutes.

Grandmother's Brown Betty

Serves 8
350°
45-50 min.

Combine in large bowl:
8 tart apples, sliced
½ c. raisins
½ c. honey
½ c. apple juice or water
¼ c. brown sugar
3 T. flour
1 t. cinnamon
Turn into greased 7x11" baking pan.
Combine in bowl:
½ c. quick-cooking rolled oats
½ c. whole wheat flour
½ c. wheat germ
½ c. shelled sunflower seeds
¼ c. honey
4 T. margarine
Mix well. Spread over apple mixture.
Bake at 350° for 45-50 minutes.

Anne Braun, Liberal, Kan.

Birchermüsli: Blend 2 c. yogurt, ½ c. raisins, ½ c. chopped nuts, 1 c. oatmeal, ½ c. sugar, 2 T. orange juice, 1 c. sliced fresh peaches, 1 c. sliced apples, 2 sliced bananas, ½ c. blueberries. Vary fruits according to availability.
—*Elaine Sommers Rich in Mennonite Weekly Review*

Frozen Lemon Cream

Serves 9

Beat until stiff:
1 can (1⅔ c.) evaporated milk, thoroughly chilled
Slowly add:
¾ c. sugar
Then add:
3 T. lemon juice
grated rind of 1 lemon
Beat until very stiff.
Roll into crumbs:
12 graham crackers
Put half of crumbs in bottom of 9x9" pan.
Pour in cream. Add remaining crumbs on top. Cover tightly and freeze until ready to serve.

Elmira Fry, Elizabethtown, Pa.

Homemade Ice Cream

Serves 12

Combine in 1-gallon freezer:
1 qt. thick vanilla pudding
2 qts. milk
1 can sweetened condensed milk
1 T. vanilla
Turn freezer until ice cream is stiff.

Options:

Substitute 1 qt. cream, if available, for sweetened condensed milk. Reduce milk to 6 c. Add ½ c. additional sugar to pudding.

Chocolate: Make chocolate pudding and add ⅔ c. chocolate syrup.

Fruit: Substitute 3 c. strawberries, peaches, blueberries, or pineapple for 3 c. milk.

Butternut: Make butterscotch pudding, using brown sugar. Add 1 c. toasted nuts.

Annie Lind, Windsor, Vt.

Snow Ice Cream

Serves 8 children

Stir together lightly:
2½ qts. clean snow
½ c. milk or cream
1 t. vanilla
1 c. sugar
Eat right away.

Betsey Zook, Leola, Pa.

Pumpkin Ice Cream

Serves 10

Scald in double boiler:
2 c. milk
Combine in bowl:
4 egg yolks or 2 eggs, beaten
1 c. sugar
⅛ t. salt
2 c. mashed cooked pumpkin
2 t. cinnamon
1 t. nutmeg
½ t. allspice
¼ t. ginger
½ t. vanilla
Add to hot milk and cook 4 minutes longer. Cool.
Add:
1 c. cream
1 c. pecans or other nuts (optional)
Pour into freezer container. Crank until stiff.

Irene L. Bishop, Perkasie, Pa.

Applesauce Pudding: Combine cookie or graham cracker crumbs with a little sugar and cinnamon. Layer alternately with applesauce into a glass serving bowl. Chill before serving.
—Ruth Gish, Mt. Joy, Pa.

Lime Frost

Serves 6

Prepare as directed on package:
1 pkg. lime gelatin
Chill until nearly firm. Combine in blender:
lime gelatin
1 pt. slightly softened vanilla ice cream
1 T. lime juice
Blend until mixture begins to hold shape. Pour into 6 sherbet glasses and chill. Serve with whipped topping and a lime slice for garnish.

Options:

Use other flavors of gelatin.

Prepare gelatin with 1 envelope unflavored gelatin, ½ c. frozen orange juice concentrate, and 1½ c. water. Dissolve according to package directions.

Lon and Kathryn Sherer, Goshen, Ind.

Graham Cracker Crust

T·S

Makes 1 pie crust
375°
8 min.

Combine and press into 9" pie pan:
1⅓ c. graham cracker crumbs
¼ c. sugar
¼ c. melted margarine
¼ t. nutmeg
Bake at 375° for 8 minutes.

LaVonne Platt, Newton, Kan.

Basic Fruit Gelatin

Reserve canned fruit juices for this gelatin. It's cheaper, not as sugary, and just as fast as the flavored product.

Serves 4-6

Combine in saucepan:
1 c. fruit juice, drained from canned fruit
1 envelope unflavored gelatin
Stir to begin dissolving gelatin. Then heat almost to boiling point until liquid is clear. Remove from heat and add:
1 c. cold fruit juice or water
1 T. lemon juice
1 T. frozen orange juice concentrate
Chill until set.

Options:

When partially set, fold in fresh or drained canned fruits as desired.

If using fresh unsweetened fruits and tart juice, add 2-4 T. sugar to hot gelatin mixture.

When partially set, fold in 1 c. whipped cream or cottage cheese.

Replace second cup fruit juice with 1 c. chilled yogurt.

Omit lemon juice and/or orange concentrate if using strong-flavored fruit juices.

Dorothy King, Dalton, Ohio

When a gelatin dessert or salad calls for 2 packages flavored gelatin, use one envelope unflavored gelatin for the second package. Fold in fruits or vegetables as usual. End product is less sweet and less expensive, but just as tasty.
—Iona S. Weaver,
Collegeville, Pa.

Pineapple–Orange Gelatin

Serves 6

Combine in small saucepan:
1 envelope unflavored gelatin
1 c. cold water
Add:
3 T. honey or sugar
Warm mixture just until gelatin dissolves. Add:
2 T. frozen orange juice concentrate
juice drained from unsweetened pineapple chunks plus water to make 1¼ c.
Chill until syrupy. Fold in:
1 c. drained pineapple chunks
2 oranges, peeled and diced
1 banana, sliced
Chill until set.

Ruth Gish, Mt. Joy, Pa.

Cheesecake

Serves 6
375°
30 min.

Preheat oven to 375°.
Prepare 1 8" unbaked graham cracker pie shell.
Combine in bowl or blender:
2 eggs
8 oz. cream cheese or cottage cheese, or a mixture
⅓ c. honey or sugar
¼ c. dry milk solids
2 t. vanilla
1-2 T. lemon juice
Pour into crust and bake 30 minutes
Cool 1 hour.
Add topping, if desired, and chill

Options:

Add one of these to cheese mixture
—1 t. almond extract (omit vanilla)
—¼ c. chopped almonds or walnuts
—1 small can crushed pineapple
—1½ t. grated lemon peel to both crust
   and filling
—2 T. cheddar cheese, finely shredded
—¼ c. yogurt

Use one of these as topping:
—Combine 1 c. yogurt or sour cream,
   2 T. sugar, 1 T. vanilla, 1 t. cinnamon,
   and/or ¼ t. nutmeg
—Add drained strawberries, pineapple,
   peaches, cherries, blueberries, or
   nuts to yogurt or sour cream topping
—Thicken any of above fruits with
   cornstarch and use as topping

Double recipe for larger cheesecake
made in springform pan.

LaVonne Platt, Newton, Kan.
Danita Laskowski, Goshen, Ind.

Cottage Cheese Pie

Serves 6-8
350°
1 hr.

Preheat oven to 350°.
Have ready 1 unbaked 9″ pastry or
graham cracker pie shell.
Combine with mixer or blender:
   2 egg yolks (reserve whites)
   1½ c. cream-style cottage cheese
   ⅓ c. sugar or honey
   2 T. flour
   ¼ t. salt
   ¼ t. cinnamon
   1 c. milk
   2 T. lemon juice
   grated lemon rind
Beat until stiff but not dry:
   2 egg whites
Fold into cheese mixture. Pour into
unbaked pie shell and sprinkle top with:
   1 T. sugar
   ½ t. cinnamon
Bake 1 hour, or until filling is almost firm
in center. A slightly soft center will set as
pie cools. Top with a fruit sauce if
desired.

Yogurt–Cheese Pie

*Contributor is a Mennonite
grandmother who says, "Our cookery
has rated among the best for years
but there are aspects to it that disturb
me—so many recipes are high in fats
and sugars." Her recipe passes the
test as a nutritious dessert.*

Serves 6

Prepare and cool:
   9″ graham cracker pie shell
   (see p. 196)
Combine in small saucepan:
   ⅓ c. milk
   1 envelope unflavored gelatin
Stir to soften gelatin. Warm over low heat,
stirring constantly, until gelatin
dissolves.
Combine in blender or mixing bowl:
   1 c. cottage cheese
   1½ c. plain yogurt
   ¼ c. sugar or 3 T. honey
   dissolved gelatin mixture
Whirl or whip briefly. Chill mixture 20-30
minutes until it begins to set. Pour into
pie shell and chill.

Options:

Sprinkle with nutmeg.

Put 1-2 c. fresh berries or sliced bananas
into pie shell before pouring in yogurt
mixture. Chill and serve within 8 hours.

After filling sets, top with any thickened
fruit.

Instead of pouring filling into pie shell,
layer with fruit into parfait glasses.

Iona Weaver, Collegeville, Pa.

*In icings, use up to ⅓ c. dry milk
solids to 1 c. confectioners
sugar.*

Refrigerator Cheesecake

A low-calorie, high-protein dessert perfect for finishing off a high-carbohydrate, low-protein meal.

T·S

Serves 6

Prepare graham cracker crust, or line 9" pie pan or 8x8" baking pan with graham cracker crumbs.
Combine in saucepan:
   1 pkg. unflavored gelatin
   ½ c. cold water
Warm over low heat until dissolved.
Combine in blender:
   dissolved gelatin
   1¼ c. water
   2 c. (1 lb.) cottage cheese
   1½ c. dry milk solids
   ½ c. sugar
   ⅛ t. salt
Whirl until liquified. Add:
   ¼ c. lemon juice
Blend until well mixed. Pour into crumb crust. Chill until set.

Options:

Use any toppings suggested for Cheesecake, *p. 196*
Use just a few cracker crumbs for low-calorie version.

Helen Burkholder, St. Catherines, Ont.

Quick Pie Crusts: If you make pies often, save time by cutting a quantity of fat and flour together in advance at a ratio of ¼ to ⅓ c. fat to 1 c. flour. Add salt. Store crumbs in tightly covered container in refrigerator or cool cellar. To make 2 crusts, measure out 2 c. crumbs and toss with 4 to 5 T. water.
—Edna Longacre, Barto, Pa.

Coconut–Custard Pie

T·S

Serves 8
350°
50-60 min.

Preheat oven to 350°.
Combine in blender:
   4 eggs
   6 T. margarine
   ½ c. flour
   2 c. milk
   ¾ c. sugar
   1 t. vanilla
Add:
   1 c. coconut
Blend several seconds. Pour into a greased and floured 10" pie pan, or two 8" pans. Bake 50-60 minutes. Pie forms its own crust.

Lois Zehr, Ft. Dodge, Iowa

Shoofly Pie

Here's a good recipe from the Orie Miller home for the famed Pennsylvania Dutch specialty. Rich, yes—but also cheap! Delicious served warm with cold milk to drink.

Serves 6
375°
35 min.

Preheat oven to 375°.
Prepare 1 unbaked 9" pie shell.
Cut together with pastry blender:
   1 c. flour
   ½ c. brown sugar
   2 T. shortening or margarine
Reserve ½ c. crumbs for topping.
Combine in mixing bowl:
   1 c. molasses
   1 egg, slightly beaten
   ¾ c. cold water
   1 t. soda in
   ¼ c. hot water

Add crumb mixture and beat together. Pour into unbaked pie shell. Sprinkle reserved ½ c. crumbs on top. Bake 35 minutes.

Elta Miller, Lititz, Pa.

Peach Kuchen

Serves 6
400°
15/30 min.

Preheat oven to 400°.
Combine in bowl:
1½ c. sifted flour
¼ t. baking powder
½ t. salt
2 T. sugar
Cut in:
⅓ c. margarine
Pat mixture over bottom and sides of a 9" pie pan or skillet.
Arrange in pastry:
8-12 peach halves, canned or fresh
Sprinkle over:
¼ c. sugar combined with
1 t. cinnamon
Bake 15 minutes.
Combine:
1 egg, beaten
1 c. sour cream, sour milk, yogurt, or combination
Pour over peaches and bake 30 minutes longer.

Options:
Drizzle peaches with honey instead of sugar.

Use 2 c. fresh diced rhubarb. Increase sugar over fruit to ½ c.

Hilda Janzen, Newton, Kan.

Make your own confectioners sugar. Whirl 1 c. granulated sugar and 1 t. cornstarch in blender about 1 min. or until powdered.
—June Suderman,
* Hillsboro, Kan.*

Pumpkin Pie

Serves 6
425°/375°
10/30 min.

Preheat oven to 425°
Have ready 1 9" unbaked pie shell.
Combine in blender or mixing bowl:
1 c. cooked, sieved pumpkin
½ c. sugar
1 t. cinnamon
¼ t. ginger
¼ t. nutmeg
¼ t. cloves
1 t. vanilla
1 c. milk
2 egg yolks
Beat until stiff:
2 egg whites
Fold egg whites into pie filling. Pour into unbaked pie shell. Bake 10 minutes, then reset oven to 375° and bake about 30 minutes or until filling is set.

Options:
Substitute yellow squash, sweet potatoes or carrots for pumpkin. No need to mash vegetable first if using blender—just drain well. Spicy flavor sells any kind as pumpkin.

If using frozen pumpkin which may be watery, decrease milk to ¾ c.

Elizabeth Showalter, Waynesboro, Va.
Ruth Hershberger, Harper, Kan.

Milk Flitch (an old Pennsylvania Dutch pie with a variety of odd names, made for children from leftover pie crust): Into pie crust sprinkle brown sugar and flour. Dot with butter. Almost cover mixture with milk. Bake until brown and bubbling. Some like it dry, some like it runny—not measuring assures it will never be monotonous.
—Ruth Eitzen, Barto, Pa.

Whipped Topping—I

T-S

Makes about 2½ cups

Chill small mixer bowl and beaters several hours before using.
Put into bowl:
    ½ c. ice water (may be chilled in bowl)
    ½ c. dry milk solids
Beat at high speed until peaks form, about 5 minutes.
Add:
    3 T. lemon juice
Beat in gradually:
    3 T. sugar
Chill 1 hour.

Miriam LeFever, East Petersburg, Pa.

Whipped Topping—II

T-S

Makes about 2 cups

Shortly before serving, mash until smooth:
    1 medium ripe banana
Beat to stiff froth:
    1 egg white
Add banana to egg white 1 teaspoon at a time, beating constantly.
Add:
    1 t. sugar
Beat until light. Serve on fruit or puddings.

Viola Dorsch, Musoma, Tanzania

> **Sprinkle cakes or cupcakes with granola before baking.**
>
> **Granola topping for coffee cake: ¼ c. granola, 2 T. brown sugar, 1 T. melted margarine.**

Grandma Witmer's Crumb Cake

Serves 12-15
350°
40 min.

Preheat oven to 350°.
Combine in large bowl:
    4 c. flour
    ½ t. salt
    2 c. sugar
Cut in to make crumbs:
    1 c. shortening (may use part margarine)
Reserve ⅔ c. crumbs and set aside.
In separate bowl, stir together:
    1 t. soda
    1 t. cream of tartar
    1 c. buttermilk or sour milk
Add:
    2 beaten eggs
Add liquid mixture to crumbs. Mix together and pour into greased and floured 9x13" pan. Sprinkle reserved crumbs on top, plus a dash nutmeg. Bake 40 minutes.

Ellen Longacre, Bally, Pa.

Carla's Hot Milk Sponge Cake

A light cake using almost no fat.

Serves 9-10
325°
30-35 min.

Preheat oven to 325°.
In mixing bowl, beat well:
    2 eggs
Add:
    1 c. sugar
    1 t. vanilla
Beat until light. Combine separately:
    1 c. flour
    1 t. baking powder
    ¼ t. salt
By hand, fold dry ingredients into egg mixture.

Bring to boil in small saucepan:

½ c. milk
1 t. margarine

Add slowly to batter, stirring gently. Pour into well-greased and floured 7x12" or 9x9" cake pan. Bake 30-35 minutes.

Option:

When cake is partially cool, spread with ½ recipe Coconut Topping, *p. 202*. Broil as directed.

Carla L. Funk, Laird, Sask.

Everyday Fruitcake

Combine 3-4 dried fruits: apples, apricots, figs, peaches, pears, dates, and golden or dark raisins. Snip larger fruits into small pieces.

2 small loaves
325°
1 hr.

Preheat oven to 325°.
Combine in bowl:

1 c. whole wheat flour
½ c. brown sugar
1 t. baking powder
½ t. salt

Mix ¼ c. of this mixture with:

2 c. dried fruit assortment
(see above)
¾ c. walnuts or pecans, chopped

Set aside.
Stir together in large bowl:

3 eggs, beaten
¼ c. honey
½ t. vanilla
2 T. frozen orange juice
concentrate

Add dry ingredients. Mix well. Fold in fruits and nuts. Spoon mixture into 2 3x6" or 1 4x8" loaf pan, well greased and bottoms lined with waxed paper. Bake 1 hour or until well browned. Cool on rack 10 minutes, then turn out loaves and remove waxed paper.

Evelyn Liechty, Berne, Ind.

Roman Apple Cake

Serves 12-16
350°
35-40 min.

Preheat oven to 350°.
Combine in mixing bowl:

1 c. sugar
2¼ c. flour
¼ t. salt
⅜ t. baking powder
1½ t. soda
½ t. cloves
1 t. cinnamon

Beat in:

⅔ c. shortening
2 eggs
⅔ c. milk
1½ t. vanilla

Add:

3 c. raw apples, pared and
chopped

Mix well. Pour into greased and floured 9x13" pan.
Cover with *topping*:
Crumble together:

1 T. melted margarine
2 t. cinnamon
⅓ c. brown sugar
2 t. flour
½ c. chopped nuts or coconut
(optional)
¼ c. rolled oats

Bake 35-40 minutes.

Miriam LeFever, East Petersburg, Pa.

Split a cake and fill with pudding or custard. Add sliced bananas if desired.

Jelly Frosting: Combine in top of double boiler ½ c. tart jelly, 1 unbeaten egg white, and dash of salt. Beat while cooking until jelly disappears. Remove from heat and continue beating until frosting stands in peaks. Lovely to look at as well as eat!
—Geraldine Mitsch,
Aurora, Ore.

Black Walnut–
Banana Cake

Marvelous flavor—a reward for patient people who pick up, dry, and shell black walnuts.

Serves 10-12
350°
45-50 min.

Preheat oven to 350°.
Cream together:
  1½ c. sugar
  ½ c. margarine or shortening
Beat in:
  2 eggs
  1 c. thinly sliced bananas
  1 t. vanilla
  ¾ c. sour milk, combined with
  1 t. soda
Sift together and beat in:
  2 c. flour
  1 t. baking powder
Add:
  1 c. black walnuts, ground or
  finely chopped
Pour into greased and floured 9x9" cake pan. Bake 45-50 minutes.

Ruth Hynicker, Elizabethtown, Pa.

Gingerbread
With Wheat Germ

Serves 9
350°
45-50 min.

Preheat oven to 350°.
Combine in mixing bowl:
  2 c. unsifted flour
  1 t. baking soda
  ¾ t. salt
  1½ t. cinnamon
  1 t. ginger
  ¼ t. cloves
  ¼ c. sugar
  ½ c. wheat germ

Add:
  1 c. buttermilk or sour milk
  ¾ c. molasses
  ⅓ c. oil or melted margarine
  2 eggs, beaten
Beat just until batter is smooth. Turn into well-greased 9x9" cake pan. Bake 45-50 minutes or until tests done. Serve hot with applesauce blended with yogurt or a whipped topping.

Rosemary Moyer, North Newton, Kan.
Elizabeth Showalter, Waynesboro, Va.

Oatmeal
Cake

A rich, moist cake; serve in small pieces.

Serves 16-18
350°
35 min.

Preheat oven to 350°.
Combine and let stand 20 minutes.
  1 c. quick oatmeal
  1¼ c. boiling water
Cream together until fluffy:
  ½ c. shortening
  1 c. brown sugar
  1 c. white sugar
  2 eggs
  1 t. vanilla
Add oatmeal mixture. Beat well.
Sift together:
  1½ c. flour
  1 t. soda
  1 t. baking powder
  ½ t. salt
  1 t. cinnamon
Add to creamed mixture and beat well. Pour into greased and floured 9x13" cake pan. Bake 35 minutes or until tests done.
Coconut Topping:
Combine:
  ½ c. brown sugar
  ⅓ c. margarine
  ¼ c. cream or milk
  ½ c. chopped nuts
  1 c. coconut
Spread on hot cake and broil 2-4 minutes until brown. Watch closely.

Applesauce–Nut Cake (cooperative method)

Contributor likes to cook with a friend.
Invite a child to help with this recipe.

Serves 10
350°
35-40 min.

Preheat oven to 350°.

Person 1:
Combine and set aside:
1 c. sweetened applesauce
1 t. lemon juice
Measure and mix together:
2 c. flour (may use ¼ whole wheat)
1 t. soda
1 t. cinnamon
½ t. ground cloves
½ t. salt
Chop and set aside:
½ c. dates

Person 2:
Cream together:
½ c. margarine
1 c. brown sugar
Add:
2 eggs
Beat well. Measure:
1 c. walnuts, chopped OR
sunflower seeds
½ c. raisins
Grease and flour 8x12″ pan.

Now get together:
Add applesauce and dry ingredients
alternately to creamed mixture.
Beat well. Stir in nuts, dates, and raisins.
Pour batter into pan.
Bake 35-40 minutes.

Jane Short, Elkhart, Ind.

Serve freshly baked cake warm
and unfrosted. Serve leftover
cake a day later with fruit sauce
or whipped topping.

Oatmeal Cookie Mix

	1 gal.	2 gal.
Put through a coarse sieve:		
white sugar	1½ c.	3 c.
brown sugar	1½ c.	3 c.
sifted flour	3 c.	6 c.
salt	2 t.	4 t.
soda	2 t.	4 t.
baking powder	1 t.	2 t.
Cut in:		
shortening	2 c.	4 c.
Add:		
rolled oats	6 c.	12 c.

Mix well. Store in cool place.

Makes 4 doz.
350°
12 min.

Oatmeal Cookies:
Combine in bowl:
2 eggs, beaten
2 t. vanilla
4 c. oatmeal cookie mix
Mix well. Drop teaspoonfuls onto
greased baking sheet, flatten with fork,
and bake at 350° about 12 minutes.

Options:

Add chopped nuts, raisins, coconut,
chocolate chips, or sunflower seeds.

Add 1 t. cinnamon to egg mixture.

Put 2 cookies together with a blend of
peanut butter and honey or jelly.

Hilda Janzen, Newton, Kan.

Cake Toppings

Use a thin glaze drizzled on the
cake instead of thick icing.

Before baking, sprinkle a 9x13″
cake or 2 dozen cupcakes with
a mixture of ¼ c. finely chopped
nuts and ½ c. brown sugar. Add
coconut if desired.

Broiled coconut icing uses less
sugar than other icings.

High-Protein Peanut-Butter Cookies

Makes 6-7 doz.
375°
8-10 min.

Cream together until fluffy:
- 1½ c. shortening
- ½ c. granulated sugar
- ½ c. brown sugar
- ½ c. honey
- 1 c. peanut butter
- 3 eggs
- 1 t. vanilla

Sift together and add:
- 2½ c. whole wheat flour
- 1 c. dry milk solids
- ½ c. soy flour
- 1 t. salt
- 1 t. baking powder
- 2 t. baking soda

Chill dough. Roll into 1" balls and place on greased cookie sheets. Flatten with fork dipped in flour. Bake at 375° for 8-10 minutes.

Priscilla Ziegler, Lancaster, Pa.

Whole Wheat Peanut-Butter Cookies

Makes 5 doz.
375°
8-10 min.

Cream together:
- ½ c. shortening
- 1 c. peanut butter
- 1½ c. sugar
- 1 egg

Add to creamed mixture:
- 1 c. wheat germ
- 2 t. vanilla
- 6 T. water

Combine and add:
- 1½ c. whole wheat flour
- 1 c. dry milk solids

- ½ t. salt
- 1 t. baking powder
- 2 t. baking soda

Roll into 1" balls. Place on greased cookie sheet and flatten with fork dipped in flour. Bake at 375° for 8-10 minutes.

Marcia Beachy, DeKalb, Ill.

Dietetic Date Cookies

Makes 5 doz.
350°
10-12 min.

Combine in saucepan:
- 1 c. raisins
- ½ c. snipped dates
- 1 c. water

Boil 3 minutes, stirring constantly. Cool.
Cream together:
- 2 eggs
- ½ c. margarine
- 3 t. liquid sweetener
- 1 t. vanilla

Sift together:
- ¼ t. cinnamon
- 1 c. flour
- 1 t. soda

Add dry ingredients to creamed mixture alternately with date mixture. Beat well. Chill several hours. Drop from teaspoon onto greased baking pan. Bake at 350° for 10-12 minutes.

Geraldine Roth, Morton, Ill.

New Zealand Whole Wheat Crisps

Makes 3 doz.
350°
10-12 min.

Combine:
  ½ c. melted margarine
  1 T. corn syrup
  ⅔ c. sugar
Add:
  1 c. whole wheat flour
  ⅛ t. salt
  1 t. soda dissolved in
  2 T. water
Mix well. Stir in:
  ⅔ c. coconut
  ⅔ c. chopped nuts
Drop by level tablespoonfuls 2" apart on ungreased cookie sheet. Bake at 350° for 10-12 minutes.

Ruth Hunsberger, Doylestown, Pa.

Molasses Crinkles

Makes 4 doz.
350°
12-15 min.

Cream together:
  ¾ c. shortening
  1 c. brown sugar
  1 egg
  ¼ c. dark molasses
Sift together and add:
  2¼ c. flour
  ½ t. salt
  2 t. soda
  1 t. cinnamon
  1 t. ginger
  ½ t. ground cloves
Mix thoroughly. Chill dough several hours. Shape dough into balls 1" in diameter. Roll in granulated sugar and place 2" apart on greased baking sheet. Bake at 350° for 12-15 minutes.

Wheat Germ Balls

Tester's husband says, "They're good! You make them and I'll eat them." A fair exchange of energies?

Makes 3½ doz.
350°
12-15 min.

Combine in mixing bowl:
  2 c. flour
  1 c. toasted wheat germ
  1 c. shortening
  ¾ c. sugar
  1 egg
  1 t. grated orange rind
  1 t. vanilla
  ½ t. salt
Beat at low speed until well mixed. Chill dough. Roll into 1" balls. Roll in ¾ c. wheat germ. Place on cookie sheet and bake at 350° for 12-15 minutes.

Mary Lou Houser, Lancaster, Pa.

Coconut–Date Balls

Makes 3 doz.

Combine and cook over low heat, stirring constantly:
  2 eggs, beaten
  ½ c. margarine
  ½ lb. dates, finely cut
Boil 2 minutes. Remove from heat and add:
  1½ c. crisp rice cereal
  ½ c. nuts, chopped
  1 t. vanilla
Cool; shape into little balls. Roll in coconut.

Barbara Longenecker, New Holland, Pa.

Date Oatmeal Cookies

Makes 6 doz.
350°
10-12 min.

Cream together:
  ½ c. margarine
  1 c. sugar
  3 eggs
Beat well. Sift together:
  1½ c. flour
  1 t. baking powder
  ½ t. salt
  1 t. soda
  1 t. cinnamon
  ½ t. allspice
Add to creamed mixture alternately with:
  ½ c. milk
Stir in:
  2 c. rolled oats
  1 c. chopped dates
  ½ c. coconut
  ½ c. nuts (optional)
Drop by teaspoonfuls on greased cookie sheet. Bake at 350° for 10-12 minutes.

Lena Brown, Grantham, Pa.

No-Bake Cereal Cookies

Makes 2-3 doz.

Combine in saucepan and heat to boiling:
  ½ c. brown sugar
  ⅓ c. light corn syrup
Stir in:
  1 t. vanilla
  ¾ c. peanut butter
Mix until smooth. Stir in:
  3 c. ready-to-eat cereal flakes
  1 c. flaked coconut (optional)
Drop by teaspoonfuls onto waxed paper.

Rosemary Moyer, North Newton, Kan.

Crunchy Drop Cookies

Makes 6 doz.
350°
10-12 min.

Cream together:
  1 c. shortening
  1⅓ c. brown sugar
  2 eggs
  2 t. vanilla
  6 T. milk
Combine and add:
  2½ c. flour
  1 t. baking soda
  ½ t. salt
Stir in:
  4 c. granola
Drop by teaspoonfuls onto greased cookie sheets. 350° for 10-12 minutes.

MCC Dining Hall, Akron, Pa.

Chocolate Chip Oatmeal Cookies

Makes 6-8 doz.
375°
10 min.

Cream together:
  1 c. shortening (may use half
      margarine and half lard)
  ¼ c. peanut butter
  ½ c. sugar
  ½ c. brown sugar
  2 eggs
  1 t. vanilla
Add:
  1½ c. flour
  1 t. soda
  ½ t. salt
  2 c. rolled oats
  1-2 c. chocolate chips
  1 c. chopped nuts (optional)
Mix well. Drop by teaspoonfuls on greased cookie sheet. Bake at 375° for about 10 minutes.

Elsie Epp, Marion, S.D.
Miriam LeFever, East Petersburg, Pa.

Chocolate Chip Cookies

Makes 5-6 doz.

375°

8-10 min.

Cream together:
- **1 c. margarine or shortening**
- **1 c. brown sugar**
- **1 c. granulated sugar**

Add:
- **2 eggs**
- **2 T. hot water**
- **2 t. vanilla**

Beat until fluffy. Sift together and add:
- **1 c. white flour**
- **1½ c. whole wheat flour**
- **⅔ c. soy flour**
- **1 t. salt**
- **1 t. soda**

Add:
- **2 c. or 12 oz. chocolate chips**
- **1 c. chopped nuts (optional)**

Drop by teaspoonfuls on greased cookie sheet. Bake at 375° for 8-10 minutes or until light brown.

Priscilla Ziegler, Lancaster, Pa.

Oatmeal Cookies With a Purpose

Makes 5-6 doz.

325°

10-15 min.

Purpose:
Constructive fun for children

Requirements:
1. Cookie dough
Cream together:
- **1 c. margarine or shortening**
- **1 c. brown sugar**

Add:
- **2 c. rolled oats**
- **1 c. dry milk solids**
- **½ c. water**

Beat well. Sift together:
- **2¼-2½ c. flour**
- **3 t. baking powder**
- **1 t. salt**

Fold into creamed mixture and mix well. Divide into small portions and chill.
2. Clean kitchen table.
3. Pie plates and cookie pans.
4. Rolling pins from toy bake sets or small round bottles.
5. Animal cookie cutters.
6. Aprons or old towels to protect children's clothing.
7. Children of either sex, ages 2 and up, with clean hands.

Extra Requirements (for parent, neighbor or grandparent):
1. Patience.
2. Loving-kindness.
3. Smiles.
4. Praise, given out liberally.
5. Wisdom, to help children share tools.
6. Pretend dark glasses.

Method:
1. Sprinkle flour on table for each child.
2. Distribute pieces of dough.
3. Demonstrate how to roll dough to ¼" thickness, cut out cookies, and transfer them to baking pans.
4. Preheat oven to 325°.
5. Wear pretend dark glasses to avoid seeing trail of flour from table to floor, or path of dough from fingers to mouth.
6. Pop pans into oven as soon as filled. Bake 10-15 minutes.
7. Put each child's cookies in separate container.
8. When all dough is baked, present each child with his or her container.

Results:
1. Sparkling eyes.
2. Happy faces.
3. Grimy hands.
4. Bulging cheeks.
5. Sweet voices saying, "Mm, good, it's yummy yummy in my tummy."
6. Spontaneous hugs from flour-covered arms.
7. A few cookies.

Helen Bergmann, Virgil, Ont.

Gingerbread Treats

Use mild molasses or combination of dark molasses and corn syrup.

Makes 4 doz.

350°

10-12 min.

Mix together:
  1 c. hot water
  1 c. molasses
Combine separately and add:
  3 c. flour
  ½ t. baking soda
  1 t. baking powder
  1½ t. ginger
  ½ t. salt
Add:
  ¼ c. melted shortening or oil
  1 c. raisins
Mix well. Drop by teaspoonfuls onto greased baking sheet. Bake at 350° for 10-12 minutes.

Eleanor Hiebert, Elkins Park, Pa.

Peanut Bars

Makes 2 doz.

350°

30 min.

Cream together:
  ½ c. margarine
  ½ c. brown sugar
  ½ c. granulated sugar
  1 egg
  ½ t. vanilla
Add:
  1½ c. quick-cooking rolled oats
  ¾ c. whole wheat flour
  ½ t. baking soda
  ¼ t. salt
Stir in:
  1 c. peanuts, coarsely chopped
  ½ c. seedless raisins

Pat mixture evenly into a greased 9" baking pan. Bake at 350° for 30 minutes Cool in pan. Cut into bars.

Option:

Substitute other nuts as available

Carolyn Blosser, Akron, Pa

Raisin or Date Bars

Makes 3 doz.

400°

25-30 min.

Combine in saucepan:
  2½ c. raisins
  ¾ c. water
  ¼ c. sugar
  3 T. lemon juice
  2 T. cornstarch
    OR
  3 c. chopped dates
  1½ c. water
Cook over low heat until thick. Cool.
Combine in bowl:
  ¾ c. margarine
  ¾ c. brown sugar
  1 t. salt
  ½ t. baking soda
  1¾ c. flour
  1½ c. rolled oats
Mix well until crumbly. Firmly press half of crumb mixture into 9x13" greased pan. Spread cooled filling over top and cover with remaining crumb mixture, patting down lightly. Bake at 400° for 25-30 minutes. Cut into bars while warm.

Mary Lou Houser, Lancaster, Pa.

Butterscotch Brownies

Makes 2 doz.
350°
30 min.

Preheat oven to 350°.
Melt:
    ¼ c. margarine
Add:
    1 T. dark molasses
    ¾ c. sugar
    2 eggs, beaten
    2 t. vanilla
Stir well. Sift in:
    ½ c. plus 2 T. dry milk powder
    ½ t. baking powder
    ¼ t. salt
Add:
    1 c. wheat germ
    ½ c. walnuts or pecans, chopped
Stir only enough to blend, using no more than 20 strokes. Spread in greased 8x8" pan. Bake 30 minutes.

Lena Brown, Grantham, Pa.

Old-Fashioned Sugar Cookies

Mrs. Wiebe, now 84, says this was the only cookie recipe her mother, Elizabeth Thierstein Claassen, used as she raised 14 children.

Makes 10 doz.
375°
10-12 min.

Cream together:
    1⅔ c. sugar
    1 c. lard, margarine, or shortening
    2 eggs
    1 c. sour cream
Stir in:
    2 t. baking powder
    9½-10½ c. flour
    1 t. lemon extract (optional)
    1 t. vanilla

Chill dough. Roll out, sprinkle with a little sugar, and roll over again lightly. Cut into small rounds. Bake at 375° for 10-12 minutes.

Martha Wiebe, Whitewater, Kan.

Peppernuts

Contributor says, "We developed the Peppernut variation last Christmas and gave a lot away to people who had no idea something that tasted so good could be so healthy." Around the holidays, peppernuts are always available in Prussian Mennonite homes to fill children's pockets and dunk in grown-ups' coffee.

400 °
10 min.

Cream together in large mixing bowl:
    2 c. honey
    ½ c. margarine
    1 egg
Add:
    ¾ c. hot water
    ½ c. finely chopped nuts or
        sunflower seeds
    1 t. cinnamon
    ½ t. ginger
    ¼ t. cloves
    1½ t. baking powder
    ½ t. soda
    4 c. sifted whole wheat flour
    4 c. unbleached white flour
Roll into long pencil-like sticks ¾" in diameter and freeze overnight between layers of waxed paper or dish towels. The next day, slice ⅜" thick and place on greased baking sheets so they do not touch each other. Bake at 400° for 10 minutes. Peppernuts will be hard after they cool. Spicy taste ripens by storing in a closed container several days.

Option:
Substitute corn syrup and molasses if honey is unavailable or too expensive.

Lois Barrett, Wichita, Kan.

Gardening and preserving

Dill Pickles

A true more-with-less pickle—cheap, fast, sugarless, crisp, and flavorful, and all ingredients except salt and vinegar can be home-grown.

Makes 10-12 qts.

Fill each of 10-12 sterilized quart jars with the following:

small whole cucumbers or larger cucumbers cut in spears
1 grape leaf
1 sprig fresh dill
¼ onion
1 clove garlic (optional)
1 small red pepper
OR ¼ t. dried red pepper flakes (optional)

Heat a canner half full of water.
Combine in saucepan:

13 c. water
6 c. vinegar
1 c. salt

Bring to boil and pour brine into filled jars. Seal. Process jars for 5 minutes in boiling water. Ready to eat in 2 weeks.

Zelma Martin, Lancaster, Pa.

Bread and Butter Pickles

Makes 12 pts.

Cut into thin rings:
   **30 medium unpared cucumbers
      (1 gallon sliced)
   8 medium onions**
Cut in fine strips:
   2 large red or green peppers
Place vegetables in large bowl or kettle. Dissolve in ice water and pour over:
   ½ c. salt
Let stand 3 hours. Drain.
Combine in large kettle:
   **5 c. sugar
   5 c. vinegar
   2 T. mustard seed
   1 t. turmeric
   1 t. whole cloves**
Bring to boil. Add drained vegetables and heat to boiling point. Do not boil. Pack into sterilized jars and seal.

Mennonite Community Cookbook, *used by permission.*

Cucumber Relish

Makes 6-7 pts.

Grind through food chopper:
   **12-14 cucumbers
   1 bunch celery
   2 onions
   2 green peppers
   2 sweet red peppers**
Let stand overnight.
Drain and add:
   2 T. salt
Mix well.
Bring to boil in large kettle:
   **3 c. sugar
   3 c. vinegar
   1 t. celery seed
   ½ t. tumeric
   1 t. mustard seed**
Add vegetables and cook 30 minutes. Fill into jars and seal.

Judy Classen, Akron, Pa.

Gardening

*Kidney beans are very easy to grow. Let them hang on the bush until pods begin to dry. Shell and wash in cold water. Spread them out on paper to dry for a few days, until they split when hit with a hammer. I put them in a big plastic bag in my freezer to help keep them fresh, and just scoop out what I need. Before kidney bean pods become dry on the stalk, we pick some and cook as a vegetable like lima beans. The shells are slightly yellow at this point and the beans a deep pink. To prepare, cook in water and add chopped onion and cream if desired. When creamed, they go nicely over potatoes instead of gravy.
—Kate Kooker, Ardmore, Pa.*

*Sunflower seeds, a traditional Russian Mennonite snack food, are easy to grow and fun to eat. To shell for use in cereals, cookies, or salads, try this: Put ¼ to ½ cup seeds in the blender; whirl at lowest speed for ten seconds. If all the seeds aren't shelled, repeat for a few more seconds. Stir cracked seeds into a bowl of water. Repeat the process until several cups of seeds have been cracked. Then let seeds and water set until kernels settle. Strain off the shells which float. (Use this as birdseed, since all may not be cracked.) Pour off the water. Spread the seeds out onto a cookie sheet. When dry, sort and clean the kernels. Store in cool, dry place, until ready to use in recipes.
—Kamala Platt, Newton, Kan.*

End-of-the-Garden Pickle

Makes 18 pts.

Soak several hours in brine of ½ c. salt and 2 qts. water:

2 qts. small whole cucumbers

Cook separately in salted water just until crisp-tender:

1 pt. pickling onions
2 qts. carrot slices
1 qt. celery, sliced in ½" pieces
1 qt. cauliflowerets
1 qt. yellow wax beans
1 qt. lima beans
4 sweet red peppers, cut in strips

Drain vegetables. Rinse and drain cucumbers. Place all vegetables in large enamel dishpan.

Combine in very large kettle:

1½ qts. water
1½ qts. vinegar
6 c. sugar
¼ c. pickling spices tied in a bag

Bring to a boil and simmer 5 minutes. Remove spice bag. Add vegetables to hot syrup. Bring quickly to boiling temperature. Pack into hot jars and seal.

Option:

For a Pennsylvania Dutch Chow-Chow, add 1 qt. cut corn and 2-3 c. cooked kidney beans.

Olive Wyse, Goshen, Ind.
Nora Bohn, Goshen, Ind.

If it is possible in your climate to mulch with bales of hay so that the ground does not freeze hard, you can have fresh root vegetables all winter. Plant leeks, carrots, salsify, parsnips, beets, and turnips in July so that they reach ideal size by the time frost kills the tops. Vegetables will remain in delicious condition below the ground.
—Rosa Mullet, Pantego, N.C.

Creole Sauce

Makes about 3 cups

Heat in large skillet:

2 T. oil

Cook until soft, but not brown:

1 c. onion, chopped
½ c. celery, chopped
1 clove garlic, mashed

Add:

2 c. cooked or fresh Italian plum tomatoes, chopped
1 bay leaf
pinch dried thyme
½ t. basil
¼ t. oregano
⅛ t. celery seed
1 T. chopped parsley
1 t. salt
dash sugar
freshly ground pepper

Cook uncovered over low heat about 1½ hours, or until sauce is reduced by half. Stir occasionally. During last 20 minutes of cooking time, add:

1 large sweet pepper, diced

Store in refrigerator until ready to use. Serve with rice, chicken, beef, pork, or seafood. Make in large quantities to can or freeze when tomatoes are in season.

Evelyn Liechty, Berne, Ind.

To harvest green soybeans: When pods are plump but still green, clip off plants at ground level. Leave roots to enrich the soil. Pile the plants under a tree and strip off the pods. Wash pods; drop into boiling water and cook 3 to 5 minutes, or until beans will pop out easily. Cool pods and shell out beans. Freeze without further blanching. To serve, cook ten minutes and season with butter, salt, and pepper.
—Rod and Mary Lou Houser, Lancaster, Pa.

Chili Sauce

Makes 10-12 pts.

Cook until soft:
  1 gal. tomatoes, cut up
  2 medium onions, cut up
Press through collander to remove skins
and seeds.
Add:
  1 c. sugar
  ½-1 c. vinegar
  5 t. salt
  1 t. cinnamon
  1 t. dry mustard
  ½ t. curry powder
  ½ t. nutmeg
  Cayenne or chili powder to taste
Cook down to desired consistency. Pour
into pint jars, seal and process in hot
water bath for 5 minutes.

Helena Pauls, Inman, Kan.

Spaghetti Sauce For Canning

Makes 12 qts.

Cut all in pieces:
  ¾ bu. tomatoes, unpeeled
  3 large sweet potatoes, unpeeled
  2 bunches celery
  3 sweet red peppers
  1 hot pepper
  8 medium onions
  3 cloves garlic
Cook together in large kettles for 2½
hours. Put through a food mill.
Add:
  1½ c. sugar
  ¾ c. salt
  1 c. oil
Heat again to boiling. Pour into jars and
seal. Process in boiling water bath ½
hour.

Ada Beachey, Goshen, Ind.

Tomato Ketchup

*Using blender yields a smoother
ketchup.*

Makes 8 pts.

Prepare by one of two methods:
  **4 qts. tomato pulp seasoned with
  4-5 large onions**
1. Pour boiling water over tomatoes;
peel, quarter, and squeeze out some
juice with hands (reserve to drink).
Process tomatoes and onions in blender.
2. Quarter and cook tomatoes with
onions. Pour into food mill, allowing thin
juice to run off. Then transfer food mill to
another bowl and press out thick pulp.
Measure pulp. Combine in large kettle:
  4 qts. tomato pulp
  2 T. celery salt
  4 t. salt
  3 c. sugar
  2 c. vinegar
  ¼ t. red pepper (optional)
  **4 t. mixed pickling spices tied
  in bag**
Bring to boil. Reduce heat and cook
slowly 1-1½ hours, stirring occasionally.
Remove spice bag.
Combine in small bowl:
  5 T. cornstarch
  ¼ c. water
Stir into boiling tomato mixture. Boil 5
more minutes. Seal in hot sterile jars.

Karen Rix, Fonda, Iowa

*Growing your own soybeans
has several advantages over
purchasing them in a
health-food store. It is more
economical, soybeans provide
nutrients for your soil and you
can harvest some while they are
green. The taste difference
between green (or fresh-frozen)
and dried soybeans is reason
enough to warrant growing your
own.*
—LaVonne Platt, Newton, Kan.

Freezer
Vegetable Soup

Makes about 10 qts.

Brown in large heavy kettle:
4 lbs. ground beef
Add:
1 qt. corn
1 qt. green or yellow string beans
1 qt. peas
1 stalk celery, finely chopped
½ head cabbage, finely chopped
6 onions, finely chopped
2 c. white or red cooked beans,
** or both**
6 carrots, finely chopped
6 sprigs parsley, chopped
salt, pepper, and herbs to taste
water or stock to cover
Cook until vegetables are tender. Divide
into containers and freeze.

Option:

Children enjoy alphabet noodles added
to this soup.

Minnie O. Good, Denver, Pa.

Oven
Apple Butter

Makes 6 qts.
350°
3 hrs.

Combine in large greased roast pan:
5 qts. applesauce, unsweetened
10 c. sugar
1 c. vinegar
2 t. cinnamon
1 t. cloves
Bake at 350° for 3 hours, or until thick. Stir
every 20 minutes. Pour into jars and seal.

Edna M. Reed, New Cumberland, Pa.

Quick
Strawberry Jam

Makes about 4 cups

Mix well and let stand 4 hours or
overnight:
2-3 c. mashed strawberries
** (depending on desired**
** thickness)**
3 c. sugar
Bring to a hard boil. Reduce heat to
medium. Boil 10 minutes.
Add:
1 3-oz. package strawberry
** gelatin**
Mix until well dissolved and bring to
boiling point again. Remove from heat
and let set a few minutes. Stir again. Put
in jars and keep in refrigerator or freezer.

Options:

Strawberries with pineapple gelatin.

Raspberries with raspberry gelatin.

Grapes with grape gelatin.

Peaches with peach, lemon, or
pineapple gelatin.

5 c. rhubarb, chopped, with raspberry or
strawberry gelatin.

Ellen Burkholder, Pembroke, Ont.
Helen Burkholder, St. Catharines, Ont.

*Raise green leafy vegetables
such as collards, kale, mustard,
rape, spinach, and Swiss chard
in a lavishly enriched portion of
soil. Keep it well watered.
Greens grown fast in ideal
conditions in a cool season
have a delicious flavor not to be
compared to the taste of greens
grown indifferently in hot dry
soil. Plant greens very early in
the spring and late in August for
a fall crop.*
—Rosa Mullet, Pantego, N.C.

Easy Sauerkraut

1. Sterilize quart jars. You will need 2 lbs. of cabbage or a medium-sized head for each quart.
2. Shred each head of fresh cabbage in dime-thin pieces after removing outer leaves. Use cores and outer leaves in stock pot.
3. Sprinkle 4 t. salt over each shredded head. Mix well with hands.
4. Pack tightly into jars until juice forms and reaches top. Screw lids on loosely. Set jars in a pan to catch juice as cabbage ferments.
5. After 7-10 days the brine level will drop suddenly, indicating kraut is done. Keep in refrigerator a few weeks, or for longer storage press kraut down with a wooden spoon to remove the gas bubbles and add more brine made of 4 t. salt to 1 qt. water to fill jars.
6. Set jars in canner with warm water. Bring all to boiling, cover, and boil 30 minutes; seal. This is a mild, fresh-flavored kraut.

Alice W. Lapp, Goshen, Ind.

We haven't found a fast way to shell out dry beans, so we work on them when we're sitting and talking with friends. We put the shelled beans we plan to eat (not those to be used for seed) in a 200° oven for several hours to keep them from getting weevils in storage.
—Don and Priscilla Ziegler, Lancaster, Pa.

Kale and Swiss chard will not freeze until temperatures go down to about 15°. My parents raised them in fall for an early winter vegetable.
—Helene Janzen, Elbing, Kan.

Apple-Honey Butter (oven method)

Makes 10-12 pts.
300°
3 hrs.

Core, cut and cook until soft:
7 lbs. apples
Press through food mill to make 1 gallon applesauce.
Combine in large enamel roaster
applesauce
1½ lbs. honey
1 c. cider or vinegar
1 c. crushed pineapple
Bake at 300° for 3 hours, stirring occasionally. Pour into jars and seal.

Ruth Gish, Mt. Joy, Pa

Freezing

When onions are inexpensive, buy in quantity, chop, and freeze in small portions. When green peppers are plentiful, cut in strips or dice and freeze on cookie sheets. When frozen, scoop into containers, and return to freezer. Handy for casseroles.
—Miriam LeFever, East Petersburg, Pa.

Chop a quantity of parsley and pack into several peanut-butter jars. Keep in freezing compartment of refrigerator. A tablespoonful flakes off easily anytime you want it.
—Edna Longacre, Barto, Pa.

We always seem to have one overripe banana left from each bunch. I freeze these right in the peel. When several have accumulated I use them in baking cake or breads.
—Esther Martin, Neffsville, Pa.

Freezing pumpkin: Cut pumpkins in half, take out seeds, turn upside down on cookie sheets and bake until soft. If you have enough pumpkins, fill your oven to save heat. When tender, scoop out pumpkin and blend till smooth with as little water as possible. Freeze.
—Patricia Franke,
  Wolcottville, Ind.

Freezing apples for pie: Peel, quarter, and slice a few apples at a time. Drop immediately into cold salted water. Place in freezer container. Salt water prevents apples from darkening.
—Anna Ruth Banks,
  Smithville, Tenn.

Freezing corn on the cob: Clean ears by trimming ends and removing silk. Do not wash or use water on them. Freeze in plastic bags. To serve, drop ears into boiling water. Cook 6 to 8 minutes after water returns to boiling. Tastes like fresh corn.
—Sarah Claassen,
  Beatrice, Neb.

Freezing beet tops, spinach, and other greens: Cut off leaves, wash, blanch, cool immediately in ice water, drain, and freeze. To serve, cook with just a little water. Add salt and butter or a cream sauce.
—Esta M. Eby, Mohnton, Pa.

Near the end of the summer, collect odds and ends from the garden and freeze mixed vegetables for soup. Slightly overripe vegetables will be acceptable used this way.
—Dorothy Miller, Barto, Pa.

If you don't want to make your own ketchup, you can still save about one third by buying it in a number 10 can. Open the can and pour the ketchup into quart-size square plastic containers and freeze. Keep one container in the refrigerator. From it you can easily fill a plastic ketchup dispenser to use on the table or carry to picnics. Plastic dispensers are easier for children to control than glass bottles.

Drying

Dry apples for a snack food. Put peeled, cut-up apples in the sun with a screened cover. Or dry in the oven at very low heat for 4 to 6 hours. Old adjustable window screens make perfect oven racks and enable apples to dry on both sides at once.
—Phyllis Leaman,
  Lancaster, Pa.
—Janice Pauls,
  MacPherson, Kan.

I often dry bananas. My local produce market sells me a case of darkened bananas which are still beautiful inside for ⅓ the retail price. I peel the bananas, cut them lengthwise in quarters, and then crosswise in half. I place them on two old oven racks and dry in oven on very low heat for 24 to 48 hours. A pilot light or light bulb hung in the oven on an extension cord is enough heat— if it's too hot juices come out of the fruit and it's not as tasty. Eat as snack food.
—Kathy Histand,
  Sellersville, Pa.

Dry mint leaves in the shade on screen or newspaper and pack into jars. A dozen or more mint varieties are available, each with particular flavor.

Plants are available from friends or herb nursery houses. Plant several around faucet beside the house for hardy perennial availability. Best flavor is in the newly formed leaves and growing tips at the end of the stalks. Pinch these off for tea. Lateral buds will push out to multiply your crop.
—Don Ziegler, Lancaster, Pa.

When tangerines are in season, wash skins well and air them several days until completely dry. Then break into pieces, or powder by processing in blender. If you want them thinly sliced, cut before drying. Store in attractive jars. Dried peels improve with age and keep well for years. Murcot Honey is a good variety of tangerine to use. Add dried peel to foods such as mincemeat, fruit cakes, puddings, pickles and red beets.
—Evelyn Liechty, Berne, Ind.

I must live on a sugar-free diet and enjoy canning my own grapefruit. Peel the grapefruit and pull sections apart. Use kitchen shears to cut off edge along the core, then gently peel back the skin. Drop sections into pint jars, fill with water and a little liquid sweetener if desired, then seal and process 10 minutes in boiling water bath. It does take time, but I have more time than money. When I buy grapefruit on sale it costs me 10 cents a pint to can.
—Lela Miller, Albany, Ore.

To can tomato sauce without cooking it down: Cook tomatoes as for tomato juice. Pour tomatoes into food mill and let juice run through without turning handle. Transfer food mill to another container and press through pulp for a thick sauce. Can thin juice for drinking or use in soups, pulp for tomato sauce to use in spaghetti sauce or casseroles.
—Anna Mary Brubacher, St. Jacobs, Ont.

Any jar with a top that fits dome lids and rings can be used for canning. Use jars from mayonnaise, instant tea, and coffee, etc.
Reuse jars with matching one-piece vacuum lid for open-kettle canning of tomato juice, ketchup, pickles, and cooked jellies and jams. These are lids with a built-in ring of rubber on the inside, such as you get with dry-roasted peanuts, bottled juice, or wheat germ.
—Phyllis Leaman, Lancaster, Pa.

Often when I want to use beans I don't have them soaked and ready, so I can 7 quarts at a time in my pressure canner. Soak 5 pounds navy beans overnight. In the morning divide the beans into 7 quart jars, add 1 teaspoon salt to each jar, and fill to the neck with water. Process in pressure canner for 1 hour at 10 pounds. Beans are ready for soup, baked beans, or whatever you want.
—Ada Beachy, Goshen, Ind.

Canning beef: Cut meat in 2-to-3-inch squares. Pack into jars, not too tightly. Add 1 teaspoon salt to each jar. Don't add water. Seal and process in pressure cooker at 10 pounds for 90 minutes. Save tallow and render by frying to make soap.
—Irene P. Chrisinger, Mt. Pleasant, Iowa

Snacks and miscellaneous

North American snack habits take criticism from all directions. Instead of spending more time denouncing the products we already recognize as wasteful, let's work positively toward a list of good snacks:

apples
bananas
bread or toast, whole grain
carrot sticks
celery,
    as is or spread with
    cheese or peanut butter
cheese
cherry tomatoes
cookies,
    made with whole grains
    and minimal sugar
crackers, whole grain
dates
dried apples
fruits and real fruit juices
fruit and nut breads
granola
honey on bread
milk
nuts
oranges
peanut butter
peanuts
popcorn
popsicles,
    homemade with minimal sugar
pretzels
puddings,
    homemade with minimal sugar
raisins
sunflower seeds
roasted soybeans
yogurt

Most of the above go well in lunch boxes or on car trips. Last summer our family took a week's trip with another family in a station wagon. The most popular snack in the car, while it lasted, was a huge plastic container of carrot and celery sticks and other raw vegetables. No one got sticky, thirsty, or irritable with a half-upset stomach. Apples, had they been in season, would have been as good.

It's easiest for me to encourage our children in wholesome after-school snacks if I have a bowl of fruit or the makings of sandwiches out on the table when they walk in. I like to take a break myself and sit down to cut apples or spread toast while we talk. If I ignore their hunger, they begin going through the cupboards themselves. Then they're likely to come up with chocolate chips I was saving or declare that nothing but ice cream will satisfy. You can discourage eating poor snack foods by simply not having them on hand, but it's also important to have good things invitingly displayed.

Roasted Soybeans— I

Soak beans overnight. Cook 1 hour in salted water.
Preheat oven to 350°.
Dry beans in a towel, rubbing briskly to remove outer covering and split beans in half. Single-layer the beans in shallow pans. Bake 30 minutes, turning once or twice. Sprinkle with salt while warm.

Mabel Kreider, Lancaster, Pa.

Roasted Soybeans— II

Soak soybeans overnight. Next morning put beans in a towel and dry thoroughly. Put beans in heated heavy skillet and stir until golden brown. Just before removing from skillet, add 1 T. margarine or peanut oil and sprinkle with ½ t. salt. Drain on paper.

Miriam LeFever, East Petersburg, Pa.

Roasted Soybeans— III

Soak beans overnight. Place in a kettle with celery stalks and leaves, chopped

onions, and salt. Cook over low heat 3-4 hours. Drain well.
Spread on a cookie sheet with 1-2 T. oil. Roast in 200° oven 4-8 hours until nutlike in flavor and texture. You can use the warm broiler of a gas stove while other baking is being done.

Marianne Miller, Topeka, Kan.

Roasted Wheat Berries (from Ethiopia)

Heat a small amount of oil in skillet. Add wheat berries (whole wheat) and pop like popcorn.
They don't actually pop, but will puff up. Serve hot with salt.

Catherine Kornweibel, Easton, Pa.

Seed Snacks— I

Save squash and pumpkin seeds. Boil in water 5-10 minutes. Drain well.
For each cup of seeds, combine and sprinkle over:
1 T. melted margarine
1 t. Worcestershire sauce
Sprinkle with salt or seasoned salt. Bake at 350° for 30 minutes or until nearly dry.

Kathryn Leatherman, Goshen, Ind.

Seed Snacks— II

Sprinkle squash or pumpkin seeds with turmeric, cumin, coriander, cayenne, and salt. Fry in small amount of oil.

Kamala Misra, Bhubaneswar, India

Roasted Chestnuts

To avoid chestnuts exploding, make a small cut on side of each nut with a paring knife. Place nuts in single layer on cookie sheet. Roast at 400° for about ½ hour. Shake pan occasionally. Different sizes require different time; sample before taking out.

You can also roast chestnuts in the fireplace, or boil in salted water for several hours.

Doris Hamman, Lansdale, Pa.

Roasted Sunflower Seeds

Take these on a car trip, pack little bagfuls in lunch boxes, and hide some in a high cupboard to sprinkle on salads. But calorie watchers, beware—once you start, it's hard to stop!

Makes 2 cups
325°
30 min.

Combine in shallow baking pan:
2 c. hulled sunflower seeds
1 T. oil or melted margarine
1 t. Worcestershire sauce
¼ t. salt
garlic and onion salt to taste
Mix well. Toast at 325° about 30 minutes, stirring occasionally, until seeds are golden and crunchy.

Option:
Combine all in heavy skillet and toast over low heat, stirring often.

Author's Recipe

Peanut-Butter Popcorn

Pop enough corn to make 2 quarts.
Cook to a rolling boil:
½ c. sugar
½ c. light corn syrup or honey
Remove from heat and add:
½ c. chunky peanut butter
½ t. vanilla
Pour over popcorn, stirring to coat.

Janet Landes, Phoenix, Ariz.

Raw Vegetable Dip

T·S

Makes 1¼ cups

Mix well and chill:
1 c. mayonnaise
1 t. horseradish
1 t. dry mustard
1 t. curry powder
dash lemon juice
2 T. sour cream
Serve with fresh unpeeled zucchini rounds or sticks plus other raw vegetables such as carrots, celery, cucumber, or cauliflower.

Options:
Add yogurt and/or blended cottage cheese.
Vary flavor with chopped herbs in season.

Ruth Heatwole, Charlottesville, Va.

Apple Snack

Peel, core, and halve:
2 qts. apples
Shred apples coarsely and put on buttered cookie sheet. Bake at 225° until dry. Remove from cookie sheet with pancake turner; break into pieces. Store in air-tight container.

Lina Gerber, Dalton, Ohio

Mint Tea

"This method captures the full nose-tingling essence of mint," says Don.

Makes 2 qts. concentrate

Stuff a 2-qt. jar until full with:
clean mint leaves
Add:
1 c. sugar
Run hot water over outside of jar to prevent breakage, then pour in:
boiling water to fill
Agitate jar to dissolve sugar. Cover loosely and let stand several hours or overnight. Strain contents. Use resulting concentrate by pouring into ice-filled tall glasses. Concentrate may be frozen.

Don Ziegler, Lancaster, Pa.

Fresh Meadow Tea

Makes 1 gal.

Bring to boil:
2 c. sugar
4 c. water
Pour over:
2 c. mint leaves, packed
2 sliced lemons
Let stand overnight. Strain off concentrate and store in refrigerator. When ready to serve, pour into a gallon container and fill with water and ice.

Marilyn S. Dombach, Mt. Joy, Pa.

Orange Ice Delight

Quick high-nutrient breakfast: Orange ice delight and a slice of whole wheat toast.

Makes 1 pt.

Whirl in blender:
1 egg
⅓ c. concentrated orange juice
1 c. milk
4-6 ice cubes, partially crushed
1-2 t. sugar or honey (optional)
Makes 1 pint

Option:

Substitute for orange concentrate: 1 banana plus ½ t. vanilla. or ½ c. sliced strawberries.

Virginia Birky, Salem, Ohio
Minnie Good, Denver, Pa.

Cottage Cheese Dip

T·S

Makes 2 cups

Combine in blender:
1 lb. creamed cottage cheese
1 t. onion juice or minced onion
salt, pepper and paprika to taste
Whirl until smooth. Vary flavors and serve with crackers or vegetables as suggested in Raw Vegetable Dip. *p. 220*

Lorraine Kroeker, Lexington, Neb.

Nippy Garbanzo Spread

Makes 2 cups

Sauté:
    2 T. margarine or olive oil
    1 onion, finely chopped
Combine in saucepan:
    **1½ c. cooked chick peas
        (garbanzos), mashed or
        ground**
    sautéed onion
    2 beaten eggs
Heat, stirring until thickened and dry.
Add to taste:
    salt
    cayenne pepper
    mayonnaise
Spread on bread or crackers.

Joan Gingrich, Lancaster, Pa.

Cheese Ball

Makes 1¾ lbs.

Have cheeses at room temperature.
Combine in bowl:
    8 oz. cream cheese
    **1 lb. sharp yellow cheese,
        shredded**
    ¼ t. garlic salt
    2 T. finely minced onion
    ½ t. salt
    **½ c. finely chopped black walnuts
        or other nuts**
Form into balls or logs. Sprinkle with chili
powder or roll in chopped parsley or
nuts. Chill. Serve with crackers.

Elizabeth Showalter, Waynesboro, Va.

Fancy Tea Crackers

T·S

Makes 2-3 doz.
375°
3-5 min.

Combine with fork:
    1 egg white
    ¼ c. sugar
    **¼ c. chopped cashews or
        other nuts**
Arrange soda crackers on baking sheet.
Pile a little nut mixture on each cracker.
Bake a few minutes at 375° until lightly
browned. Serve with hot tea.

Viola Wiebe, Hillsboro, Kan.

Soft Margarine

Soften 1 lb. margarine to room
temperature. Whip with ½ c. milk; return
to refrigerator. Use on sandwiches or
wherever soft margarine is desired.
Makes it easy for children to spread their
own bread.

June Suderman, Hillsboro, Kan.

Wheat Crackers

Makes about 1¼ lbs.
425°
7-10 min.

Combine in bowl:
    3 c. white flour
    1 c. whole wheat flour
    1 t. baking powder
    ½ t. salt
Cut in:
    **¾ c. margarine or
        lard-margarine combination**
Beat lightly:
    1 egg

Pour egg into 1 c. measure. Add:

enough milk to make 1 c. liquid

Mix to form a ball. Knead lightly, about 20 strokes.

Preheat oven to 425°.

Divide dough into 4 parts, roll out thinly on floured board and place on greased cookie sheets. Cut with pie crimper or pizza cutter to desired cracker size. Prick dough all over. Sprinkle generously with salt. Bake 7-10 minutes or until lightly browned. Store in airtight container.

Options:

Increase proportion of whole wheat flour to white.

Add ¼ c. wheat germ.

Margaret Ingold, Goshen, Ind.

Soda Crackers

Makes about ½ lb.
375°
10-12 min.

Preheat oven to 375°.

Combine in bowl:

2 c. flour
1 t. salt
½ t. soda

Cut in:

2 T. margarine

Stir in:

⅔ c. sour milk or buttermilk

Round dough into a ball and knead a few strokes. Divide dough into several pieces and roll out very thin on a floured board. Lay sheets of dough on ungreased flat baking pans. Sprinkle with salt and prick with fork. Cut into 1½" squares with sharp knife or pizza cutter. Bake 10-12 minutes, or until lightly browned.

Option:

Add 1 c. shredded cheese for cheese crackers.

Viola Dorsch, Musoma, Tanzania

Wheat Thins

Makes ⅔ lb.
350°
10 min.

Preheat oven to 350°.

Combine in mixing bowl:

2 c. whole wheat flour
2 T. wheat germ
1 t. salt
1 t. baking powder
2 T. brown sugar
2 T. dry milk solids

Cut in with pastry blender:

6 T. margarine

Combine separately and stir in:

½ c. water
1 T. molasses

Knead a little until smooth. Grease two cookie sheets (10x15") and sprinkle each with cornmeal. Divide dough in half. Roll out half of dough directly onto cookie sheet with floured rolling pin, rolling dime-thin. Sprinkle lightly with paprika, garlic, onion, or seasoned salt. Run rolling pin over once more. Prick with fork. Cut in squares or triangles. Bake 10 minutes or until lightly browned.

Donna Koehn, Blaine, Wash.

Sandesh

*Many of the famous sweets of India
are made from fresh milk curd, a
high source of protein. One of the
simplest is Sandesh.*

Makes 2-3 doz.

Bring to a boil:
**2 qts. milk
4 T. lemon juice
  OR 1½ c. whey from
      cheese-making**
Stir as milk begins to boil.
When milk separates into curds and
whey, remove from heat. (If milk does not
separate, add small amounts of lemon
juice and continue boiling until it does.)
Strain mixture through muslin-lined
colander. Place curds in saucepan.
Add:
½ c. sugar
Cook over low heat, stirring constantly,
until mixture is thick (10-15 minutes).
Pour onto buttered platter and spread to
¼" thickness. Top with podded whole or
crushed cardamon seed. Cool and cut
into diamond shapes.

LaVonne Platt, Newton, Kan.

Hinkelsteins
(oat sticks)

*A nourishing lunch-box or after-school
snack. Excellent keeping quality.*

Makes 100 sticks
375°
15-20 min.

Preheat oven to 375°.
Combine in large bowl:
**3 c. whole wheat flour
2½ c. oat flour (process rolled
      oats in a blender)
½ c. soy flour
2 t. salt
2 c. chopped dates
¾ c. coconut
½ c. sesame seeds
½ c. sunflower seeds
½ c. chopped nuts**
Stir thoroughly, making sure dates are
coated with flour mixture.
Add:
**½ c. oil
4½ T. honey
  OR 5 T. molasses
1⅛ c. milk**
Mix well. Divide into two greased 10x15"
jelly roll pans. Pat firmly and evenly. Cut
into 1x3" pieces with pizza cutter. Bake
15-20 minutes or until browned. Remove
sticks around the edges if they brown
before center is done.

Ruth Hollinger, Goshen, Ind.

Cheese Sticks

Makes ⅔ lb.
375°
10 min.

Combine:
1 c. grated sharp cheese
½ t. salt and dash pepper
1¼ c. flour
Cut in with pastry blender:
⅓ c. margarine
Sprinkle with:
3 T. milk
Toss with fork. Form into ball. Preheat oven to 375°.
Turn dough onto floured board and roll out ⅛" thick. Sprinkle liberally with sesame seeds. Run rolling pin over again. Prick dough with fork all over. Cut into 1x2" sticks, or 2" squares and then into triangles. Place on ungreased cookie sheet. Bake 10 minutes or until golden.

Miriam LeFever, East Petersburg, Pa.

Yogurt Popsicles

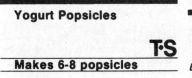

Makes 6-8 popsicles

Stir together:
1 pt. plain yogurt
6 T. (½ small can) frozen orange juice concentrate
1 t. vanilla (optional)
Freeze in popsicle molds or small waxed paper cups. Insert sticks into paper cup molds when partially frozen. To serve peel off paper cup.

Option:
Substitute frozen grape or pineapple concentrate.

Mary Lou Cummings, Quakertown, Pa.

Applesauce Candy

Makes 64 squares

Combine in saucepan:
1 c. applesauce
1 c. sugar
Bring to a boil and cook 2 minutes.
Dissolve in applesauce:
1 pkg. fruit gelatin
Add:
¾ c. nuts, finely chopped
Pour into 8x8" pan. After 24 hours, cut into 1" squares and roll in sugar. Roll in sugar the second time 24 hours later and it's ready to eat.

Options:
Cinnamon Candy: Add 1 T. cinnamon and use raspberry gelatin.
Lime Squares: Add ¾ t. peppermint extract and use lime gelatin.
Lemon Candies: Add finely grated rind of one lemon and use lemon gelatin.

Florence Mellinger, Lancaster, Pa.

Honey Milk Balls

Excellent lunch-box treats.

Makes 2 doz.

Combine in bowl:
½ c. honey or corn syrup
½ c. peanut butter
1 c. dry milk solids
1 c. uncooked rolled oats
OR 1½ c. graham cracker crumbs
Mix well, then knead by hand until blended. Shape into small balls. Makes 2 dozen.

Options:
Mold dough into a long roll and slice.
For each ball, shape dough around a nut.
Roll in coconut.

Orange Eggnog Popsicles

T·S

Makes 12 popsicles

In large mixer bowl or blender beat together:
- **1 pt. vanilla ice cream**
- **1 6-oz. can (¾ c.) frozen orange juice concentrate, thawed**
- **1 egg**

Gradually beat in:
- **1½ c. milk**

Freeze as directed in Yogurt Popsicles.

Option:

Subsitiute frozen grape or pineapple concentrate.

Virginia Birky, Salem, Ohio

Fudgsicles

T·S

Makes 8-10 popsicles

Make Quick Chocolate Pudding, *p. 187.*
Increase milk to 2½ c., cocoa to 3 T., and sugar to ½ c.
Cool.
Freeze as directed in Yogurt Popsicles.

Option:

Use 1 box chocolate pudding mix (not instant) prepared with 3 c. milk.

Donna Kroeker, Lexington, Neb.

Corn Chips

Makes ½ lb.
350°
10 min.

Preheat oven to 350°.
Combine in mixing bowl:
- **1 c. yellow cornmeal**
- **⅔ c. flour**
- **1 t. salt**
- **1 t. baking powder**
- **2 T. dry milk solids**

Stir together in separate bowl:
- **½ c. water**
- **¼ c. oil**
- **½ t. Worcestershire sauce**
- **⅛ t. Tabasco sauce**

Add liquids to dry mixture and stir with fork. Knead a little until smooth. Grease two cookie sheets (10x15") and sprinkle each with cornmeal. Divide dough in half. Roll out each\half directly onto cookie sheet with floured rolling pin, rolling dime-thin. Sprinkle lightly with paprika, garlic, onion, or seasoned salt. Run rolling pin over once more. Prick with fork. Cut in squares or triangles. Bake 10 minutes or until lightly browned.

Donna Koehn, Blaine, Wash.
Miriam LeFever, East Petersburg, Pa.

Granulated Soap

Soap takes 2-3 weeks to dry, but it can be used immediately. If lumps of soap are too large to dissolve easily during the cycle of washing, put them in a small amount of hot water first to soften them before adding the soap to washer.

Makes 13 lbs.

Preparing grease:
Heat together accumulated fat and drippings. Strain. If fat contains meat juices or lots of dark particles, allow to cool and then use fat which rises to the top. Discard dark particles which settle to the bottom.
In a large iron or stainless steel kettle (do not use glass, or aluminùm), mix together:
    1 can lye
    1 c. pure borax
    3 qts. cold water
Slowly add:
    4½ lbs. warm melted grease.
Stir, stir, stir, frequently throughout the day with a wooden spoon. When the mix becomes firm and can no longer be stirred easily, wear gloves and crumble the soap. A pastry blender can also be used to break up particles.
Do not double recipe. Use about ½ c. to a washer load of clothes.

Mary E. Groh, Albany, Ore.

Paste for Children's Play

Makes 5 cups

Combine in top of double boiler:
    1 c. sugar
    1 c. flour
    1 qt. cold water
Cook until thickened, stirring often.
Add to preserve:
    1 T. alum
    ½ t. oil of cloves
Seal into jars. Paste will set to stiffer consistency. Lasts indefinitely if kept sealed.

Nora Bohn, Goshen, Ind.
Herta Janzen, Calcutta, India

Play-Dough

Mix together in bowl:
    2 c. flour
    2 T. alum
Heat to boiling:
    1½ c. water
    ½ c. salt
    1 T. oil
    food coloring
Stir liquids into dry ingredients. Knead until smooth. Store in airtight container.

Ada Beachey, Goshen, Ind.

Homemade Laundry Soap

Makes 9 lbs. soap

Clean grease, using either method:
1. Boil grease in an equal volume of water. Remove from heat; chill by adding 1 qt. cold water for each gallon of liquid. Remove firm fat from top.
2. Melt fat and strain through muslin. Place in iron, enamel, or stoneware container (never use aluminum):
   5 c. cold water
Slowly add to cold water:
   1 can lye
Stir to dissolve and allow to cool (may take several hours). Melt grease; allow lye solution and grease to come to correct temperatures:
—sweet lard or soft fat at 85° with lye solution 75°
—half lard, half tallow at 110°, with lye solution 85°
—all tallow at 130°, with lye solution 95°
Pour lye solution into melted fat in a thin stream with slow, even stirring. Too rapid pouring or stirring causes separation. Stir slowly 10-20 minutes until mixture is thick as honey. Pour into wood or cardboard box lined with damp cotton cloth. Cover with old blanket or rug to retain heat. Let stand 24 hours. Remove soap, cut into bars, and store where air can reach it. Dry in even temperature 2 weeks to age.
To use in automatic washer, you must have soft water. Shred soap finely on a grater, or cut in pieces, and melt in small amount of hot water before adding to washer.

Ada Beachy, Goshen, Ind.
Gladys Stoesz, Akron, Pa.

Index

Index to Recipes